PENGUIN BOOKS

# GOD OF SIN

Ushinor Majumdar has been an investigative journalist (assistant editor) with *Outlook* magazine since 2015. He has written in-depth stories on economic offences, security, governance and also reported from conflict zones in central India. He collaborates on cross-border investigations and his reports have been published in international media outlets. Apart from that he writes regularly on the judiciary, crime, current affairs and has reported on major natural calamities. Ushinor has previously reported for *Tehelka* magazine and *Hindustan Times* and is a member of the Foundation for Media Professionals.

# Contents

# PART ONE

# 1

# Arrested Divinity

A clock in Jodhpur police headquarters chimed the midnight hour, flipping the calendar from 30 August to 31 August 2013. The sound halted the conversation. Everyone turned to look at the clock and then at each other. They decided to wait for some more time—a grace period. The armed constables snoozing outside went back to sleep for another hour.

At 1 a.m., five officers—three men and two women, in crisp uniforms, armed with their service revolvers—clipped down the stairs and into two waiting police vehicles, ready with drivers. Three armed constables shut the doors and climbed into the back.

Ten pounding hearts raced through the empty streets of Jodhpur. Jairam and Parmal, seated in the back of the police Bolero, clasped their automatic weapons, their eyes fixed on Mehrangarh Fort. It peeked through the intermittent gaps in the newer buildings till it completely vanished from sight. The cars whizzed past the military complex and hit the highway to Indore.

The three armed constables were chosen because they knew how to drive and could double up as substitute drivers. The journey ahead was long and there would be no time to stop and rest. In fact, they would not get any major breaks for the next two days and two nights.

Additional deputy commissioner of police (Addnl DCP), Jodhpur West, Satish Chandrajania, sat in the Tavera with Inspector Subhash Chandra Sharma and an armed constable.

In the Bolero, the husband–wife couple of sub-inspectors Satya Prakash Vishnoi and Mukta Parikh sat with the bundle of nerves that was Chanchal Mishra, assistant commissioner of police (ACP), Jodhpur West.

~

Chanchal Mishra was recruited to the Rajasthan Police Service in 2011. She underwent the rigorous two-year training at the academy, during which police officers are given lessons in intelligence-gathering and analysis, maintenance of law and order, and other policing essentials. Following their time at the academy, many realize where their interests lie.

Even before the training began, Mishra had decided that she was interested in investigating crime. Once at the job, she knew it would be a while before she was given a big case to crack. She was to be proven wrong within a month of being posted.

On 21 July 2013, Mishra joined at the rank of deputy superintendent of police and was posted as assistant commissioner of police in Jodhpur West—a fairly busy place that required constant attention. A month later, she was thrust into what was not just her first case but what may well turn out to be the biggest and most high profile one of her entire career.

Mishra was given the charge of investigating allegations against the controversial godman Asumal Harpalani, aka Asaram Bapu. The godman was accused of sexually assaulting a minor, Mita,[1] who along with her parents had been a devotee of the godman. She was also a student at a school run by a religious trust supervised by the godman.

Chanchal Mishra had conducted a detailed initial probe that examined the case from every possible angle. Finally, she served a notice to the godman to appear for an interview, with the deadline of 30 August 2013.

Sub-Inspector Bhanwar Singh of Jodhpur police went to Asaram's ashram in Indore to deliver the notice. Asaram's aides first tried to turn him away saying[2] their guru was in *ekantwas* (isolation). Bhanwar Singh, who had travelled by train from Jodhpur and was both exhausted and irritated, decided to wait patiently. He negotiated with the aides for a while. Asaram's aides knew this was no ordinary visitor; he had the force of law with him. So, one of them went inside with a message for the godman. He returned a little later to say that his knocks on the door of Asaram's room had yielded no response.

Bhanwar Singh calmly told them that if they did not want to call the godman outside, he would barge in and deliver the notice himself. He needed a receipt for the notice, to acknowledge that it had been delivered. The case was gaining momentum and he was well aware that the decision to ask Asaram to join the

---

[1] Name changed to protect identity.

[2] http://www.dailymail.co.uk/indiahome/indianews/ article-2403334/Asaram-Bapu-keeps-police-waiting-seven-hours-summon-sex-assault-allegations.html accessed on 15 May 2018

investigation had been made only after sufficient prima facie evidence had been collected.

Asaram consulted with one of his lawyers on the phone and decided to accept the summons.

In the meantime, political posturing around the case had begun. Bharatiya Janata Party (BJP) leader Uma Bharati was the first to offer support to the godman on 22 August 2013, saying that the charges were 'politically motivated'.[3] Other party leaders joined in, including the then national vice president, Prabhat Jha, who was also a member of the Rajya Sabha. Jha told reporters that it was a 'well-planned Congress conspiracy'.[4]

Narendra Modi, at the time, was chief minister of Gujarat and head of the BJP's campaign committee. A month later, he would formally be announced as the party's prime ministerial candidate, but was already viewed as such by a large section of the party and many common citizens as well.

Many of Asaram's followers and well-wishers tried to garner support for him by using the line that a 'Hindu spiritual leader' was being targeted. Modi made an official statement to BJP leaders and party members that they could not support the godman. The party line was to be that the allegations were being investigated and Asaram would be dealt with as per the law. At the time, the Congress government was in power in Rajasthan and at the Centre but public support had decidedly shifted away from the Congress.

---

[3]  https://www.business-standard.com/article/pti-stories/sexual-assault-case-against-asaram-bapu-may-be-politically-113082201058_1.html published on 22 August 2013 and accessed on 14 August 2018

[4]  https://www.indiatvnews.com/politics/national/digvijay-attacks-bjp-on-asaram-bapu-issue-12167.html published on 28 August 2013 and accessed on 14 August 2018

Asaram responded to the notices by fax, saying he was 'medically ill' and unable to travel to Jodhpur. There was no medical certificate enclosed—not even from the Ayurvedic practitioners whom Asaram consulted and who would accompany him to most places. The notice had said that he was to appear for an interview with the Jodhpur police on or before 30 August 2013. He missed the deadline.

Thus began what was one of the most challenging exercises in the entire case—Asaram's arrest. Another controversial guru, Rampal Singh, also known as Sant Shree Rampal, had been arrested in 2006 and remained incarcerated until he was granted bail in 2008. Some other godmen had also been placed under arrest. But none of those arrests had involved as high profile a religious/spiritual leader as Asaram. None of them had involved a small team of police officers, led by a rookie cop, traipsing into a powerful godman's ashram and prying him out of it.

~

Nobody slept through the night. The atmosphere was charged with excitement and dread. They were stepping into unknown territory. All the officers were aware of Asaram's political and financial clout.

There were a few rest-stops to freshen up, drink tea and switch drivers. Sometimes, the drivers would just pull up by the side of the road, splash some water on their faces, stretch their legs for less than a minute, and be off again. They had some seven hundred kilometres to cover—one way—and return. If they did manage the arrest, they would have to come back by this very road, and quickly. Rest was a luxury they could hardly afford.

It was dusk by the time the two cars drove into Indore and made their way straight to the office of the inspector general (IG) of police.

The IG greeted the team with the one question that everyone asked.

'Are the charges true? Did he do it?'

'As yet, that's what our investigation shows,' Mishra replied with a smile. She had become accustomed to being asked this question. They had some evidence, yet she knew she had to keep her mind open for any other possibility. It was a conflict that weighed on her mind, but she knew that all avenues had to be kept open.

The Jodhpur police and the Rajasthan police headquarters in Jaipur had briefed the IG in Indore. They had to interrogate Asaram, did not expect him to cooperate and were ready to arrest him and take him to Jodhpur.

The IG's second question was, 'Are you really going to arrest the godman or will you simply leave after disrupting the law and order situation here?'

It was a simple question but a critical one for the police in Indore, since the aftermath of such an eventuality would be his responsibility alone.

'We are prepared to take him back with us,' responded Mishra.

The IG provided escorts and sent them on their way.

During the day, the IG had deployed 900 policemen, including district and reserve forces, around the godman's ashram in Indore. He had made other arrangements that would prove to be crucial later. There were large numbers of women police personnel, drawn from the 'mahila battalions' of the Indore police. They were tasked with ensuring that the women devotees did not impede Asaram's arrest.

The police had received intelligence inputs that the godman was in the middle of a satsang attended by at least three thousand of his disciples. It was difficult to place an exact number. Aware of the police team's impending visit, supporters from in and around Indore had poured into the ashram. Due to his massive popularity in Madhya Pradesh and the Hindi belt of north India, it was not difficult to assemble a large crowd.

Nobody knows who came up with the figure of three thousand attendees, much like the numbers thrown around at political rallies by intelligence agents. I have asked them how they do it. 'How do journalists do it?' would be their counter question. I have no answer to that, nor do many other journalists, for that matter. Some ask the 'tentwallah' for a chair count. Then double or triple it based on speculation about the crowd who would be standing.

Whatever the actual numbers, the satsang area was packed. During his sermon, Asaram announced that they would not allow the Indore police or the media to enter the premises.

Back in Jodhpur, almost every television set was tuned to news stations, as was the case in many other parts of the country. Journalists were at the gates of the ashram, waiting for the day's development, hoping for high drama. Many expected a stampede followed by a baton charge and bursts from water cannons. Cameramen wore bandannas around their necks, ready to pull them up to their noses to protect themselves from tear gas.

Family members of the police team from Jodhpur sat in front of their TV sets, watching the spectacle. When they saw the police vehicles arrive at the ashram gate, they nervously speculated about the vehicle in which their relatives were seated.

At the ashram's entrance, the police from Jodhpur saw Madhya Pradesh police personnel deployed all around the perimeter of the ashram. There was a concentration of uniforms around the gate. Soon, pandemonium broke out. The mediapersons rushed towards the gate. Some of the godman's followers pushed past them to get to the police team. Many followers from inside the ashram also arrived at the scene. Someone called the ashram staff to inform them of the investigating team's arrival.

Interestingly, the devotees manning the gate refused to let the Indore police enter. They only spoke with the officers from Jodhpur.

'We will not let the media in.'

'That's not our concern. We are here to talk to Asaram,' replied one of the officers.

The guards finally moved aside to let the Jodhpur team in. The police team could have broken down the gate and stormed in, but nobody wanted a scene. The media tried to push its way in but were stopped at the gate. Live reports and ticker updates flashed angrily across TV channels.

The Jodhpur team ditched one of their cars, piled into the Tavera and drove through the gate at 9.30 p.m. The ashram has a perimeter of a few kilometres, and like Asaram's other ashrams, is built like a small township. The premises are divided into sectors for offices, an Ayurvedic shop, a *yagyashala* (for rituals), a *gaushala* (cowshed), a large satsang hall that can accommodate a few thousand people, and a two-storey building that serves as residential quarters for the godman and ashram staff. All these buildings are connected by tarred roads.

Asaram's son, Narayan Sai, was waiting for the police team in a lawn in the residential area of the ashram. He greeted them with '*Hari Om*' and introduced himself. He was surrounded by an entourage of lawyers and ashram staff.

The police presented the FIR to Narayan Sai, explained the charges to him and said they would need to talk to Asaram. For fifteen minutes, Narayan Sai and his entourage quizzed the police team about the charges against the godman. Asaram's Ayurvedic doctor, Nita Vaidya, also talked to the police. Mishra's response was, since Narayan Sai was not the accused, the police would not discuss the case with him.

Finally, Narayan Sai said, 'He is busy at the satsang and is in the middle of delivering his sermon. I have sent him a message but you will have to wait till he finishes and comes here.'

In order to avoid any disturbance, the police team decided to wait it out. The few thousand disciples could have easily turned into a dangerous mob, if Mishra and her team had tried a filmy style extraction of the godman as he was delivering his sermon. Besides, the police team had discussed that it would be better to try a peaceful method first, in order to elicit a measure of cooperation from Asaram.

The satsang was blaring through megaphones and speakers installed everywhere in the ashram. The police team could hear Asaram announce their arrival to his disciples.

'The police are here. They are here to take me away. Should I go with them?' Asaram asked.

'No Bapu,' they howled.

'Okay, if you don't want me to go, then I won't go.'

Despite an impending police interview and the possibility of arrest, Asaram remained characteristically flippant, not betraying a hint of nervousness.

The police team tried to lighten their mood with jokes while waiting for Asaram. It was a young team and besides, they had bonded during the long drive from Jodhpur to Indore.

'I don't think he will go,' said one.

'I don't think they will let us go either. We are five, they are five thousand,' said another.

About half an hour after the police's arrival, Asaram emerged from the satsang, draped in white, and greeted them individually with 'Hari Om'. Narayan Sai introduced Mishra as the investigating officer. Asaram directed his staff to offer them nuts and '*pey*'—a warm decoction served to guests at the ashram.

'We have had dinner and don't want anything right now. We would like to begin the interrogation,' Mishra told Asaram.

'*Tu toh karma yogini hai. Tere chehre pe karm ka tej hai* (You are a karma yogini, there is an aura of duty on your face),' Asaram said to Mishra.

Irritated with the banter, Mishra asked him to take a seat for interrogation.

'*Main toh tere nana jaisa hoon; tu meri nawasi jaisi hai* (I am like your grandfather; you are like my granddaughter). *Tu toh itni chhoti ladki hai, tu mujhe interrogate karegi* (You are such a young girl, how will you interrogate me)?' was Asaram's reply.

Keeping her cool, Mishra smiled and repeated her request.

'I have just returned from the satsang, let me clean up first. I am ill and so I also have to take some Ayurvedic preparations before I sit with you,' Asaram responded.

In the meantime, a government doctor had arrived from Indore city to conduct the mandated medical check-up prior to the interrogation.

The doctor followed Asaram into his hut, examined him and returned to certify that he was 'fit for investigation'. The report was added to the file.

Asaram, however, did not return immediately. Mishra and the other officers, who were waiting outside his quarters called out to him to come back out.

They also asked Narayan Sai to help them persuade Asaram to come out and talk to them. Narayan Sai went to the window, called out to his father and spoke with him. He assured the officers that Asaram would come in a while.

This charade was repeated a few times. During these exchanges, the father and son—both self-proclaimed godmen—spoke in their native Sindhi language, unaware that Sub-Inspector Satya Prakash spoke Sindhi as well. He reported to the rest what they had been discussing. It unmasked the godman's earlier flippant demeanour.

'We have to somehow stall them for the night. How many disciples have you arranged to come here in the morning? Have you spoken to the *akhada*s [wrestling facilities] to send people?' Asaram had told his son in Sindhi.[5]

He was clearly trying to get reinforcements to intimidate the police team. Intelligence inputs had earlier indicated that the ashram staff and Narayan Sai had contacted akhadas to request naga sadhus to come to the Indore ashram with the intention of using them to prevent the police from arresting Asaram.

The one thing the police officers realized was if they delayed the arrest till morning, they would not be able to leave with the godman.

Outside the ashram, the devotees who had attended the satsang had been spurred into action. They dragged out the green rugs which they were sitting on and took them to the road outside the premises. They proceeded to lie down on the mats to form a human roadblock outside the front gate.

The Indore police had posted plain-clothes policemen outside another gate closer to the godman's residential quarters.

---

[5]   As reported by the three policemen present on the scene.

They told the Jodhpur team that they had a ten-minute window in which they had to leave. The ashram staff had mistaken the plain-clothes men to be devotees blocking the gate and had not removed them.

With a deadline of ten minutes, the Jodhpur team had to think on its feet. Meanwhile, the godman had turned off the lights in his quarters.

'If you don't open the door in the next five minutes, we will call for a JCB (demolition machine) and break it down,' Mishra announced.

The lawyers again tried to stall the police team, but the latter were adamant that they wanted the godman to come out first.

Mishra's threat worked. Asaram came out chanting 'Hari Om', plopped down on a chair in a prayer room inside the building and told Mishra to ask what she wanted to. That is when Narayan Sai left the scene but Nita Vaidya and four–five *sevikas* remained at the head of the crowd which had swelled to around a hundred by then.

'Take off your shoes. Bapu stays here so this is a temple. You can't go in with shoes,' said one of the sevikas.

Saying the shoes were part of their uniform, the police officers refused to take them off. They also asked for chairs, which were brought for them. The atmosphere had grown hostile and tense.

That was when Inspector Sharma and Sub-Inspector Satya Prakash picked up the godman and began to walk with him to the Tavera that was waiting close by. The driver saw them and turned on the ignition. Mishra and Addnl DCP Chandrajania got into the car. An attendant came forward with some of Asaram's belongings and a bucket of 'Bapu's Ayurvedic medicine'. They seemed to have been prepared for this eventuality.

Initially, Asaram resisted, but was told that he could either cooperate or the police would have to adopt other methods.

Mukta Parikh was about to follow them into the Tavera when the five or six sevikas present lay down in front of the car. She walked over to them and physically started removing them, clearing a path for the car, which veered around the sevikas. Some of them tried to run after the car and Parikh had to hold them back by force.

The car surged ahead and started to pick up speed. They had to get out but they could not leave Parikh behind at the mercy of thousands of Asaram's angry supporters.

Satya Prakash climbed from the middle seat into the back and opened the rear (fifth) door of the moving SUV. With one hand, he gripped the back of a seat and stretched the other towards his wife. Parikh had started to run, and as the car slowed down, Satya Prakash leaned out and managed to pull her into the moving vehicle.

The devotees outside had realized that the police were leaving with their guru. They dashed towards the moving car but the police personnel, mostly women, (deployed to control the large number of female devotees) were prepared for them. They had tied ropes to trees which they were using to keep the hysterical devotees at bay. Till then, Mishra and her team had no idea about the size of the crowd since they had not gone to the satsang venue.

The car carrying Asaram Bapu sped past the mob towards the gate where the plain-clothes policemen from Indore were stationed. It was a narrow gate, the opening just wide enough for people to walk through. The occupants of the police SUV did not know how they would make it past the narrow gate. They just had instructions to get there. Perhaps there was a vehicle waiting for them and they would have to make a quick switch on foot.

After issuing the ten-minute deadline to Mishra and her team, the Indore policemen had called for a JCB demolition truck, thanks to a quick-thinking IAS officer. The truck had demolished the gate and a part of the wall so that the car could drive through. The mission was to ensure that the car left the area without unnecessary delay.

The road back to Jodhpur passes through several towns and villages where they could encounter Asaram's devotees. Besides, if they did not reach Jodhpur within twenty-four hours from the time of the arrest, the law required them to get a transit remand from a court in Indore. That would mean that they would have to wait till the next morning because it was quite late in the night. They feared a longer time period would have also tipped off Asaram's followers, who would have been waiting along the road and might have created obstacles.

The Jodhpur police headquarters organized tickets for the team to travel by air. The tickets arrived on their phones en route to the airport.

They reached the airport past midnight and were greeted by wide-eyed security personnel who did a double take on seeing the godman, known to travel with entourages of a different kind and used to being treated as a VIP with a mere wave of his hand and a serene smile.

Mishra and her colleagues made it past the entrance hurriedly and checked in for their flight. They began the interrogation in a secluded lounge. Asaram denied all the charges that he was confronted with.

'She [Mita] was like you, like a granddaughter to me. I haven't done any of this. I only tried to counsel her. What would she gain by becoming a teacher or a CA? I advised her to surrender and become a servant of god,' Asaram maintained during the brief interrogation.[6]

Mishra found his answers unsatisfactory and placed the godman under arrest at 1 a.m. on 1 September 2013. The place of arrest was the airport at Indore, heavily guarded by armed personnel of the Central Industrial Security Force (CISF), and out of reach of any fanatic devotees.

After giving cursory answers to the questions, Asaram drank his milk-based Ayurvedic preparation out of the small pail he had brought with him, and which had been checked by the medical team to see if it was a poisonous substance. He drifted off into a seemingly undisturbed sleep soon after.

The airport provided some respite for the police team, now down to the original five, accompanied by CISF personnel— the armed guards and drivers had to drive back all the way to Jodhpur. They lounged around the waiting hall, some draping themselves across the seats for a brief nap. Others headed to the coffee stall to stay alert.

~

Thanks to their sources in the police, crime reporters in Jodhpur had got wind of the story. Of course, it was reported with a lot of masala. There was intense speculation as to why Asaram was being flown to the city. Some reported that the godman had taken ill. The Jodhpur police team had called the government doctor from Indore for a medical examination, who had earlier filed a report saying the godman was medically fit to travel.

---

[6]   Based on an interview with Chanchal Mishra.

As the news flashed on TV, Asaram's followers bought up most of the air tickets for the morning flight from Indore to Delhi, on which he was being transported. As a result, the police team did not get seats on either side of the same aisle.

Some of the followers were crying, some wanted to take selfies with their Bapu, some wanted to simply touch him. Most were angry with the police team.

'*Bapu nirdosh hai* (Bapu is not guilty)!' they would repeat time and again.

Satya Prakash and Satish Chandra Sharma sat with the godman, who stared out of the window. The other three had to control the followers. Both trios had seats towards the back of the plane. The cabin crew first tried to calm the passengers down, and then turned to the police team for assistance.

Asaram's followers were continuously getting up from their seats and either asking for blessings or trying to get photos of him. There was not much else they could do. Through all this commotion, the godman remained motionless and speechless.

Two of the air hostesses approached the police officers with a request. 'Excuse me, madam. My mother is a big follower of Asaram and listens to his *pravachan* (sermons),' said one. 'Can we please take a selfie with him to send to our mothers?'

Chanchal Mishra laughs as she recalls the moment.

'Judging by their uniform and gait, I always thought air hostesses are very sophisticated and ultra-modern. But, here these women were no less than any of the other diehard followers of Asaram!'

Mishra was to later make a note of this unexpected request in her investigation file. It was an example of the extent of Asaram's influence. Even when the man was under arrest, his followers were undeterred. They were more interested in getting a piece of the godman; they were hardly concerned about the crimes he stood accused of.

The plane landed at the Indira Gandhi International Airport in New Delhi. While deboarding, Asaram's followers tried to touch the godman and lie at his feet as he walked down the aisle and off the plane. A security vehicle was waiting on the tarmac. The five officers and their charge were whisked away to the VIP lounge. They were to board a connecting flight to Jodhpur.

Outside the airport, reporters and hundreds of Asaram's followers had gathered. But, they could no longer trail him. The CISF was already on alert and additional personnel had been deployed. When Mishra and a colleague strolled out briefly, CISF personnel stopped them and suggested they remain in the secured area. They were already faced with a restive waiting crowd.

The police planted a story that they might head to Jaipur with the godman. Many of the godman's followers boarded a flight to Jaipur instead. As a result, the flight carrying Asaram from Delhi to Jodhpur was fairly uneventful. By then, the police team had been awake for two days and two nights straight.

The waiting area outside the tiny airport in Jodhpur was teeming with cars, bikes and people, the crowds spilling over for kilometres on the road to the city. A large police contingent was stationed there for security.

When the team finally exited the airport in two cars, reporters, bystanders and the godman's followers flocked to them to get a glimpse of Asaram. Cameras were shoved into the vehicles as they tried to navigate their way out of the airport.

Just as they entered the city, a crowd of Asaram's followers suddenly came in the path of the cavalcade. A sudden application of brakes caused the police car at its head to turn turtle. Another stopped to assist it but the rest, including the one carrying

Asaram, had to keep moving to their destination to avoid a crowd building up around it.

The media was stationed outside the police headquarters and the women's police station. Asaram was taken to a guest house instead, where the police prepared the paperwork and conducted another round of interrogation before producing him before a magistrate at a court in Jodhpur.

The magistrate remanded him to police custody for a single day rather than the four days that had been asked for. Asaram was led away for a medical examination that included a 'potency test'.

The single day that Asaram spent in police custody coincided with 'Aja Ekadasi'. Asaram told the police that he observed the rituals associated with this event and would fast all day. The Aja Ekadasi fast requires a devotee to abstain from drinking water, a *nirjala upvaas*. Some orthodox believers will not even swallow their sputum and also keep a *satvik* fast the day before.

The investigators needed him to be at his functional best and, given his age, a fast in custody could lead to several complications. The police did not want his health to deteriorate while he was under their watch.

The potency test that is conducted on all those accused of rape is a three-stage test. It includes physical stimulation, which, graphic as it may sound, does not require actual touching of genitals. The second step is examination by a urologist and a psychiatric evaluator. There is another step in many rape cases called a Penile Colour Doppler, in which blood flow to the penis is checked through an invasive procedure.

Before the test, there were several news reports that Asaram was likely to be impotent. Impotency is often used as a substitute for erectile dysfunction.

When the team of three doctors approached the godman for the first stage of the test, he was affronted by the idea and did not want to allow it. It was an invasion of modern science on the spiritual life he professed to have led. The medical team explained that it was not an invasive procedure.

'*Yeh deh toh nashwar hai* (The body is mortal),' said the godman,[7] and gave them permission to proceed. He could have refused and sought a legal remedy instead.

One of the doctors used a feather to stroke the godman's penis and it responded to the attention immediately. The erection was achieved without drugs or other stimulation. This medical evidence would be classified as 'circumstantial' evidence for the court of law to show that he was physically able to have sex.

The testing of potency has been the subject of some controversy in India. In certain environments, a male organ may not respond to physical stimuli, which will then require the use of drugs, invasive procedures or tests. Many forensic experts recommend the use of collecting 'trace evidence' from the genitalia of the accused and the survivor, reserving potency tests for those who claim to be impotent.[8] In Asaram's case, the potency test was likely[9] to lead to a debate in terms of legally establishing the then new definition for rape following the 2013 amendment to Indian criminal law. The medical examination of Mita had not proven sexual assault.

---

[7] https://timesofindia.indiatimes.com/india/Asaram-cleared-potency-test-without-any-drugs/articleshow/22243949.cms accessed on 28 April 2018

[8] https://www.sciencedirect.com/science/article/pii/S2090536X16300715 published in December 2016 and accessed on 14 August 2018

[9] http://nipccd.nic.in/reports/posco/pol.pdf at page 114 accessed on 13 August 2018

During his statement to the police, Asaram did not deny that he had met with Mita or that he had spoken to her in private, when nobody else was present. He denied having assaulted her. Asaram accompanied the police team to the scene of the crime and identified the place where he met Mita.

The magistrate in Jodhpur did not extend the police remand to beyond the single day.

# 2

# God on Trial

The police did not have an easy time preparing the charge sheet. What helped was that Mita appeared to be intelligent and seemed to possess 'an IQ higher than that of the average child', as Chanchal Mishra told me later. Mita's responses to questions put to her by the police were accurate, even though Narayan Sai claimed[1] that she was mentally unstable. 'Her educational records (mark sheets) also reflect her intelligence,' Mishra told me.

At the Kamla Market police station in Delhi, the police had asked Mita if she could write the FIR, which she did. She was video-recorded doing so by the Delhi police. Following the FIR, the police took her for a medical examination at Lok Nayak Hospital in Delhi. The old legal definition of rape required

---

[1] https://www.business-standard.com/article/news-ians/after-police-custody-asaram-jailed-for-14-days-roundup-113090200943_1.html published on 2 September 2013 and accessed on 29 April 2018

medical proof that rape was committed. Absence of evidence would create 'reasonable doubt' in the eyes of the law. Asaram's followers continued to claim that there was no rape because there was no vaginal penetration.

This was a hurdle for Mishra. Most people, even within the police department, were classifying it under Section 354 of the Indian Penal Code (IPC), which deals with sexual harassment. Mishra's seniors decided to play the devil's advocate and said that the offence should be booked under Section 354. She had to convince them with reasoned arguments in order to include rape in the charge sheet.

'That is the kind of evidence in rape cases and the medical only corroborates it,' said Mishra. 'The medical did not show rape because there was no [vaginal] penetration. But, whatever other things she said were put down in the medical report, including the sexual assault. That is also a legal document and later it became a document with which her future statements and depositions could be compared. The intent of the lawmakers was to introduce this kind of sexual assault under rape and they wanted to differentiate it from the definition of sexual harassment under Section 354 of the IPC. There has to be some sort of a clear line between the definitions of Section 354 and Section 376. Earlier, everything other than penetration was prosecuted under Section 354. In the Nirbhaya case, the penetration using a rod was not covered under Section 376, which is why the law was amended. Now, any object that is used for any kind of sexual penetration is a clearly defined offence under Section 376.'

Mishra's single day of interrogating Asaram was countered by cross-examination that lasted for a year. Several of Asaram's lawyers, including Siddharth Luthra, Surana, Laddha, questioned her. Due to this, the work in the field office where she was posted suffered. Behind her back, other officers would call her 'pravasi' (foreign resident) commanding officer and comment that perhaps she should remain in Jodhpur. She would be in frequent contact with P.C. Solanki, Mita's lawyer. When Mita would break down after gruelling sessions in court, her family would call Mishra to counsel her and provide moral support. Mita's father would also consult her at times.

While the investigation was still under way, the police also had to arrest four co-accused—Shilpi, Sharath Chandra, Prakash and Shiva—and realized the challenge their arrest would pose because they were not high profile like their godman was. The TV cameras had relentlessly followed Asaram everywhere since the sexual assault complaint. The four co-accused could easily melt away.

Mishra hoped that they would surrender. Asaram's bail would be considered only after the charge sheet was filed in court. Without the four co-accused, the charge sheet could not be submitted which would in turn delay Asaram's chance at getting bail. Asaram's advisers seemed to understand this.

On 2 September 2013, a day after Asaram was brought back to Jodhpur, Shiva appeared at Jodhpur and made himself available for questioning. He was interrogated and placed under arrest.

Shilpi, Sharath and Prakash filed applications for 'anticipatory bail' before the district and sessions court in Jodhpur, which was not granted by the sessions court, nor later by the Jodhpur bench of the Jaipur High Court. Within fifteen minutes of the anticipatory bail being denied at the high court, Shilpi surrendered before the Jodhpur sessions court.

Shilpi has an MSc in psychology, and is the daughter of an income tax officer. Like Mita, her family members too were Asaram's disciples and she grew up to become a follower herself.

After completing her education, she forsook the option of a career for the chance to serve her guru. Shilpi had been made warden at the Chhindwara gurukul in July 2013, weeks before Mita approached her with a complaint about feeling dizzy.

Questioning Shilpi proved to be an uphill task for the police. They would try to coax answers out of her and meet with staunch denial in response. She withstood all their interrogation tactics—they raised their tones, played 'good-cop-bad-cop', flung facts at her. She remained unmoved. She had a narrative and stuck to it. Whenever her story was contradicted, she calmly responded with, 'No, it wasn't like that.'

The investigators suspected that Shilpi believed in ghosts and demons. She had told them that the ashram had given them literature about exorcism through occult practices, which the police were unable to find at the ashram. When asked for a location, she declined to disclose where she had kept the copies.

Sharath Chandra is an MTech from Hyderabad. Nobody from among his family were Asaram's followers. He chanced upon a satsang, was impressed and became a follower. Asaram had told the court earlier that he himself had nothing to do with the Chhindwara ashram. Following Sharath's interrogation, the police were able to chart out how Asaram ran the gurukul through a trust.

Chhindwara is a tribal-dominated district though the same cannot be said about its urban centre. It was ruled by the Gonds till it was colonized by the British.

The Chhindwara gurukul is run by a trust that was originally called the Sri Shakti Trust, which also owns the land and building where the gurukul stands. In the 1990s, Asaram acquired the trust and its properties and built an ashram there in 1997.

Even so, the godman maintained in court that he had nothing to do with the gurukul. The gurukul's director, Sharath's interrogation indicated that the trust that owned the gurukul was run by Asaram and the police could dig up the documents that proved the same. This was necessary to show that Asaram had raped the survivor while she was under his care and protection.

Asaram's gurukul is run according to his wishes and fundamentally serves as a residential school for the children of his followers. The full name of the Chhindwara gurukul is Sant Sri Asaramji Gurukul Higher Secondary School.

How Asaram came to acquire this trust and the land it owns is not known. The Jodhpur police did not go into it because for the purpose of the rape case, they simply needed to prove that Asaram operated the trust. But, elsewhere, other authorities were working on discovering the source of Asaram's funds.

Sharath and Prakash surrendered on the same day and time. They believed that once they cooperated with the police and a charge sheet was filed, Asaram would be granted bail. Prakash had a limited role and was present in Manai during the sexual assault. As the case progressed, it seemed that Prakash and Shiva would, in all probability, be acquitted. When it eventually happened, the police thought it must be because of a technical reason.

But, the investigators are convinced that the conspiracy could not have been hatched without Shiva being a part of it. The conspiracy involved getting Mita to Asaram after convincing her father to do so. All communication between the girl's father and Asaram took place through a mobile phone that was in Shiva's possession. Shiva would receive the calls and when Asaram was available and agreed to speak, he would pass the phone to him. At other times, Shiva directed the family where to come and when. Similarly, all communication between Sharath and Asaram was also filtered through Shiva. He was aware that Sharath and Shilpi had claimed that Mita was possessed by a spirit. The story about the possession was admitted by many, including Ranjit Deora (the disciple at whose house Asaram stayed). That story could not have been communicated to Asaram, except through Shiva. The police prepared an elaborate chart of all the phone calls between Sharath, Shiva and the girl's father.

On 6 November 2013, the charge sheet was finally submitted and the charges were framed by the court in Jodhpur in February 2014. That was also when the high court directed the Jodhpur court to hold day-to-day hearings for Asaram's trial.

The two main contentions that Asaram's defence lawyer picked up were the call detail records and the date of birth. The lawyer pointed out that call records do not necessarily mean that Sharath, Asaram and the girl's father were talking about her when they made the calls. The call recordings did not prove it.

Mishra pointed out that in May and June, there were no calls between Asaram and Sharath. In July, after school had reopened and Shilpi had joined, there were a few calls. But, between 6 August and 15 August 2013, there was a sudden spike in the number of calls between Sharath, Shilpi, the father and Asaram. The time frame coincided with that of the events that led to the sexual assault.

Mishra told the court that because of the sudden, unnatural spike in the number of calls between the accused and the co-accused, they inferred that these calls were related to the conspiracy to lure the girl to Asaram. The Protection of Children from Sexual Offences Act (POCSO) requires the accused prove their innocence, and so Asaram and the co-accused needed to provide proof of what those phone calls were about.

During the trial, Asaram's legal team claimed that there were discrepancies in Mita's age records. Mishra and her team had sought documents from two schools. The first was the gurukul. After the sexual assault, Mita did not return to the school, where she had studied from seventh to twelfth standard, and sought a transfer certificate. The said transfer certificate, issued as per the records of Asaram's gurukul, reflected a date of birth that proved she was a minor in August 2013. Besides, there were the admit card and mark sheet of her tenth standard board exams, which also showed the same date of birth and further proved that she was a minor when Asaram sexually assaulted her. The records of the primary school that she had studied at before joining the gurukul showed the same date of birth.

Asaram's legal team challenged and made detailed objections to each and every document adduced to prove that the girl was a minor in August 2013.

During the cross-examination, Asaram's lawyer asked Mishra why she had not gone beyond these two schools to earlier schools.

'I needn't have,' replied Mishra.

'The law with regard to victim and accused is settled,' says P.C. Solanki, Mita's lawyer.

Rule 12 of the Juvenile Justice Rules of 2007 (which was the law in question at the time) lays down the law for establishing the age of a minor.

'In case of a dispute with regard to age, the court will inquire into the age. The first proof is the certificate of matriculation,' Solanki continues.

Mita's date of birth in the gurukul's school records and her CBSE (Class X) records showed that she was a minor on the date of the sexual assault.

'In the absence of a matriculation certificate, the law requires a certificate issued by a school, excluding playschools,' explains Solanki. 'In the absence of that too, a certificate issued by a municipality, panchayat or local authority. Beyond that, a medical examination to establish the age of the person claiming to be a minor.'

Mishra had provided two layers of proof and had not looked beyond it because the law did not require her to. Asaram's defence said that she should have conducted a medical examination to determine the girl's age. 'This too is not required when we have adduced documents to the effect,' Mishra responded.

Asaram's defence team also grilled Mishra about why the police had not approached the girl's primary school. They stressed that there was no record for her first standard. Mishra said that was because Mita was directly admitted to the second standard instead of the first, after the school admission panel found her to be 'quite intelligent during the interview'. In effect, they had given her a double promotion.

Mishra told me she had experienced the same phenomenon herself. 'The school I studied in suggested to my parents that I skip the third standard. They thought that I could cope with fourth standard and could catch up with some of the third standard material by myself. This happens in small, private schools all the time,' she said.

When Asaram's defence team pressed Mishra about why she had not got the records from the playschool, she said she didn't need to as per the law, which specifically prohibits playschool records.

Asaram's defence team also argued that the date of birth records for Mita's brother were inaccurate and, by inference, her records must be inaccurate too. Mishra simply said that she did not have to probe anyone else's proof of date of birth except that of Mita.

Mishra's cross-examination went on from 9 July 2015 to 11 July 2016. She made it a point to be present at almost every court hearing. Those who observed Asaram in court during the various stages of the trial did not see him express any remorse or regret. His followers have maintained their faith in his innocence throughout and he has himself never admitted to any wrongdoing.

Asaram's team had produced some documents that contested Mita's date of birth. Hence, her date of birth records were re-investigated after the charge sheet was filed. By that time Mishra and her immediate superiors had been transferred out of Jodhpur. Additional Superintendent of Police Pahad Singh was given charge of the investigation. The document submitted by Asaram's team was from a playschool in Uttar Pradesh, run by another godman, who also happens to be a politician. Pahad Singh's investigation declined to consider the playschool record, which was explicitly prohibited by the law. He concluded that the date of birth in the charge sheet was based on legally accepted documents.

Though the counter date of birth document had been presented by Asaram's defence team, the trial court in Jodhpur did not accept it. The Supreme Court directed the trial court to take it on record. An appellate court can give the direction to take a document on record but it is up to the trial court to adjudicate on the document, its authenticity or its importance in establishing facts in the face of overwhelming evidence to the contrary.

Based on this direction, the trial court called for several records, which included ration cards, driving licences and several other statutory and other documents of Mita and her family members.

Amongst the documents produced by Asaram's team was a controversial insurance policy that the father had bought for his family. That policy document supposedly pegged the girl's age higher than in the school documents. It did not stand the test of court and a case for fraud was registered against the agent who supposedly made this policy.

Does an investigating officer need to be convinced of guilt or innocence either way? How does he or she maintain an objective stance?

'An investigating officer should not be convinced of what is written in a complaint either way,' says Mishra. 'I did not judge whether it was true or false. I had to dig up evidence for every angle and one cannot assume either guilt or innocence. After following the trail and the evidence points in a certain direction, it becomes clear.'

The most convincing factor in this case was the family's devotion towards Asaram. 'Their conduct was of hardcore followers. They had no motive for instituting a false case against their guru, whom they were devoted to. The father used to attend many of the satsangs and take neighbours and friends with him. He had enough resources to educate his children at a reputed English-medium school in his home town. But, instead, he chose to send her to his guru's school because he thought they would learn the same *sanskar* [culture] that he believed in. It was not just Mita but her younger brother too that the father sent to study at Asaram's gurukul,' says Mishra.

'How can one assume that a father will abuse his daughter to trap his own guru? For what motive? There was no contradiction between the statements of the girl and her parents, who were questioned individually. Eventually, all three—the father, his wife and the daughter—maintained their resolve and did not waiver through the nearly five years it took. No conspiracy can be so strong. The father was broken on the inside through the entire process, but he never broke down.'

A few times during the trial, the father told the investigators and Solanki that the trial had ruined him. There was a physical, mental, financial and spiritual cost of the entire ordeal—every word they had said was being judged too—but they never expressed any desire to back down or reach some sort of a compromise with Asaram.

During the investigation, nobody had threatened Mishra. But, when certain witnesses in the cases against Asaram and his son and heir, Narayan Sai, were attacked or killed, the police chanced upon intelligence that there could be an attempt on Mishra's life. The alleged assassinator, who claimed to be a hardcore follower of Asaram, had supposedly confessed to the Gujarat police that Mishra was on his hit list.

Meanwhile, Asaram's modus operandi was widely reported in the media. When he spotted a woman who he found appealing, he would allegedly ask his sevikas to fetch her. The sevikas would approach the woman, if required prise her from her family with the lure of an exclusive 'anushthan' (ritual) with their guru, brainwash her and then deliver her to the godman. This was corroborated by almost all the former aides of Asaram who testified against him in Jodhpur and later at a court in Gandhinagar in a separate rape trial.

Asaram had first seen Mita at Haridwar in May 2013. Shilpi was transferred soon after from the Motera ashram to the

Chhindwara gurukul as a warden in July 2013, where she was
directly in charge of Mita. In August 2013, when the girl fell ill,
Shilpi immediately declared that Mita was possessed and told
both the girl and her father that Asaram would himself carry out
the exorcism.

~

The witnesses, former aides of the godman, who testified were
common to the two rape trials and some had also deposed in
the Justice (retd) D.K. Trivedi commission that, between 2008
and 2013, had probed charges of occult practices against the
godman. The accusations were made by the parents of the
Vaghela cousins, Abhishek and Deepesh, whose mutilated
corpses were found on the bed of the Sabarmati river near
Asaram's headquarters, the ashram in Motera near Ahmedabad.

In 2014, Asaram's devotees attacked[2] Dinesh Bhagchandani,
who used to be a close aide of the godman and had even been a
shareholder in a shell company controlled by the godman. The
attackers were fleeing after flinging acid at Bhagchandani when
onlookers overpowered them. One of them supposedly had a
chit on his person—a hit list with the names of six witnesses.
This included Raju Chandak, who had been with the ashram
since 1982, and Amrut Prajapati and Rahul Sachan, both
Asaram's personal Ayurvedic physicians. The other names
included Rahul Patel, a volunteer with Asaram; the husband of

[2] https://www.indiatoday.in/magazine/the-big-story/story/
20150706-asaram-bapu-narayan-sai-rape-case-bail-witness-attack-
819966-2015-06-25 published on 25 June 2015 and accessed on
3 May 2018

the 'younger sister' who accused Asaram's son Narayan Sai of raping her in the Surat ashram; and Mita's brother. The last person was Narsingh Watani, a former follower of the godman. Chandak had been attacked in 2010 after he had deposed before the Justice Trivedi commission.

One of Bhagchandani's assailants was Kishore Bodke, a former personal attendant of the godman. He disclosed that Asaram's follower, Basavaraj Basu, had handed the targets to him. Some months later, another follower, Kartick Halder, was arrested[3] in Chhattisgarh. Halder is supposed to be the most extreme of them all and was accused of shooting at four witnesses—Mahendra Chawla, Akhil Gupta, Amrut Prajapati and Kirpal Singh. Three were killed while Chawla escaped with bullet injuries and a permanent, partial disability. Halder also shot at the former warden of Asaram's Chhindwara gurukul, Omprakash Prajapati, and his wife, Seema.

Halder had been a resident of the Motera ashram since the year 2000. During his interrogation, he revealed that he planned to buy an assault rifle and described himself as a 'fidayeen' (suicide attacker) for his Bapu.

Sachan went missing in November 2015. Before that, he had been in touch with a New Zealand–based lawyer of Indian origin, Bennet Castelino, who appealed to the Supreme Court on his behalf for enhanced security following attacks on witnesses in the cases against Asaram, as well as a Central Bureau of Investigation (CBI) probe into the attacks. Sachan had been attacked in the Jodhpur court premises by Satyanarayan Gwala earlier in 2015.

---

[3] https://www.abplive.in/india-news/ats-arrests-sharp-shooter-who-killed-3-witnesses-in-asaram-case-306027 published on 15 March 2016 and accessed on 3 May 2018

After parting ways with Asaram in 2013, Sachan had returned to his native Uttar Pradesh but was unable to stay with his parents out of fear that the godman would trace him there. He made ends meet through a small Ayurvedic practice.

Sachan reached out to Castelino through a website run by the lawyer. One sentence that he told him became the crux of their petition to the Supreme Court. 'I want to live at least till I complete my testimony in the Surat and Ahmedabad cases,' Sachan's affidavit to the apex court stated.[4]

Sachan testified that Asaram used medicines to boost his sexual prowess. The godman would mark out his victims by shining a torch at them during satsangs or smaller events, even at his own ashram, where the women were staying. Three of his female aides would then coax the woman to visit the godman and manipulate her into thinking of the guru as the supreme entity in her life. Sachan provided specific testimony about witnessing Asaram sexually assault women in Rajasthan, Gujarat and Haryana in 2003. Sachan told the court of Asaram's belief that when a spiritually enlightened man had sex with his disciples, it could not be considered assault or exploitation.

Sachan put Castelino in touch with others who became witnesses and told him that he could facilitate contact with a hundred more potential witnesses. The witnesses were cautious of Castelino but Sachan's introduction eased things. 'I understood that even their security personnel cautioned the witnesses against meeting me, but Rahul ensured that things went smoothly,' Castelino said.

---

[4] https://www.outlookindia.com/magazine/story/seeing-is-a-deadly-sin/298231 published on 19 December 2016 and accessed on 20 March 2018

Since Castelino was Christian, some have accused him, particularly faceless trolls on social media, of harbouring an anti-Hindu agenda. However, he has a track record of taking religious institutions to task over perceived wrongdoings. In the 1990s, when he lived in Mumbai, Castelino had taken on the church for corruption. Years later, after migrating to New Zealand, Castelino suspecting paedophilia by members of the Catholic Church, wrote to the Pope and started campaigns against it.

On 21 November 2015, Sachan contacted Castelino for what would be the last time. Then his phone went silent. It is not known what happened to him. Eventually Castelino approached the Allahabad High Court asking for a CBI probe. At the time of writing this, sources in the central probe agency told me that they believed that Sachan was alive and may have left the country.

Mahindra Chawla also gave lengthy testimonies to trial courts in Jodhpur and Surat against both Asaram and Narayan Sai. In 2016, I met Chawla's lawyer, Utsav Bains, who represented him in the Supreme Court. He's one of the few Indian lawyers who has an investigative bent of mind and likes to find out facts for himself, at times even launching himself in the field to do so. This is a difficult feat in India and lawyers mostly restrict themselves to arguing in court. Rare is the lawyer who gets neck-deep into finding facts for his clients, that too those for whom he is working on a pro bono basis. In 2012, his investigation contributed to breaking up a sexual exploitation and trafficking racket at a childcare home in Rohtak, Haryana.

Bains also represented Akhil Gupta's father, Naresh Gupta, and his wife. They had approached the apex court for a witness protection programme, especially since Chawla had been attacked despite being granted security. His guards were missing when Halder shot at him. Sachan also had security cover when he went missing.

Bains had rallied some of the witnesses to the apex court, which took notice of the lawyer's arguments. The court issued[5] a notice to the state government and said it would frame guidelines for witness protection in India, which led the central government to draft proposed guidelines for witness protection.

Before the charge sheet was submitted, Asaram asked the Supreme Court for a media gag, which was refused. The godman had had his share of negative coverage 2008 onwards, when the mutilated corpses of the Vaghela cousins were discovered.

Asaram did not make it easy for the police while in custody. He frequently complained of severe pain due to trigeminal neuralgia and his health and age were one of the main arguments in seeking bail. On one occasion, he complained of being so sick that he was unable to get up from his bed to even go to the bathroom. The court pulled up the policemen who escorted Asaram to jail every day and believed him to be fine.

The next day, Asaram came out of the jail in good spirits and singing a bhajan. He had his hands up in the air and belted out lyrics with vim, '*O jogi re, kya jadoo hai tere pyaar mein.*' At one point he also raised his hands close to his mouth and twiddled his fingers as if he were playing a flute. Just before he

5   https://www.outlookindia.com/website/story/missing-asaram-case-witness-sc-issues-notices-to-all-states-to-frame-witness-pro/300595 published on 21 August 2017 and accessed on 22 July 2018

boarded the police van to go to prison, he spotted a policeman surreptitiously recording this scene on a camera. The video went 'viral' on social media.

The neural condition that Asaram complained of led him to demand better healthcare in custody. The apex court denied him bail but since the Jodhpur prison did not have the requisite equipment to examine him, it gave permission for the godman to be transported to New Delhi for an examination by doctors at the All India Institute of Medical Sciences (AIIMS).

At the hospital, before his examination, the nurse who brought him breakfast reported Asaram comparing[6] her to butter and inquiring if she was from Kashmir because her cheeks were as red as apples. It is not known in what context this was said, but when a rape accused makes such remarks, there is usually only one way of interpreting them.

The day after the verdict was delivered, Asaram assumed the role of prisoner number 130 at Jodhpur jail. Life would not be very different from what it had been since September 2013. Inmates are no longer known as numbers based on a judicial expansion of human rights. Jail authorities also do not stress on their wearing the standard uniforms unless senior officials are visiting. In April 2018, Jodhpur jail had around forty-five guards working in three shifts to handle 1,450 inmates. That meant that at any given time,

---

[6] https://www.deccanchronicle.com/nation/current-affairs/270916/at-aiims-asaram-bapu-compares-nurse-to-butter-her-cheeks-to-kashmiri-apples.html published on 29 September 2016 and accessed on 20 April 2018

there were around fifteen staff members on duty who were in charge of prisoners and the jail's security.

On 27 April 2018, Asaram released[7] an audio statement to his followers from within the prison. It was uploaded to the website of his organization. '*Achchhe din ayenge* (Good days will come),' Asaram had told[8] his followers through the audio clip. The godman thanked his followers for not turning up in Jodhpur on the day of the verdict. He indicated that they would appeal the verdict, which had been given by a lower court. There were higher courts, and 'the truth cannot be concealed'.

The administration was furious. How did he breach security? Did he have a phone? How did he manage to get the message out?

Reporters made their way to the prison and tried to meet the jail superintendent, who decided to address the media before wild speculation took a toll on his image. Lalit Parihar, a Jodhpur-based journalist, arranged for me to meet Vikram Singh, who was in charge of Jodhpur Central Jail. Singh had recently been promoted to deputy inspector general of prisons, which meant he had charge of over forty-six jails in the Jodhpur–Bikaner range. He was Jodhpur jail's superintendent through most of Asaram's stay there.

After a few minutes' wait, an entry in the prison's register, and we were directed to Singh's residential quarters outside the walls of the jail. He was giving interviews to a television news

---

7    https://indianexpress.com/article/india/good-days-will-come-asaram-says-in-viral-audio-clip-5154945/ published on 28 April 2018 and accessed on 14 August 2018

8    https://khabar.ndtv.com/news/india/asaram-says-good-days-will-come-in-viral-audio-clip-1844218 published on 28 April 2018 and accessed on 14 August 2018

crew and responding to each of their queries without batting an eyelid.

Yes, Asaram had made the call, but as an inmate of the jail, he had the right to make a certain number of calls to some specified phone numbers. As far as the prison authorities were concerned, he had called one of those numbers but they did not know that someone else would be recording it or playing it live through the internet. The state's home department was not pleased and had asked for a departmental probe into the matter. After the television crew wound up, Singh eased up a little and we started a chat about the godman's stay, even as some other journalists sat around.

'Many influential people had come to visit Asaram in jail,' said Vikram Singh, but stopped short of naming them.

'Asaram's followers would approach MLAs and MPs [lawmakers]. They would call me and say, "*Dekh lena* (Please see what you can do)." We have to work both according to the rules and also according to them,' said Singh.

Some of his followers would go to the extent of committing some petty crime in Jodhpur just so they would be thrown into prison and get a glimpse of the godman. But, the prison authorities would figure out which ones were followers and keep them away from the godman to dissuade other followers from trying this tactic to get a 'darshan'.

In March 2018, Salman Khan was convicted for hunting a protected species of deer. He strode into Jodhpur jail as if he was there to shoot for a film, and waved generously to fans among prisoners and staff who had come to greet him.

Once the other formalities were over, the jail superintendent took him to meet Asaram—the two most high-profile inmates of the prison.

The actor discussed several things with the godman and discovered they had one thing in common—trigeminal neuralgia or 'suicide disease', the neural disorder both of them allegedly suffered from.

In 2011, it was widely reported[9] that the Bollywood film star had been suffering from the disease for seven years. The pain was apparently so severe that its management requires high-dosage painkillers and antidepressants to deal with. In August that year, Khan underwent[10] a five-hour-long neurosurgery after he started experiencing difficulty chewing and swallowing food. Despite the surgery, he continued on medication for some time.

In jail, he sympathized with Asaram and told him about the shooting pain in his mouth and on his face and how the surgery abroad had helped. He advised Asaram to get the same surgery.

Jail authorities allowed Asaram's staff to visit the godman. They would come to consult with him about various functions that had to be discharged for the trusts and other organizations under the godman's name. The godman was not around, nor was his son, and decisions had to be taken for the management of the trusts.

Asaram's family never came to meet him, except Narayan Sai, who met his father before his own arrest in November 2013. He even held a press conference from their ashram in Pal, near Jodhpur city.

---

[9]   https://web.archive.org/web/20140715123125/http://www.
      hindustantimes.com/news-feed/archives/salman-suffering-from-the-
      suicide-disease/article1-737044.aspx accessed on 28 May 2018
[10]  https://timesofindia.indiatimes.com/entertainment/hindi/bollywood/
      news/Salman-Khans-jaw-pain-returns/articleshow/12108139.cms
      accessed on 29 May 2018

Most of Singh's time administering the prison was spent dealing with Asaram. 'Not a few hours, but let's say 50 per cent of the time goes towards him,' said Singh.

'How so?' I asked.

'Well, you are also here because of him.'

Asaram's stay at the jail was not violent except for an altercation between him and Parsaram Bishnoi, a co-accused in the 2011 murder of Bhanwari Devi. One day, there was a clash between Bishnoi and another inmate near the hospital. Asaram was close by and smiled during the altercation. Bishnoi assumed that Asaram was responsible for staging the entire incident and threatened the godman. This frightened Asaram and he requested the prison authorities for help. The prison authorities moved Parsaram from the hospital and into the barracks.

Outside the prison, a slap or jostling is turned into a gang war in some media reports, Singh had told me. The same was made of Asaram's altercation with Bishnoi and soon it was reported in some quarters that Bishnoi had assaulted the godman. 'It was an exaggeration,' Singh said.

Prakash was the only one among the five co-accused who was granted bail but nobody filled his bail bond, nor did he seek to leave the godman's side and remained in prison throughout the trial. Apparently, whenever Asaram was unhappy about something, he would use Prakash as his punching bag.

Asaram's routine in jail is akin to that of a retired person. He mostly wakes up early and goes for a morning walk, followed by yoga and a bath before heading for breakfast. While Asaram was an undertrial, his meals would come from the ashram at Pal, for which the trial court had granted him permission. The law does not give any such special privilege to a convict. They have to partake of the food that is prepared for inmates unless there is a special case, permitted by a court.

The ration for undertrial prisoners is slightly less than for convicts but there is a high wastage in the Jodhpur jail. Not all the rotis made are consumed and have to be thrown away. Several years ago, the jail had organized for these to be delivered to a cowshed. The practice was stopped after some cows allegedly died after consuming the stale rotis.

'But the food here is very good. I have not seen any of the inmates lose weight after eating here. You should try some if you get an opportunity,' Singh quipped.

Prakash would read aloud to Asaram from newspapers (usually *Rajasthan Patrika*) and scriptures including the Bhagavad Gita after breakfast. This was not because Asaram had any problem with his vision; he had in fact told members of the jail staff who wore spectacles that he could fix their vision problems too. No such miracle had taken place till the time of writing this.

On most afternoons, Asaram takes a nap if he does not have to be present in court, and wakes up for a brisk walk in the evening. He is exempt from working in the jail because of his age. He was around 81 at the time he was pronounced guilty by the Jodhpur trial court and the prison's oldest inmate. But he was not the only person serving time for sexually assaulting a minor. Singh said that most of the inmates were those accused of sexual assault on children and women.

The jail authorities say that unlike other inmates, Asaram has never been caught with any contraband nor has he demanded any special favours. While he awaited trial, the court had allowed him meals cooked in the ashram and his Ayurvedic medicines to be delivered to the prison.

In the evening, the prison is locked down, and the wardens or the superintendent sometimes sit with Asaram for a chat before his dinner of two rotis and milk. The topics vary from spiritual discussion to political issues.

'He still has a positive opinion about Modiji,' said Singh, touching on a topic that features in almost all political discussions in the country. 'Asaram described Modi as "*karmath*" (one who executes his duties).'

The barracks in the jail have electric fans to combat Rajasthan's desert weather. It is an irony that one of the main items produced by the inmates are coolers. Asaram was given a special quarter in the prison. Earlier, the special court under the repealed Terrorists and Disruptive Activities (TADA) law used to be held within the jail premises. That courtroom was now defunct and had been turned into a quarter for the godman. His verdict was also delivered in that same courtroom. It was as if the court in Jodhpur had come to his doorstep to deliver the verdict.

This courtroom-turned-quarters has a bed and a small television set. But, Asaram does not seem to have much interest in television and dissuades his aide Prakash from watching it too.

While the trial was pending, Asaram did engage with others about the crime he was accused of. He apparently told some of the jail staff, 'Why would I call a girl from 1,800 km away, and make her parents sit outside while I assault her?'

That question seemed to make sense to several people who were not his followers. During the course of research, I met a few volunteers of the Rashtriya Swayamsevak Sangh (RSS). In Jodhpur, one such RSS functionary did not believe that the charges were genuine. After Gurmeet Ram Rahim's conviction in a rape case, the Akhil Bharatiya Akhara Parishad (an umbrella

council of fourteen Hindu religious bodies) had declared
Asaram and Ram Rahim as 'dhongi sadhus' (fake godmen) in a
list released in August 2017. It was followed up with three other
lists, all of which included Asaram.

Asaram was not daunted by this list. Shortly after his name
appeared on it, a TV camera followed him up the steps to the
trial court at the Jodhpur district court.

Reporter: 'Sir, the list says you are neither a saint nor a
preacher. What do you say, which class of godman are you?'

Asaram: 'I am in the category of donkeys.'

Those who did not admit the authenticity of the charges
against Asaram believed that the prime reason for his conviction
was for being 'vachaal', which literally means one with a loose
tongue.

'He made many political statements. A spiritual leader
should not meddle in political matters and see, they eventually
had him packed off to jail. Then he threatened others, who have
ensured that he remains in prison for the rest of his life, that
too the rest of his natural life,' a Rajasthan government official
told me. 'He once said about a powerful politician, "Main usko
bhasm kar doonga (I will turn him into ash)." Such statements
have had a rebound effect.'

The Jodhpur trial being over, Asaram was likely to be moved
to Gujarat to face trial in another rape case in Ahmedabad, based
on a complaint by another former follower. While the Jodhpur
trial progressed, he attended the proceedings in Ahmedabad
through videoconferencing.

# 3

# Life till Death

Jodhpur was simmering for some days before the verdict, both literally and figuratively. There was anticipation in the air as the day of the verdict drew near.

None can predict what will happen in a judgment till the moment it is delivered. Many lawyers try to keep their clients grounded and undercommit, hoping to overdeliver. The more seasoned lawyers stay away from their phones.

In a high-profile case, which has been building up for years, it's slightly different. A very senior lawyer who had worked his way up from trial courts once told me that on the night before one of the most important cases of his life (a famous murder case), he felt a pain in his chest.

'We rushed to the emergency ward of a hospital but were told it was only a panic attack. My client never came to know of this episode. My wife prayed all night. I had to take a nerve relaxant and sleep. The next day, I was half an hour late for court and all the way to the courtroom I kept thinking that the judge would hold it against me,' he said. 'The verdict was not in my favour but once that finality has come upon you, you just move on. Even though it's your client's case, you put your heart and soul into it.'

P.C. Solanki had put a little more than four years of his life into the day-to-day hearings that the Asaram trial had generated. A lot of sleepless days and nights had gone into it. The phalanx of lawyers who appeared for Asaram, backed by their respective juniors, at various stages was impressive: Ram Jethmalani, Mukul Rohatgi, K.T.S. Tulsi, Vikas Singh, S.K. Jain, Salman Khurshid, Siddharth Luthra, Soli Sorabji, Shekhar Naphade, Raju Ramachandran, C.V. Nagesh, K.K. Manan, J.S. Choudhary, Mahesh Bora, M.R. Singhvi, Sajjan Raj Surana, N.K. Bohra, Rajendra Choudhary, Onkar Singh Lakhawat, Vaid Prakash, Shokat Ali, Somnath Ladha, Sudeep Pasbola, Bhavit Sharma, Umaid Shrimali, Pradeep Choudhary, Nishant Bora and Umardhan Lakhawat.

This list is important because it shows the kind of legal scholarship and court craft that Solanki was up against. In other courts, some of the witnesses had lawyers appearing out of a pure fighting spirit, pitting their own meagre savings against the might of some of the highest-paid lawyers to practise in India. Sometimes they would manage to get a senior advocate to appear in the Supreme Court. Chawla's lawyer Utsav Bains, who represented some of the other witnesses too, would sometimes engage a senior advocate to appear. Other times, the seniors would be engaged elsewhere; Bains's client certainly did not have the money to tear them away.

Mita and her family stuck with Solanki. Some months before the sexual assault took place, he had conducted a session on the POCSO law for recruits at a police training academy. By the time the case was over, he knew every comma and full stop of the law and why it was there.

None could accuse Solanki of being an 'anti-Hindutva' agent, as many of Asaram's followers said in public about anyone who they saw as working against the godman. Solanki's mother, Aaichuki Devi, had brought him up to believe in god and Hindu traditions. From a young age, he would attend programmes at an RSS shakha and was a state joint secretary of the Akhil Bharatiya Vidyarthi Parishad (ABVP) as a student at Jodhpur's Jai Narain Vyas University. His railway mechanic father had educated all his three daughters—two of whom became gazetted officers—and the son read for a master's in law.

Solanki had long been an admirer of Ram Jethmalani and looked forward to meeting him some day. He never expected that it would be as opposing counsel. In court, Jethmalani pressed for bail for Asaram and argued that it was not rape because medical examination did not reveal penetration, which Solanki argued was not essential under the POCSO law.

Jethmalani also took strong objection that, in this case, medical examination was conducted before the FIR was lodged, which, he told the court, was against the settled law. Solanki pointed out that Section 27 of POCSO allowed the investigator to conduct a medical exam even without lodging an FIR. Jethmalani demanded a copy of the bare act, read the concerned section and sat down speechless.

Solanki appeared and argued at the trial as well as at the higher courts, where Asaram's lawyers filed applications. In the Supreme Court, Asaram filed an application and former union minister and senior advocate Salman Khurshid appeared on his behalf. Khurshid made oral arguments for interim bail, citing the godman's poor health. He produced a medical certificate for trigeminal neuralgia, and said that Asaram required immediate gamma surgery, a facility that was not available in Jodhpur jail.

Solanki objected that no bail application had been shared with him and said that Asaram should be examined by a medical board.

The Supreme Court constituted a board under doctors of the state-owned medical college in Jodhpur, who said they did not have the equipment to examine the said condition. So, Asaram was sent to AIIMS which ruled that his disease did not require gamma surgery and his bail was denied by the Supreme Court.

When BJP lawmaker Subramaniam Swamy appeared on Asaram's behalf as a pleader, Solanki insisted the court could not proceed unless Asaram personally told the court that Swamy could appear on his behalf. So, Swamy had to wait in court for an hour till Asaram was produced.

Senior lawyer Raju Ramachandran also argued a bail application on behalf of Asaram before the Jodhpur High Court while the trial was going on. He said that the trial, despite day-to-day hearings, was considerably delayed. Solanki pointed out that ultimately Asaram was responsible for the delay because his trial lawyers were conducting lengthy cross-examinations in court. At the time, Chanchal Mishra was being cross-examined and it had already lasted for months, and eventually a whole year. Mita, too, had been cross-examined for close to a month. The high court agreed with Solanki.

Solanki later made a chart comparing how long the examinations and cross-examinations of the major witnesses took, to show who was responsible for the delay. Every defendant has the legal right to cross-examine and scrutinize all the aspects of the trial, but Solanki's point was to show that his prosecution had not caused the delay at any point.

| Witness | No. of days in examination-in-chief | No. of days in cross-examination |
|---------|-------------------------------------|----------------------------------|
| Mita | 4 (11 April to 21 April 2014) | 23 (13 May to 13 June 2016) |
| Mita's father | 2 (2 January and 3 January, 2015) | 16 (5 January to 22 January 2015) |
| Mita's mother | 2 (16 July and 17 July 2014) | 17 (8 October to 25 November 2014) |
| Chanchal Mishra | 11 (9 July to 22 July 2015) | 49 (29 July 2015 to 11 July 2016) |

While Mishra's cross was effectively for forty-nine days, she was in court and her cross-examination went on for a year and was recorded in 176 pages. The prosecution's evidence lasted for two years and five months, of which a substantial share was cross-examination of witnesses by Asaram's lawyers.

The evening before the judgment, Solanki sat down at his desk. There was no policeman or security guard anywhere on the lane, though a police official later told me that they had had a plain-clothes man keeping watch. When Solanki called me to his house after dinner, the street was empty.

I walked over to find him dictating an application on behalf of his client. His man Friday, Vipul, was typing away furiously at a desktop personal computer. Solanki creased his lips into a perfunctory smile, gestured to me with his fingers to sit down, and went back to the dictation.

Solanki's friend and journalist, Lalit Parihar, strolled in a little while later. We smiled and greeted each other without

any words. We silently showed each other jokes on WhatsApp
to pass the time till Solanki took a break. The four of us were
squeezed into Solanki's six-foot-by-ten-foot air-conditioned
chamber, made smaller by law books in a glass-fronted wooden
bookcase and neatly piled stacks of hardbound files.

There was no hint of nervousness on Solanki's face. If he
was feeling tense, it was not discernible in his demeanour.

'So, what are you expecting tomorrow?' I ventured. I could
feel Parihar's eyes boring into the side of my head.

'Guilty,' said Solanki.

'Sentence?'

'At least ten years on each count,' he responded. (He was
miles off, as we learnt later.)

Solanki went back to his application. Once in a while,
he would want to look at his notes, get up, walk over to the
eighteen hardbound volumes of case files on the other side of
the room. He would stroke one and inspiration would seem to
hit him. He was trying to work out the grounds for a demand
for compensation.

'Mita's family has spent lakhs of their money travelling to
Jodhpur. They have lost out on business, society, relationships
and so forth. They would come here and be cooped up in a hotel
room or visit my chamber here and that meant that her father
was unable to keep a close hand on his business for a long time,'
he said.

The family would stay in a single room, the constricted
space often causing friction. The commonality of purpose
prevailed through the entire time, a period of nearly five years,
though. The die had been cast.

Solanki recollected his conversations with them, looked
at his handwritten notes—no doubt from a conversation with

them—and continued to dictate. The four of us sat there for a long time, well past midnight, till the dictation ended. Even Parihar, a night romper, was bleary-eyed by then.

'Sir, how do you plan to get to court tomorrow? The streets will be crowded,' Parihar asked.

'I've got a bicycle especially for this occasion,' answered Solanki.

He didn't break into a smile. Still, we wondered aloud if he was joking.

'It's an imported bicycle.'

'It's the day of the judgment. Aren't you worried about security, at least tomorrow?' I asked Solanki and exchanged a glance with Parihar. One of Asaram's supporters had attacked a witness outside the courtroom.

Solanki did not bat an eyelid. When journalist Priyanka Dubey was in Jodhpur to report on the case for the *Caravan* magazine in 2016, she sat pillion with Solanki on his scooter, as did I. He had taken us (on separate occasions) on his scooter. The hour of the night and the empty streets did not seem to bother him. In many other lower-risk cases, I have seen lawyers with three or four security officers assigned to protect them. Some are humble, and tell the security officers to walk unobtrusively. Then there are some who like to have an entourage of safari suits around them. Nobody has done a study to find if it gets them more cases.

Parihar checked his watch, announced it was 1 a.m. and was about to get up when Solanki sat him down.

The court would be convened at 8 a.m. and the verdict delivered immediately afterwards. There was some confusion if the court would be convened at the district court premises and moved to the jail, or it would convene at the jail. Solanki was not in a mood to clarify any of these trivial details that could make a nervous wreck out of a cameraperson looking to capture crucial moments.

The media had already decided to split its attention—the majority of the reporters were to set up and wait outside the jail premises; the others would update from the court premises and shift to the jail, as per the situation.

Around 2 a.m., I was wondering how I would make it to court in time, when Solanki announced that since I was an out-of-towner, I should be at his residence by 7 a.m. That was our cue to leave. Outside the house, Parihar climbed astride his motorcycle and paused.

'If he does get on a bike, please shoot a short video and send it to me,' he said as he kicked his motorcycle to life and sped off.

At 3 a.m., Solanki sent me a message on WhatsApp and was off to sleep. At 7 a.m., Vipul was sitting in the waiting room adjacent to Solanki's chamber on the ground floor of his residence. He was all nervous smiles but his boss was nowhere to be seen.

Solanki's mother appeared, offered me water, tea, breakfast and much else. She came outside and shot a look at her eight-year-old grandson, who was playing in the yard of a neighbour's house across the narrow lane. The neighbour kept a watchful eye on him too.

'No school today?' asked an acquaintance who was passing by.

'*Aaj yudh ka din hai* (It is the day of battle),' said the boy.

Solanki had decided to keep his son at home that day. He was under the spotlight and everyone knew his family. He didn't want to be worrying about them.

When Solanki did appear he seemed enmeshed in a whirlwind of activities. He arranged the documents he would need, got copies of his application for compensation. This went on for nearly an hour till he was finally ready.

Parihar called me to ask if I had reached.

'Is Solankiji really coming on a bicycle? Do you see a bicycle?' Parihar asked.

Outside, Solanki's Alto had been uncovered, cleaned and prepared. He rarely took his car out onto congested Jodhpur roads. Besides, the few routes out of his neighbourhood led either through the busy Ghantaghar (clock tower) area or its adjoining market. The scooter was much more practical.

'*Phir bhi*. By chance, if he gets on a bicycle, I want a video,' said Parihar.

Around 8 a.m., Solanki emerged. His papers and files followed, and were loaded into the car. Before leaving, he hugged his son.

'Best of luck, buddy,' the child told his father. ('I never call him Papa. He is my friend,' he had told me a month earlier.)

Solanki bent down and touched his mother's feet and she put her hand on his head to bless him. Neighbours had gathered to see off their warrior, with the majestic Mehrangarh Fort looming in the background.

We took our seats in the car and headed for the courtroom. The streets were still quite empty. Solanki drove past the clock tower and pulled up next to the Mukteshwar Gangeshwar temple at Nayee Sadak. He brought his palms together in reverence, moved his lips in prayer, and drove on.

The court premises, shared with the Jodhpur bench of the high court of Rajasthan, had more security than usual. Uniformed police constables at the gate looked at us, their gaze intensifying as they recognized the lawyer from TV. Solanki returned their smiles.

He parked close to the courtroom, tore out a crisply starched lawyer's band from its plastic bag and tied it around his neck. In one motion, he shrugged the black coat on to his shoulders and strode off towards the court building.

Some journalists had gathered outside, since they were not allowed inside. A camera or two had been placed. They wanted a quick sound bite from Solanki but he shook his head, walked into the building and climbed up the stairs to the first floor.

A reporter had applied to the court asking it to allow journalists to cover the verdict from inside the jail premises. It was denied.

Keeping the media outside proved to be a circus enough.

Some journalists were already sending live pieces from outside the courtroom. There were some police cars, a police van, an escort for the judge's car, and other vehicles. Amandeep Singh Kapoor, DCP, Jodhpur East, was tasked with supervising security. The commissioner trusted him because Kapoor had ensured everything went smoothly when Salman Khan was in his town for the blackbuck poaching case. Many people had lined up to see the star, hoping that Khan would be incarcerated there. Security needed to be tightened once the court pronounced a guilty verdict. Khan had stayed there for some days before his sentence was suspended, pending appeal. Kapoor had monitored the security every step of the way.

~

The police sought Asaram's cooperation for the day of the verdict. He sent out a message, including through media advertisements, asking his followers to stay away from Jodhpur.

'Nobody needs to come to Jodhpur city on the 25th. Bapu will meet everyone in Pal ashram (10 km south of the city limits) on the 26th and he will address everyone else through TV broadcasts from there,' the followers had been told.

The city was devoid of followers, not that they hadn't tried to sneak in. The police were wary of a repeat of what had happened at Panchkula just seven months prior, when Gurmeet Ram Rahim's followers had gathered in the thousands and rioted at the 'guilty' verdict.

There was a Section 144 order imposed by the authorities in Panchkula but had since become the subject of a dispute before the court on the wording employed in the order.

Supporters of Dera Sacha Sauda had gathered in Panchkula, waiting for a darshan of their godman, when he would appear in court for the verdict in the rape trial. Nobody knew of course why they had arrived four days ahead. They were camping close to the Panchkula district and sessions court, which houses the CBI court that eventually pronounced Gurmeet Ram Rahim guilty.

As the followers ran amok, it led to a massive breach of law and order and left several people dead and injured since the police had to resort to force to control the situation. There were videos of fanatic followers who became violent and also videos of some of them being shot down by security personnel.

Jodhpur city police wanted to avoid such violence at any cost. On 3 August 2015, the Jodhpur bench of the Rajasthan High Court issued a notification transferring Asaram's trial to the jail premises. From 5 August 2015, all proceedings were to be held in the Jodhpur Central Jail, where the godman was being held.

Not only were Asaram's supporters creating chaos in the city, but the more violent among them had slipped in amongst the larger mass of non-violent supporters and attacked witnesses and threatened to harm others, including senior police officers such as Ajay Pal Lamba, the DCP who had supervised Chanchal Mishra's investigation.

Asaram's legal team filed a writ petition challenging this notification for the trial to be held at the jail. Since there were day-to-day hearings at the trial, lawyers appearing in the case were tied up for a substantial portion of each day in attending proceedings. This also required several hours of preparation every week. For them, it meant letting go of many cases that would come their way,

Shifting the trial to the jail would also include travel away from the court, cutting off more hours from other cases. For the lawyers, that would cause further loss in fees.

On 11 September 2015, the Rajasthan High Court passed an interim order holding its notification of 3 August 2015 in abeyance.

During a subsequent hearing, the high court observed that Asaram's lawyer had assured the bench that the godman would appeal to his supporters to not gather near Jodhpur jail, the court premises or in any other place in the city. The high court also noted that Asaram's appeal to his followers would be published in both state and national daily newspapers.

The high court also gave wide powers to the police and the district administration to take appropriate security measures and issue orders under Section 144 (criminal procedure code) to restrict Asaram's followers from gathering in the city and inconveniencing its residents.

In its April 2018 affidavit, the Jodhpur police noted that the order, the advertisement or security restrictions imposed did not have an effect on Asaram's supporters while the trial continued.

'These supporters continued to throng the city in large numbers to get a glimpse of Asha Ram [Asaram]. Often, they tried to run after and climb the vehicle carrying Asha Ram and tried to enter the court perimeter by breaking the security cordon of the police,' the deputy police commissioner had written in the affidavit.

'That on the dates of hearing in the trial court, while Asha Ram used to be taken to court, a huge crowd used to assemble there and created a difficult situation to maintain law and order. Even on return from court, the supporters used to block the police vehicles in which Asha Ram was being taken. However, the police personnel on duty worked hard to ensure maintenance of law and order situation. Such reports and photographs have regularly appeared in the local media. The hon'ble court has also been apprised from time to time.'

The judges did not need to be told because, first, the media broadcast these live images frequently. Second, the judges would have witnessed some of it first-hand and knew that delivery of justice under these conditions was tough.

In April 2017, his supporters had again climbed on to the van carrying Asaram to court. They hung from its sides and to the grilles on its windows. Others ran behind it wailing, while Asaram looked on.

Due to the nuisance in the court premises and on the journey to and from it, the high court passed similar orders (for Asaram to restrain his supporters) on 1 May 2017. During the hearing, the court gave a stern warning to Asaram's lawyers to advise their client to comply.

It did not have any effect, though, and on several occasions, Asaram's followers would en masse rush past the security cordon and surround the van. A police guard who had been inside the vehicle told me that it felt quite menacing and a few times, he had felt that they might topple the van or even break its doors. There would always follow a tussle between the security personnel and Asaram's followers. A few batons would take care of the situation but it was an undesirable action to resort to.

A similar situation occurred in July 2017 and it was again brought to the notice of the high court, which passed yet another order.

When the final arguments in the trial were ultimately over and the judgment had been reserved for 25 April 2018, the police started keeping a tab on Asaram's ashram and deployed its intelligence officials to monitor some of the key people involved.

Through various means, the police were able to find out that several followers planned to converge on Jodhpur for the verdict. The administration was apprehensive of a much larger number turning up. The visuals from Panchkula figured in discussions during high-level meetings.

The Rajasthan police headquarters in Jaipur was also concerned. They knew that all eyes around the country were upon them, waiting for the verdict, keen to see if the blood and mayhem would match that of Panchkula. The police wanted to ensure that the focus was on the verdict and not on their security preparation.

The only way out was to ensure that Asaram did not come out of the jail for the verdict. A not-guilty verdict would mean that followers would mill around to celebrate and create one kind of chaos. The other kind of chaos would be if he were pronounced guilty.

The police did not tell the court as much in writing, but there was a fear of some of the more fanatical followers self-immolating near the court or elsewhere in the city.

'We have to ensure the security at the court, safety of the city and maintain law and order. It will be difficult to manage every aspect if we have to deal with multiple possibilities. We have ensured deployment of additional forces from outside the city but we have to try and fortify against any possibilities,' a senior police officer told me at the time.

The Jodhpur police also referred to the chaos around the Gurmeet Ram Rahim verdict in its affidavit. They requested the court to transfer the proceedings to the Jodhpur Central Jail where Asaram was being held. They also asked that the high court direct Asaram to appeal, through the media, to his followers to stay away from Jodhpur on the day of the verdict.

The court found the request reasonable and shifted the pronouncement of the verdict from the courthouse to the jailhouse. Besides, there used to be a TADA court in that jail, and some minor arrangements would convert it into a makeshift courtroom once again.

This is the very room that Asaram had been given as a special privilege, away from the rest of the prisoners. He was not in a cell, unlike what reports had claimed.

The prison superintendent later told me that an air conditioner was installed just for the one day that the court was to convene for the verdict. This seemed contrary to the rumours that Asaram was lodged in an air-conditioned room in the jail.

With the verdict shifted to the jail, the police set about securing the city. Many hotels had already taken bookings for the time, which got cancelled at the last moment as Asaram's personal appeal went out. The police also briefed the media that it would monitor all entry points into the city.

From a few days before the verdict, the police started to check people at bus stands and railway stations. Checkposts were manned twenty-four hours a day and there would be random checks on vehicles carrying a number of passengers.

Such checks are conducted by random 'profiling'—a skill that one often sees policemen and some journalists pick up on the job. On the day of the verdict, I saw a policeman stationed outside the courthouse in Jodhpur shooing away some bystanders. I asked him if they were Asaram's followers. The confident retort was, 'No, they don't look like this. See, the man standing wearing slippers and a towel wrapped like a scarf around his neck? See, he even has a plastic bag in his hand? That is an Asaram supporter.'

The hit-and-miss approach yielded some results for the police who managed to nab a handful of people in the days immediately before the verdict who had either not got the message or did not much care for it. Their god was in jail and if there was a way to get a look at him, they would.

The western wall of the jail is adjacent to an exit of the Jodhpur railway station. It was cordoned off for two days and travellers had to go around quite a bit to access the railway station.

~

At the courthouse, where many of these scenes unfolded, a plain-clothes police constable approached me. 'Who are you? What do you want here?'

I had no pen and notepad, bag or microphone sticking out of my hand, my face was never on TV, so clearly, I did not belong among the crowd of mediapersons. He may have missed the lecture on profiling that the others seemed to have attended, or else I could have passed myself off as an Asaram supporter. My experience in Asaram's ashram in Kota back in 2013 had proved otherwise. Perhaps he assumed I was a contract killer. Nevertheless, the justified caution about security was evident.

After a while, Solanki came out and got busy with a call from Mita's father, who could be heard sobbing loudly on the other end of the line. Solanki moved away and tried to console him and they both gave each other assurances that they had done their best and come this far. After a while Solanki returned, but remained silent.

During the days leading up to the verdict, that was the only time when I saw Solanki betray such an emotion. It took him a while to recover. Two days ago, he had told me that Mita and her family wouldn't come. She was busy appearing for her exams and even if she wasn't, travelling to Jodhpur was a great security risk.

The entire family was back in their home town, glued to the television. Days before the judgment, security around their residence had been increased and additional guards deployed. They were requested to restrict their movements for a few days in the interest of their own security.

Once the judge arrived at the jail, Mita's father kept his eyes fixed to the TV and on his phone, which was stuck to a charging cable. He was awaiting a text message that would declare the end result of their multilayered sacrifices.

I found Priyanka Dubey, who had written the cover story for the *Caravan* about the Asaram case, and who was now working as a reporter for the BBC. We set off for the jail premises. Past a security barrier on Police Line road, the jail looked different. The road around the jail had been cordoned off and only mediapersons were allowed close to the prison's main entrance, apart from government employees who worked in buildings adjacent to the prison.

The cameras and mics jostled with each other outside the prison gate. Almost all English channels had sent their representatives. The Hindi channels had local reporters in Jodhpur but they had also sent their respective '*varishth patrakar*' (senior reporter) from Jaipur, who might have doubled up as their Rajasthan bureau chief. But the lead for almost all Hindi channels was the '*bahut varishth patrakar*' (very senior journalist), who had come in from Delhi.

The bahut varishth patrakar from Delhi usually puts up at the medium-swanky hotels, just below the 'three-star' variety. Alcohol will flow in the evenings, while this boss from Delhi will generally discuss politics from the head office. He is usually the man who glares into the camera, strangling a microphone and shouting the news at the camera so that you can hear the headlines in your sleep. The decibel level and force is the same, whether the news is a derailed train, anti-national students practising safe sex in universities, or the arrest of a vagrant goat who allegedly trespassed into a judge's garden. There is no discussion about the news or a live production strategy. This boss-type from Delhi decides on the spot what has to be done and the stringer/local reporter has to scramble to make appropriate arrangements.

A couple of selfie sticks identified the '*dot-com waale*' and 'mo-jo' (mobile journalism) reporters. The print reporters of Jodhpur skulked under a tree across the road from the gate and some of the so-called 'local reporters' and stringers occasionally broke away from the bahut varishth patrakar to give them company. That felt like the safer corner, with the kind of people who would verify a news from three sources before shooting off a message to the editorial WhatsApp group.

Official cars would drive towards the prison one by one into the waiting media crowd. One reporter, usually the local stringer, would accost and stall the car, while others would thrust mics and cameras at the rolled-up windows. Since they were on their way in, the officials were allowed to pass through. The quicker they went in, the (hopefully) quicker the verdict.

Once all officials settled in, the media persons did not have much to do. Back in the studios, the anchors were busy trying to stretch recaps about the arrest, the case and other nuggets awaiting a material development—anything to keep the TRPs steady.

There were two or three local lawyers, identified by white shirts tucked into black trousers, some still wearing their black coats despite the heat. The coat-wearers stood outside the prison gates clutching their files, as if it were a courtroom. Later, as they were asked to give sound bites, the files became useful props, to be waved around for the benefit of the cameras.

Just past 10.30 a.m. on 25 April 2018, a WhatsApp message from inside the prison told me (and many others there) that the accused had been convicted. A thrill went through the crowd, a murmur ruptured into a buzz as camerapersons waiting in the shade rushed back to their positions and furious live updates began. The number of smiles betrayed a lack of objectivity, but a lot had hung on this verdict for the journalists who had conducted a media trial on Asaram Bapu from day one.

The information turned out to be partially inaccurate. Asaram Bapu was convicted along with two of the accused— Sharath, the director of Asaram's residential school, and Shilpi, the warden of the same school. In their official capacities, both could be called custodians of Mita. Asaram's personal aides, Prakash and Shiva, were acquitted.

The lawyers sprang into action and started discussing (and speculating) what charges the three may have been convicted on. Some speculated about the possible sentence to be awarded, even while arguments on it had just begun inside the courtroom.

News updates raged about the scenes inside. Some said Asaram had collapsed, others claimed that he had broken down in tears, and so on.

The officials who had been inside later told me that Asaram had walked in cheerfully before the court convened. He exchanged words with his team of lawyers and took his seat. He appeared confident of being acquitted.

'All of you must join me at my ashram in Haridwar after this,' he was heard telling his lawyers.

He had looked in P.C. Solanki's direction and said, 'You must bring Solankiji with you too.'

When the court delivered the verdict, he was observed to have become calm and unresponsive. There were no hysterics or reactions of any kind. He remained silent after that.

Solanki and the public prosecutor both made arguments for the maximum sentence possible, hoping that he would get a life sentence. Pokarram Bishnoi, the special public prosecutor, also argued that the gravity of the crime and the conspiracy required a stringent punishment with the maximum sentence possible.

Solanki also pulled out the application he had prepared the night before and filed it with the court. He described the hardships that the survivor and her family had suffered. He asked that the court grant them some compensation for their suffering.

The defence lawyers argued for leniency considering Asaram's age (eighty-two at the time), deteriorating health and the long period he had already spent behind bars. It had been more than four and a half years since he had been confined to judicial custody in the Jodhpur jail.

Senior advocate Sajjan Raj Surana argued, on behalf of Asaram, that the godman had served society for a long time. Surana said that he had worked amongst the tribals in Gujarat and prevented Christian missionaries from converting people of these communities to Christianity by working for their welfare. He presented letters of praise from two past presidents, K.R. Narayanan and A.P.J. Abdul Kalam. Surana also exhibited and filed letters from former vice president Bhairon Singh Shekhawat, a former governor of a state and ex-CM of Haryana Bansi Lal.

On behalf of Shilpi, Surana argued that she was young, had her whole life ahead of her and her role in the crime was limited. Bhavik Sharma and Ved Prakash Mangla argued for leniency on behalf of Sharath.

The judge, Madhusudan Sharma, heard their arguments and retired to another room to consider them and write his sentence order. He came back with a sentence that was not expected.

Asaram's lawyers had presented various documents to prove his credentials as a godman with a global presence. The judge pointed out that as per these very documents, he had many devotees all over the world and ran more than 400 ashrams.

The judge considered that the survivor's father was also a disciple of the godman, along with the rest of his family, and had played an important role in establishing Asaram's ashram in their home town.

'He had sent both his daughter and his son to the residential "gurukul" in Chhindwara to study,' wrote[1] Sharma.

'On the pretext of chanting, Asaram called the girl and her parents to Jodhpur, drew her away from her parents and sexually

---

[1]   Asaram verdict, pages 446 to 454

assaulted her. In my humble opinion, not only did Asaram break the trust of his disciples but also tainted the image of godmen amongst the public at large,' wrote Sharma.

There are several court decisions that say that the purpose of punishment is to both secure society and punish offenders. The judge quoted judgments which also established that the punishment is not just for the crime but for justice at large. It was the court's duty to give punishment that would fit the crime.

Sharma quoted[2] a Supreme Court judgment that excessive sympathy for the convicted person would erode public faith in the rule of law. If the court does not protect the victim, he/she could turn to seeking revenge.

In the infamous rape and murder trial of Dhananjoy Chatterjee, the Supreme Court had upheld[3] the death sentence of the convict, saying:

> The measure of punishment in a given case must depend upon the atrocity of the crime; the conduct of criminal and the defenseless and unprotected state of victim. Imposition of appropriate punishment is the manner in which the courts respond to the society's cry for justice against the criminals. Justice demands that court should impose punishment befitting the crime, so that the courts reflect public abhorrence of the crime. The court must not only keep the view of the criminals but also the rights of the victim of crime and the

---

[2]  AIR 1991 SC 1463 cited in Asaram verdict
[3]  1994 (2) S.C.C.220 <Dhananjoy Chatterjee vs State of West Bengal> cited in Asaram verdict

society at large while considering imposition of appropriate punishment.

Sharma relied on this judgment to justify his reasoning for the sentence he imposed on Asaram. The six punishments are:

1.  Rigorous imprisonment of ten years and a fine of Rs 1 lakh for an offence under Section 370(4) of the Indian Penal Code (IPC). The sentence would be extended by a year in case the convict could not pay the fine.

2.  Rigorous imprisonment of one year and a fine of Rs 1,000 for the offence under Section 342, IPC. The fine would be substituted with a year's rigorous imprisonment in case the convict could not pay it.

3.  Rigorous imprisonment of one year and a fine of Rs 1,000 for the offence under Section 506, IPC. The fine would be substituted with a year's rigorous imprisonment in case the convict could not pay it.

4.  Life imprisonment for offences under Section 376(2)(f), IPC, which is to be served for the remainder of the convict's life. A fine of Rs 1 lakh that could be substituted with a year's rigorous imprisonment.

5.  Life imprisonment for offences under Section 376(d), IPC, which is to be served for the remainder of the convict's life. A fine of Rs 1 lakh that could be substituted with a year's rigorous imprisonment.

6.  Six months simple imprisonment for an offence under Section 23, Juvenile Justice Act (Care and Protection of Children) Rules 2000.

This means that the court punished Asaram with two life sentences. These are not the standard life sentences that are over in fourteen years but a life sentence that means the convict has to serve the rest of their actual, natural life in prison, his *vaikunth* (heaven), as he had once described[4] it.

Judge Madhusudan Sharma had handed Asaram the maximum sentence possible.

Apart from the life sentence, there was a sentence of ten years, two for a year each and one for six months. The sentences included three fines of one lakh rupees each and two for one thousand rupees each.

Before proceeding to describe how the judge had punished every stage of the crime possible, it is important to briefly explain the law in this regard. The exact law, crucial amendments and commentaries are easily available in the public domain.

Asaram's trial in Jodhpur was always referred to as a trial under POCSO, 2012. Once the verdict and the order of sentence were released to the public, it became clear that Asaram had been punished under the IPC and not POCSO.

Indeed, the trial was under POCSO. In the case of certain offences under this special law, the prosecution works in a different way. In the IPC, the accused is considered innocent till the prosecution proves him/her guilty. In the case of some offences under POCSO, the court presumes that the accused is guilty till he/she can prove his/her innocence.

The law as per Section 42 of POCSO reads:

Where an act or omission constitute an offence punishable under this Act and also under any other law for the time

<hr>

[4]   https://www.indiatvnews.com/news/india/i-am-ready-to-go-to-tihar-for-me-jail-is-vaikuntha-says-asaram-26818.html published on 23 August 2013 and accessed on 30 April 2018

being in force, then, notwithstanding anything contained in
any law for the time being in force, the offender found guilty
of such offence shall be liable to punishment only under such
law or this Act as provides for punishment which is greater
in degree.

The court in Jodhpur had found Asaram guilty of charges that
would carry a greater punishment under the IPC—particularly
following the 2013 amendments as a direct consequence of the
December 2012 gang rape and killing of a woman in New Delhi.
The 2013 amendment included the words '. . . shall be punished
with imprisonment for life which shall mean imprisonment for
the remainder of that person's natural life, or with death'.

The maximum punishment for that would be death and the
judge decided that 'for the remainder of that person's natural life'
is a harsh punishment. Since the law under the IPC provided for
a harsher punishment, the sentencing was carried out under the
IPC, based on Section 42 of POCSO.

Section 376(2)(f) provides for punishment for a convict
who was:

(f) being a relative, guardian or teacher of, or a person in a
position of trust or authority towards the woman, commits
rape on such woman.

That led to one count of life imprisonment. The other count
was based on the amended Section 376D which provides:

Where a woman is raped by one or more persons
constituting a group or acting in furtherance of a common
intention, each of those persons shall be deemed to have

committed the offence of rape and shall be punished with
rigorous imprisonment for a term which shall not be less
than twenty years, but which may extend to life which shall
mean imprisonment for the remainder of that person's
natural life, and with fine.

The court found that Sharath, Shilpi and Asaram had acted on
a common intention. Offences under Section 376D pertain to
gang rape. The court decided that the conspiracy of the three to
get the girl to Asaram had a common purpose. Section 376D
does not require all persons involved to have actively participated
in the act of rape itself for a punishment under this section.

The sentence under Section 370(4) refers to trafficking of a
minor for which Asaram was handed a sentence of ten years—
the maximum possible. Section 342 of the IPC provides a
maximum punishment for wrongful confinement. Section 506
carries a maximum punishment of two years, but in this case
Asaram was given a sentence of a year. Asaram was also given
the maximum sentence of six months under Section 23 of the
Juvenile Justice Act 2000 for the assault of a child under his care
and protection.

In effect, the court in Jodhpur had sentenced the accused
for assaulting a child in their care and custody, for trafficking a
minor to a place where she was sexually assaulted and the act of
sexual assault being described as gang rape since multiple people
contributed to the act.

It took a while for it to sink in that Sharath and Shilpi, the
two co-accused, had been given stringent punishments. They
were sentenced to twenty years each under Section 376D (IPC)
for enabling the sexual assault. They were also sentenced[5] to ten

---

5   Page 452 of the Asaram verdict

years each for conspiracy (120-B of the IPC) to traffic a minor (Section 370[4] of the IPC).

The judge, Madhusudan Sharma, directed that the costs of investigation and prosecution were to be calculated and recovered from the convicts. The fines collected from the convicts were to be handed over to Mita. He directed the district legal aid authorities to consider the compensation that Solanki had sought for her.

Shiva and Prakash, the closest aides of Asaram, who were privy to every move of the godman, were free to go. These were the men who knew the godman closely.

A key evidence for the conviction of Sharath and Shilpi was a complex diagram of the mobile phone conversations constructed by the investigators based on call detail records. This diagram was crucial to explaining how every time Mita's father called Sharath and Shilpi, following that, Asaram's aides would call the godman.

The cell phone that Asaram used was never recovered but it used to be in the possession of his aides. The investigators used call detail records (CDRs) of the phone numbers in order to explain how the conspiracy was plotted and executed. Nevertheless, the judge decided that the two aides were blameless.

The former aides of Asaram have each attested to many details of what went on in the ashrams and various activities of the godman and his son, including sexual liaisons and exploitation of disciples, both alleged and proved. The court decided that Shiva and Prakash did not seem to know as much as the earlier aides.

If the court was correct in its adjudication, it might also mean that Asaram had learnt from his past mistakes and put a wall between him and those closest to him regarding his indiscretions. Or, as some have alleged in other cases filed

by disciples of Asaram, the former aides conspired to taint
their guru.

Shilpi filed an appeal against the verdict of the court in
Jodhpur. On 29 September 2018, the high court of Rajasthan
(Jodhpur bench) admitted the appeal and suspended Shilpi's
sentence till its outcome. By then, Shilpi had been in jail for just
over five months.

In the high court, Shilpi's lawyers argued that 'a woman
cannot commit rape and therefore, she certainly cannot be
convicted for commission of gangrape because [a] woman
cannot be said to have an intention to commit rape'.

Section 376D of the IPC reads: '376D. Where a woman is
raped by one or more persons constituting a group or acting in
furtherance of a common intention, each of those persons shall
be deemed to have committed the offence of rape . . .'

Shilpi's lawyer further argued that the verdict had concluded
there was 'no direct evidence available on record to suggest
that the applicant-appellant sent the prosecutrix to Asaram, so
that he could sexually assault her, however, at the same time,
the trial court has concluded that on the basis of ocular and
circumstantial evidence, it is proved that the applicant-appellant
hatched a criminal conspiracy with accused-Asharam and sent
the prosecutrix to him, so that he could sexually assault her'.

The lawyer told the court that Shilpi had advised Mita's
parents to take Mita to Asaram to treat her illness. He also
argued that to prove a conspiracy, the prosecution must show
evidence that people had hatched a plan before the crime.

Mita's lawyer, P.C. Solanki, and Rajasthan's advocate
general both opposed these arguments saying that the evidence
was available on record, based on which Shilpi had been held
guilty and sentenced accordingly. They stressed that Shilpi had

convinced Mita's parents that Mita was possessed by 'evil spirits' and induced them to take her to Asaram for an exorcism.

The judge noted that Asaram's personal attendants, Shiva and Prakash, had been in touch with the parents in the days leading to the sexual assault and were charged with being part of the conspiracy. However, the trial court had acquitted them.

The judge also accepted the argument that Shilpi had not misused the conditions of bail granted to her during the trial and suspended her sentence till the disposal of the appeal.

~

While the verdict was being prepared, the media outside the prison had begun its speculation about what it could entail. Inaccurate updates kept flashing on air.

'Asaram has gone into shock.'

'Bapu fell down and started howling.'

Mostly reporters would get a one-line update and then discuss in undertones as to how to package it in the most sensational of ways. There was much context. At the time, the news of an alleged gang rape and murder of a child in Kashmir had rocked the country. The 'Kathua rape' had become a sensation at the crossroads between politics, religion and crime. Rape and crimes against women—particularly sexual assault—were on almost every news debate and op-ed pages of newspapers.

Al Jazeera put me on a live programme from outside the prison. Despite being a reporter, I was asked where this verdict falls in the backdrop of the outrage against rape in India. The Kathua incident had moved the debate well past the borders despite attempts of the gatekeepers of faux nationalism.

'Was this directed at the outrage?' I was asked.

A difficult question to answer in a few minutes considering the heavy political drama that ensued and the persecution complex of the Hindus involved—a complex that Asaram's staunch followers tried to play up in vain in his case, forgetting that everyone involved was Hindu too. I was only able to take them through some of the changes in the penal provisions since 2012.

Around the country, people watched as the actual verdict and sentence was breaking. Investigating officer Chanchal Mishra found a table and a television set at her office in Bhilwara and planted herself in front of it. Her colleagues milled around her to get a glimpse of the verdict. At the anti-corruption bureau in Jodhpur, Ajay Pal Lamba watched the verdict being flashed, though he already had updates from the prison.

As far as Mishra was concerned, her first-ever investigation—a high-profile, life-sucking probe into a powerful man—was an appraisal in itself. The verdict had endorsed her skills as a crack investigator.

The cars started to roll out of the prison one by one. A district official left, followed by the judge, with the reporters trying to stall their cars. None of them would speak, of course. I am yet to see a judge in India discuss his verdict in public.

The lawyers were whom they were actually waiting for. A defence lawyer drove out and did not seem inclined to stop and exchange words. After spending close to seven hours in the harsh summer sun of Jodhpur, the reporters were not willing to let go of anyone. One sprinted with the car, holding on to a slit in the window till the barricade on the Police Lines road gave him an opportunity to stand in front of it. The others rushed up to him. A woman reporter from an English news channel outpaced the others, and slid into the passenger seat. From that 'exclusive' seat, she interviewed the puzzled lawyer while her camera glared through the windshield.

A senior reporter, who usually breaks stories about border skirmishes on a popular English news channel, used his conflict reporting skills to wade through other reporters, flashing the brand he works for.

The sullen print media crowd under the tree smiled at this circus and spat *gutka* furiously while scribbling notes. The pace accelerated till one of the yellow, heavy-duty police barricades on wheels fell on its side. That calmed things a little but for most of the media this was the biggest story of that week and one that was drawing to a close after four and a half years of chasing it.

A month earlier, there had been a similar scene when Salman Khan was housed in the same prison. WhatsApp messages started trickling in about how Jodhpur had taken down two very influential people. There was an air of triumph that spread to parts of the city.

By evening, Solanki's house had two police guards posted outside and two inside. They allowed me in only after his mother vouched for me. A box of sweets was passed around. Solanki's older sister, a government nurse, had come to celebrate with him. She and their mother waited at the door with a plate adorned with flowers, a tiny vessel of vermilion paste and a sweet—the requirements for a basic tilak ceremony to greet Solanki.

Solanki appeared soon and his neighbours cheered. A small crowd of reporters, who knew his house, had gathered there. Someone hung a garland around his neck and Solanki bent to touch his mother's feet, the photo made its way to the front pages in several local newspapers the next day. Solanki, who had become adept at 'handling the media' plugged in microphone after microphone and joined in live debates, as I departed with a deadline for *Mumbai Mirror* and the Bengali daily, *Anandabazar Patrika*.

   Solanki called me back later that night, when everyone was asleep. I had already been given a copy of the judgment but was curious about a description of the events that unfolded in court. We sat on Solanki's terrace till almost 1 a.m., facing the Mehrangarh Fort which is just a few hundred metres away from his house.

PART TWO

# 4

# 'Mota Bhagwan': The Son of God

Asaram's arrest was a turning point for him and his followers. It was also a turning point for his son, Narayan Sai. Till that point, Narayan Sai was the 'son of god', by all counts not an easy job. He had to work on appearances befitting his job description, which meant growing into the role of a successor, for this god is mortal and must take what is known as 'samadhi' or a state of eternal meditation, what ordinary human beings call death. The son of god also has to work against the myth of his father being supreme and immortal in order to ensure a space for himself. In the exercise, he has to diffuse the propaganda around his father but not disturb it too much, lest his own position as heir-apparent is toppled in the ripple effect of fiddling with the narrative of being godmen or messengers of god, as the case may be.

As in the case of political dynasties, setting up a quasi-religious dynasty is not easy. The guru must formally introduce his son as his heir and successor. It is not easy to establish the son as the boss in a business, for though the son may command the money, he may not command the respect of his father's loyal retainers. Narayan Sai's case was not very different.

As he told police officers to whom it was also becoming evident, Narayan Sai did not have access to the empire of hidden wealth his father had created. While the lakhs of followers saw the bald old man with a flowing white beard peeking through garlands, dancing and singing to bhajans on stage, Narayan Sai saw a control freak who treated him like a child. The father's ascent from alleged bootlegger to godman, on the banks of the Sabarmati, was aided by research into the Vedas and spending time in at least two ashrams. He not only used complex words and phrases but quoted from the scriptures and explained them skilfully to his followers during his sermons.

Narayan Sai did not have the same talent. Sureshanand, a follower, would start the sermons in Asaram's absence, and even conduct full sessions at the Motera ashram. Kaushik Popatlal Vani, an ashramite, controlled the financial empire. There was a clique of businessmen who handled the godman's money ventures. Narayan Sai lived as if he were on an allowance. It is a matter of coincidence perhaps that neither of these two men are publicly available any more. The police were unable to trace Vani since the time he became crucial to their investigation in multiple cases. At the Motera ashram, I was told, 'Many have parted ways since the cases and he is no longer here,' which was hurriedly changed to, 'Sureshanandji has gone into ekantwas (isolation).'

While in his thirties, Narayan Sai had started to work on emerging from his father's shadow. He bought land in his own name, though it is not yet known how it was financed. Authorities have found that land for an ashram in Madhya Pradesh (among others) was in his own name. He culled a group of followers from among his father's, especially family members of Asaram's followers. His father could hardly grudge Narayan Sai the people he recruited for his own following. The man formed an entourage. He put the women to work building ashrams, maintaining them and allegedly sexually exploiting some of them.

'He comes across as the spoilt son of a powerful politician—the kind you see in films driving around in an open jeep—keeping up a display of money and muscle power. He's spoilt but not sharp in the head,' a government officer told me in Ahmedabad. This government officer had earlier been posted in a remote district in Gujarat where he had observed the 'son of god' at close quarters.

Narayan Sai's entourage grew by recruiting others, through enticing words placed in their ears about his own divinity. Such propaganda got him the younger generation of Asaram's followers. He moulded himself in the image of his father—clad in white kurta-pyjama and a beanie hat, like that of his father, covering his head. The kind of beanie hat that Osho appeared wearing in photographs from his later life. Narayan Sai started to create his own image too, in the likeness of Krishna. He played the flute on stage adorned in a crown and wearing the kind of clothes Krishna is depicted with in popular renditions of the Hindu god.

When Asaram was arrested, Narayan Sai burst into the limelight with vigour. He was forty-one at the time, born in January 1972. Asaram's closest aides handled all the work that needed to be done managing the godman's empire, while Narayan Sai started to appear in the media. It was Narayan Sai's photos that were published, interviews of him that were broadcast. He gave several television interviews in the wake of his father's arrest, including a detailed one to Sudarshan TV, a Hindi news channel that has broadcast many reports, interviews and features that have stressed the story put out by Asaram's people. Some may discount it, but Sudarshan TV's coverage provided both a sense of journalistic objectivism and a look into the various elements of Asaram's sect.

Narayan Sai appeared on other news channels as well and questioned the role of the media and the accusations made by it, many of which were wild and replete with hyperbole. Needless to say, he responded to them with his own set of half-truths and hyperbole.

When the story about the Jodhpur POCSO case broke, the media also dug up details that led to the Justice D.K. Trivedi commission and played them on an endless loop. In an interview,[1] Narayan Sai claimed that the D.K. Trivedi commission had given his father a clean chit. The anchor corrected him that the report was yet to be published (as it is, even at the time of writing this book). The commission's inquiry had concluded earlier in 2013.

'But the Supreme Court has given a judgment that there is no black magic at the ashram,' insisted Sai, changing track.

Narayan Sai went so far as to say that the lawyer for the parents of the two children had accepted that there was no black magic at the ashram.

When I met Subramaniam Iyer, the lawyer for the Vaghelas, he told me in detail about the commission's proceedings. Black magic or not, the children were in the care of Asaram who had no response as to how the children went missing from the

---

[1]   https://www.youtube.com/watch?v=zFP7phh14iE published on 17 September 2013 and accessed on 9 June 2018

gurukul in Motera and turned up dead, metres away from it on a dry riverbed.

The son of god did not seem to have any of the charm or persona, nor the talent for oration or the skill of taking over the situation as his father. At best, he was on the defensive, whereas the father was a front-foot player, one who led the charge.

As early as September 2013, Asaram's aides had begun to spin the theory of how Mita was older than she claimed to be. She had provided her school certificates from none other than Asaram's gurukul, where she was studying. Narayan Sai did not have answers for this and said the journalists should direct this question to the legal counsel for the ashram.

While concluding the interviews, he made a common refrain about peace and harmony and following the '*maryada* (customs)' of 'our great *samaj* (society)'. But, before that, he always asked that the media channels broadcast 'the good things we are doing for the sake of balance'.

The editor-in-chief of India News, Deepak Chaurasia, conducted an interview[2] of Baba Ramdev shortly after the Jodhpur rape allegations were made. Chaurasia asked Ramdev why he had been silent on the charges against Asaram, and how the former had played 'disco dandia' between ashrams when the Jodhpur police had sent him summons to join the investigation.

Ramdev said he knew Asaram and doubted if the allegations were part of a conspiracy, but said things would be clear once the investigation was complete.

---

[2]   https://www.youtube.com/watch?v=yYuA_icS-Sg published on 6 September 2013 and accessed on 11 July 2018

Chaurasia pointed out that previously charges had been made against Asaram. Nevertheless, said Ramdev, Asaram should have faced the media.

'*Media kya, main toh saanp se bhi pyaar karta hoon* (Why will I be angry with the media? I love snakes too),' Asaram had said while giving a bite[3] to several TV news crews outside an event, while boarding his car. This was shortly after the December 2012 gang rape in Delhi, when he had made uncharitable comments about the victim, which had led to a huge controversy.

'I have never said the media barks like a dog,' Asaram continued. 'And I have always said nice things about the victim. If you listen to my satsang for fifteen minutes, you will have a different idea of me. I have merely said that if she had chanted god's name, god would have blessed her and saved her.'

When pressed that he had mocked the media by comparing it with dogs, he responded, 'Naw naw no. I never said that the media barks like a dog. Listen to my satsang cassette for half an hour. If your problems are not solved, then meet with me. Hari Om.'

The tide had turned since the death of the Vaghela cousins in 2008 and Asaram found it difficult to manage the press. The entertainment media had been kinder with live and recorded television broadcasts of his satsangs and other events. But, he still managed to hold his own during a press conference, whereas Narayan Sai seemed to be at a loss when seated in front of a camera.

~

---

[3] https://www.youtube.com/watch?v=lw4gqMPonTM published on 23 June 2018 and accessed on 3 July 2018

One of Narayan Sai's key advisers was Monica Aggarwal. She was a smart young woman who was quite different from the rest of his female bhakts. Her parents were followers, as were her siblings, and after graduation, she committed herself as a full-time volunteer with Narayan Sai. The police believed that she managed Narayan Sai's affairs and had full access to him at all times. This made Narayan Sai's wife, Janaki Devi, jealous, as it became evident to the police later. There was a power play between the two of them, according to the wife. Aggarwal has maintained that she was with Narayan Sai purely as part of a spiritual path and her guru had tasked her with certain duties to run the operations of his ashram and organization.

Narayan Sai had barely settled into his role of an imminent successor–godman, when two sisters along with the husband of one of them approached the police in Surat on 6 October 2013. They told the police that they were former followers of Asaram and his son, and that over the course of several years, while they lived at successive ashrams, both sisters had been raped repeatedly. Asaram had sexually assaulted the elder sister first and had continued to rape her at his ashram in Motera. Narayan Sai had influenced the younger sister and sexually assaulted her once at Asaram's ashram in Surat. Later, he had recruited her for his ashram at Himmatnagar, Madhya Pradesh, and raped her multiple times there and physically assaulted her as well.

Since the charges were of a serious nature and against two powerful, influential men, the officer took them to his boss—the Surat police commissioner, Rakesh Asthana, a senior Indian Police Service (IPS) officer of the Gujarat cadre.

Rakesh Asthana was brought up and schooled in Jharkhand and after an education in St Xavier's and Delhi's Jawaharlal Nehru University, he was selected for the IPS in 1984 following his first attempt at the gruelling civil services examination. He was allotted the Gujarat cadre but when deputed to the CBI, he was posted in the probe agency's anti-corruption unit in Dhanbad as superintendent of police, and later as CBI's deputy inspector general in Ranchi.

In 1994, Asthana had begun the investigation into the fodder scam and filed the charge sheet in 1996. In 1997, he arrested former Bihar chief minister, Lalu Prasad Yadav, and the probe eventually led to Yadav's conviction on corruption charges. In 2002, Asthana had probed the Godhra train burning incident in the special investigation team (SIT) headed by former CBI chief R.K. Raghavan.

Controversy has dogged this officer as it has every other sleuth who has probed politically charged cases. At the time of writing this, Asthana was posted as special director of the CBI. There was much public opposition to his appointment to the probe agency including a challenge of the appointment in the Supreme Court of India. The Narendra Modi–led government at the Centre defended him and the Supreme Court gave him a clean chit. He has earlier worked as an officiating director of the probe agency following the retirement of Anil Kumar Sinha in December 2016. Raghavan, who led the CBI for eight years from 1993 to 2001, had endorsed Asthana's appointment as the interim chief of the agency, saying that, 'Rakesh Asthana's appointment as Interim CBI Director will be welcomed by all those who want credibility restored to the organisation, after it had suffered at the hands of a few recent chiefs.' [4] Raghavan

---

[4]  https://www.thehindu.com/news/national/Asthana-is-interim-CBI-chief/article16742603.ece published on 2 December 2016 and accessed on 25 July 2018

described Asthana as 'a dynamic officer with a reputation for integrity and professional acumen'.[5]

Asthana's role in investigating Asaram is crucial on multiple counts. He initiated and supervised the probe into the two sisters' rape cases in Surat and Ahmedabad against both the godman and his son. The probes eventually led to the digging up of economic offences by the godman's son and the assassination and murderous assaults on the followers-turned-witnesses. The major haul was of course the forty-two gunny bags of documents that exposed the entire empire that Asaram had built over the decades by misusing the trust his followers placed in him, not to mention the money they gave up to him as their guru, and in some cases, god.

In 2008, when the two Vaghela cousins, Abhishek and Deepesh, were found dead in mysterious circumstances near the Motera ashram, it led to a probe by a one-man commission. The Justice (retd) D.K. Trivedi commission heard many depositions about both father and son, including cases of sexual exploitation and assault. So, it was not that the Gujarat police was not aware of these cases, but when the two sisters approached them, it had been little over a month since Asaram was charged and arrested and he still held a lot of clout. Police officers also have to objectively sift through false cases amongst the proverbial skeletons that start tumbling out of the closet.

So, the policemen took the two sisters first to then deputy commissioner of police in Surat, Shobha Bhutada (an IPS officer of the Gujarat cadre), who in turn took them to Asthana. Since the women accused Asaram and Narayan Sai of rape, Asthana

---

[5]  Ibid.

immediately directed Bhutada to lodge an FIR to probe the rape accusations.

Asaram was already in judicial custody in Jodhpur for sexually assaulting a minor. That had given the two sisters the courage to approach the police. The older sister accused Asaram of raping her on several occasions between 1997–2006 when she was living at the godman's headquarters in the Motera ashram. The younger sister accused Narayan Sai of raping her on several occasions between 2002–06, when she had been living at Motera but the first incident was in the ashram at Jahangirpura, Surat.

The elder sister also told the police officers that Asaram's wife, Lakshmi, and daughter, Bharti, had helped the godman rape her.

The Surat police lodged two FIRs for the two separate complaints. The complaint against Asaram was lodged as a zero FIR and transferred[6] to the Chandkheda police station. A court in Gandhinagar directed an in-camera trial of the rape allegations against Asaram. The younger sister's complaint led to an FIR against Narayan alias Narayan Sai alias Mota Bhagwan, Hanuman (*sadhak* of Narayan Sai), Ganga-Sadhika, resident of Gambhoi ashram, Jamuna-Sadhika, resident of Gambhoi ashram and another six to seven residents of Gambhoi ashram in Himmatnagar, Madhya Pradesh.

The Surat police conducted its investigation into Narayan Sai and charged him, along with his trusted aide, Hanuman, of rioting while armed with a deadly weapon, rape, 'unnatural sex'

---

[6] https://economictimes.indiatimes.com/news/politics-and-nation/sexual-assault-case-asaram-brought-to-ahmedabad/articleshow/24164013.cms published on 14 October 2013 and accessed on 14 August 2018

(or sexual assault), wrongful confinement, wrongful confinement (in secret) and using 'criminal force or assault on a woman with the intent to outrage her modesty'.

I met with both the lawyers of Narayan Sai in Surat. Kalpesh Desai, a seasoned lawyer who practises in the district court, was arguing both the cases in Surat, dealing with the rape allegations and the charge of bribing the investigators. He was being assisted by Kuldeep Jadhav, who met me at the district court's parking lot. I hoped to get some details of the case and a look at their defence. The case was nearing completion, the prosecution had presented its case and the defence was finishing with its last few arguments. Desai later told me that he expected it to be over by Diwali of 2018.

Jadhav declined from commenting, citing an order of the district court barring anyone from divulging details while the case was sub judice. He said some journalists had reported factually inaccurate news reports and had been cautioned about contempt charges. Besides, he said, he did not want to give away their defence strategy.

Desai agreed to give an idea of the case and I was able to jump the long queue outside his office for a brief chat. A large, life-sized portrait of Shirdi Sai Baba hung behind his chair. Desai explained a part of how they would argue Narayan Sai's case and cleared some of the factual inaccuracies that were bugging me, mainly because I had heard different accounts of the rape incidents from some people I had met along the way. Try as I might, I could not get him to share their defence with me or some supporting evidence that might help me present their picture.

One of the rumours I had picked up during my research was that two women, former devotees, had deposed against Narayan Sai, claiming that he had 'unnatural sex' with them. The charge of 'unnatural sex' (Section 377, IPC), Desai said, was because the woman had complained of oral penetration. The rape charge had been made in 2013, but the alleged offence took place in 2001–02. So, the old rape law would apply and therefore, unlike in Asaram's POCSO case in Jodhpur, oral penetration would not be covered under the earlier version of the law.

Desai said the witnesses who gave testimony against Narayan Sai were resentful ex-followers of the godmen. 'They had differences with the two godmen and had parted ways,' he said.

It was public knowledge that the witnesses were disgruntled but it would be up to the court to decide if that was enough to raise a 'reasonable doubt'. That is because Mahendra Chawla had testified to having travelled with the younger sister when she was with another group of devotees on an evangelical mission with Narayan Sai.

'In her statement, she has claimed that Narayan Sai's aide, Hanuman, escorted her to the godman's quarters in 2001–02. But, we have witness testimonies that show that Hanuman was not even in the ashram at the time. In 2003, when Asaram had held a *shivir* (camp) in Hanuman's village, Hanuman's father had pledged his land to Asaram and it was then that Hanuman had pledged his loyalty to Asaram,' said Desai.

~

In 2017, *Caravan*, one of India's leading magazines, put Asaram on the cover of its April issue. *Caravan* is the only Indian magazine that publishes long-form narratives that go deep into a story and investigative reporting is a regular method in its reportage, not a rarity. Priyanka Dubey has found mention elsewhere in this book for her seminal coverage exposing the godman. As a former colleague at *Tehelka* magazine, she had reported detailed pieces on the allegations against Asaram. I again found her in Jodhpur when the judgment was delivered in the POCSO case.

In 2017, Dubey reported for and wrote the cover story for *Caravan*, titled: 'Crisis of Faith: The Nightmarish Struggle to Bring Asaram to Justice'. For this piece, she was able to interview the younger of the two sisters who had filed the two separate rape complaints against Asaram and his son. The following is an excerpt of the interview as it appeared in *Caravan*, which is a description of the events as told to Dubey:[7]

> In 1996, the family sent the elder sister, who was 16 at the time, to Asaram's ashram in Ahmedabad. 'She went there for a 12-day anusthaan,' she said. 'It is a process in which the devotee has to live in the ashram for 12 days, perform puja and chant mantras continuously.' At the end of this, she recounted, when their mother went to Ahmedabad to pick up her daughter, Asaram's wife, Lakshmi Devi, refused to send her home. *'Kya karegi ab sansar me jakar? Itni acchi ladki hai, yahi guru ke charnon me rehne dijiye ab ise'* (What will she do in the world now? She is such a good girl, let her live in the feet of the guru), the younger sister said her mother was told.

---

7   Excerpted with permission from *Caravan*. 'Crisis of Faith: The Nightmarish Struggle to Bring Asaram to Justice', *Caravan*, April 2017.

The mother was too much in thrall to Asaram and Sai to protest. 'What could my mother have done alone?' the younger sister asked. 'So she came back without my elder sister and they kept her in the Ahmedabad ashram.'

It was a sign of the intensity of their devotion that, despite having their elder daughter kept away from them, the girls' parents remained believers in Asaram and Sai. A few years later, in 2000, 'I went to a camp of Narayan Sai in Surat with my parents,' the younger sister said. 'I was 16 then.'

At the Surat camp, she said, Sai singled her out and asked her to visit his ashram in Meghnagar, in Jhabua. When she met him, 'he made an indication to a sevika'—a female devotee. It appeared as if this devotee 'understood that Sai had shown his interest in me.' The sevika, the victim said, 'immediately came to me and started brainwashing me,' saying that 'there is nothing in this outer world, whatever there is, it is at the feet of the guru.'

Other devotees who witnessed Sai's actions, too, understood that he had singled her out. 'So when I was standing in a queue in the ashram, some of them came up to me and asked me where I was from, and then gave me prasad,' she said. 'They said that I should eat the prasad myself and not share it with anyone, just to make me feel special.'

Later, she travelled to the Meghnagar ashram. 'When I went there it was chilly winter, and the ashram was still being built,' she said. 'I was asked to help in the construction. So I, along with six or seven other girls, actually helped in the physical construction of the ashram.'

During this period, her communications and movements were restricted. 'We were kept in confinement and my name was also changed,' she said. 'They did not allow me to go back home to meet my mother or to speak to my parents on the phone. It was torture.' The assignation of a new name helped cut victims off from the outside world. 'So even if someone from my family would have come to look for me, they wouldn't find me because they would have asked for the girl with my original name, and that girl was not there anymore,' the woman said.

In 2002, she accompanied Sai on a tour to Bihar and Nepal. (She said that Mahendra Chawla was also present on this tour.) The attention Sai paid to her intensified after this trip, she said. 'After we came back to Surat from the Nepal tour, one day he called me and asked me to come to the Surat ashram,' she said. He gave her the phone number of one of his sevaks—male devotees—and asked her to call him before she arrived. The sevak told her to come to the ashram and meet Sai without telling any of the other devotees about the meeting. 'He said that if I told other girls that Sai wanted to meet me personally, then they would feel jealous and complain that Sai does not meet them but is meeting me,' she said. 'I now realise that all this was a strategy to create a sense of false competition among the sevikas and make them feel special about meeting Sai personally.'

On reaching the ashram, she followed these instructions, and was led to Sai's cottage from a rear entrance. There, she met Sai, who 'held my hand and said, *"Sansaar me kya rakha hai. Tumhara jo bhi hai guru ka hai. Tum pichle janam ki gopi ho aur main Krishna, aur main tumhara sansaar kaat raha hoon"* (What's in the world for you? All that is yours is your guru's. You are my female devotee from a previous birth and I am the incarnation of Krishna, and I am leading you to the path of salvation).'

The Surat victim often witnessed Sai being aggressive with other women in the ashram. In particular, she said, he would hurl abuses and beat women he found talking to men. 'Once when Sai's wife was talking to the ashram manager for some work, I saw him come out and give her four slaps on her face in front of everyone,' she said. 'He was a bad-mouthed person and used to hurl lot of verbal abuse on everyone whenever he used to get angry. Whatever he used to do with women was "prabhu ki leela" [god's will] but if any woman in the ashram dared to even speak to any male, she would be beaten up.'

Towards the end of our conversation, the woman got choked up as she recounted one afternoon in 2002 when she says Sai raped her. 'I don't know how you are going to write this,' she said. Both Sai and Asaram, she said, 'used to force women to perform oral sex. They are perverts and would force women to even take the ejaculation of semen in their mouths.' She paused here, then continued. Sai, she said, 'forced me to drink his semen. I was very scared and I did not know exactly what I should do.' The two years of brainwashing made it impossible for her to resist, she said. 'We were taught not to question the guru so it was not easy for me,' she said. 'But I was very scared and I felt bad. He behaved very badly and cruelly with me.'

Around a year after the incident, when she was working as the manager of an ashram in the municipality of Himmatnagar in Gujarat, she decided to escape from Asaram and Sai's clutches.

'When I said for the first time that I wanted to leave the ashram and go back home, his other sevikas caught me up, tied my hands and feet and locked me up inside a room in the ashram,' she recounted. 'I cried through the night.' The next day, Sai came to meet her. 'He beat me up mercilessly,' she said. 'He used his legs and hands to hit me all over my body and hurled filthy abuses. He said, "*Jayegi ashram se? Kyon jana chahti hai ashram se? Kya karegi ab bahar jakar?*" (You will dare to leave the ashram? Why do you want to go from the ashram? What will you do outside?)'

After this, the woman devised a plan to escape. She phoned her brother and asked him to come to the Himmatnagar ashram to pick her up. She instructed him to tell the ashram authorities that their mother was very ill—a story that she too would give them. 'I explained everything to my brother,' she said. 'He came to the ashram after a day to pick me up. I knew that Sai would not let me go any other way. He would accuse me of theft if I ran away and would beat me and lock me up if I asked for permission.'

The strategy worked. 'Sai spoke to my brother when he came to pick me up,' she said. 'My brother told him the same story of my mother's illness. Then he allowed me to go for ten days.' She quickly packed her bags and handed over all the accounts that she was managing to another woman and left.

When she did not return to the ashram after ten days, Sai sent some sevikas to her. These devotees visited her home and pressured her to at least speak to Sai on the phone. When she called him from a public telephone, 'he yelled at me for not coming back'. She insisted that she could not return because her parents did not wish her to go.

She recounted that Sai then said she needed to return to at least settle the ashram's accounts. She explained that she had handed over all the accounts. 'But he said that I should explain them to him face-to-face,' she said.

She agreed to visit the ashram with her parents. A few days later, they set out for Himmatnagar, even though her father was unwell. 'It was seven in the evening by the time we reached Himmatnagar,' she said. 'The ashram is fifteen kilometres away from the town, so we decided to spend the night at a relative's house in Himmatnagar.' She phoned Sai and informed him that she had arrived, and would visit the ashram the next day. 'He asked me the address of where we were staying and then hung up,' she said. 'We called it a day and went to sleep.'

At around 2 a.m., 'Sai sent a jeep full of his devotees to the address where we were staying,' she continued. 'We were on the terrace and there were shops downstairs. They gathered downstairs and started shouting. They hurled abuses at me and started throwing stones at the building.' According to the woman, they yelled, '*Bahar nikalo usko, yahi chipa ke rakha hai.*' (Bring her out, she is hiding here.) 'We were all very scared,' she said. 'Then they went away. We passed the night somehow and took the first bus back home as dawn broke.' She said she and her parents continued to receive threatening messages from Asaram and Sai in the days that followed. She was relieved that they had not gone directly to the ashram, as their lives would have been at much greater risk there.

A few days later, the woman's sister, too, returned home from the ashram in Ahmedabad. 'She was also tortured a lot,' the younger sister said. 'We did meet once or twice in between while we were both staying in different ashrams, and I remember her telling me that I should go back.' Despite their similar traumas, they 'couldn't find an opportunity to talk properly in between', she said. After they were reunited in 2007, 'we shared our ordeals with each other. But we could not gather the courage to tell this to our parents, so we kept quiet.'

It was only in early October 2013, after the first case was filed against Asaram, that the sisters—each of whom is now married, with children—gathered the courage to make their own police complaints. They told their mother about the horrors they had suffered just a few days before filing the complaints; their father, who suffers from a medical condition, still does not know about them.

The younger sister said that she took the decision because of the support of her husband, and because both she and her sister felt reassured when Asaram was arrested and later denied bail. 'When the Jodhpur child-rape case broke, we were sure that the police would never be able to arrest Asaram,' she said. 'We were following the case closely on TV. We thought, even if he is arrested, he will get bail in two hours. But the Jodhpur police did arrest him from Indore, and when he was denied bail even from the high court and Supreme Court we thought we should speak up now.'

~

'When the prosecutrix herself tells us that she was raped and her husband supports her, we will obviously start an investigation and don't have to insist upon evidence up front. If the probe reveals that the FIR is false, then you can file a report accordingly, but the investigation must be initiated,' Asthana told me when I met with him at the CBI's headquarters in New Delhi.

'Whatever she narrated was put down in the FIR and then she was asked to give a statement before a magistrate. She narrated the same sequence of events to the magistrate as well and so we started with the investigation,' Asthana said.

The narration of a sequence of events at different stages is closely watched by investigators. Major slip-ups are noted. Then, many of the events are scrutinized and whatever can be, is corroborated by additional witnesses.

In this case, Mahendra Chawla and others had testified to Narayan Sai's character and also other instances of alleged sexual exploitation of female bhakts. There is also corroborating testimony of places where and when the younger sister went with Narayan Sai and so forth.

Narayan Sai was last seen in public on 28 September 2013, at an event in Chandigarh. When the complaint was lodged against him in Surat, he was believed to be in Asaram's Jaipur ashram. He had just begun to do the rounds of various ashrams after Asaram's arrest—the show must go on. Narayan Sai did not cooperate with the police investigation and was not seen after the rape complaint had been filed against him. The police served summons to him at various places beginning from 9 October 2013.

Narayan Sai had watched how the charges and case against his father had unfolded. Asaram had called for his son when the Jodhpur police sent him a notice to appear before the police officer investigating the POCSO case. The lawyers had warned them that there was a chance that Asaram may be arrested.

Narayan Sai hid in Surat for a while and then skipped town to Ahmedabad and onwards to locations in Rajasthan, Haryana,

New Delhi, Punjab and Uttar Pradesh. The police started to track the phones of several of Asaram's associates and followers and pick up some traces of his movements by listening to their conversations. A nationwide manhunt was also under way.

On 18 October 2013, the police raided a house in Shahganj in Agra. They had information that he was holed up in the house of Lakshman Sevkani, a follower of his father. By that time, Narayan Sai had changed his appearance and shaved off his hair and beard. The police first raided the wrong house and by the time they found the right one, Narayan Sai was long gone.

The police raided the Motera ashram and other places where the godman could be hiding. By then, the police had reached out to many former bhakts of Asaram, through the Jodhpur police who had already interviewed them. Some came on their own, since many were already in Gujarat. This included Amrit Prajapati and his wife who met ACP Mukesh Patel and DCP Shobha Bhutada. Prajapati provided many details about the Sabarmati ashram and what could be found where when the police went to conduct a raid. Apart from the several ashram buildings, there were also residential buildings, including one called 'Narayan Sai' apartments. I came across the name of this apartment while scrutinizing records of companies in which shares were held by Asaram and his aides. In the case of Dhanpati Marketiers Pvt. Ltd, it was the address for major shareholders—all followers of Asaram—Gokul Desai, Rajesh Kerwani and Dinesh Bhagchandani, the former aide who was later murdered by a self-styled 'fidayeen' follower of Asaram.

Before the police raided Asaram's headquarters, they realized that, in all probability, Narayan Sai would not be found there. But, the police did not want to be in a position that they had searched everywhere else in the world but the headquarters.

Besides, they did not want to create an impression that Asaram's outfit was invincible and they could not comb the ashram for Narayan Sai.

This was the second such raid at the Motera ashram. The first one, in November 2009, had followed a clash between a mob from the ashram and the police in Gandhinagar. It was a year after the Gujarat government had set up the Justice Trivedi commission to probe charges of practising occult against the godman following the killing of the Vaghela cousins in Motera. The mob had pelted brickbats at the police, one of which had left a gash on the head of the superintendent of police of Gandhinagar, Piyush Patel, who was trying to manage the situation. Patel had led the raid into the ashram and rounded up 200 of Asaram's followers. Since then, the Ahmedabad ashram residents had not tried any local mob violence or intimidation.

The Surat police, investigating the rape charges, did not want to give the feeling that the ashram was off limits. Around 60–70 policemen from Surat, joined by a small team from Ahmedabad, swung into the ashram. Sedans filled with officers including DCP Bhutada, ACP Mukesh Patel and police vans filled with constables reached the gate of the Motera ashram between 5 a.m. and 6 a.m. on 22 November 2016.

The police were prepared. Prajapati had briefed them on the layout of the ashram. As a former physician to Asaram, he had access to the remotest corners of the ashram and knew its every inch. His wife and he had stayed there for several years before they parted ways with the godman and his son.

The ashramites were taken by surprise. They had not imagined that there would be a raid at the ashram. After the last one, the godman had reached out to his politician network and had been given an assurance that it wouldn't be repeated.

Things had changed, though, since Mita's complaint in August 2013.

Shortly after the raid began, Asaram's lawyers turned up in their court uniform and threatened to take the police to court. The police were not to be bullied since they felt that capturing a fleeing rape accused did not require an arrest warrant and the ashram in Motera was where he was likely to be, given that it was the headquarters of the sect.

'Surat police conducted the raid without permission. They confiscated fifteen hard disks, several computers, five pen drives, around thirty wireless modems, one blade server, some photographs and documents,' B.M. Gupta, Asaram's lawyer later told[8] the media.

The ashramites complained to the court about police high-handedness in conducting a raid without a warrant. Their lawyers complained that the ashramites were kept from their breakfast and confined to the yard. The police said there was hostility against them while they were discharging their duties and wanted to curtail any interference with the raid. There were media reports claiming that a devotee had made off with a sackful of documents even while the raid was on. A court in Gandhinagar summoned Bhutada who had led the raid and answered the allegations against it.

Similar raids followed at other ashrams of Asaram and Narayan Sai and at the residences of their closest followers. Hanuman and Ramesh, Narayan Sai's closest aides, were travelling with him. The police went through his call records,

---

8  https://timesofindia.indiatimes.com/city/surat/Surat-police-raid-Motera-ashram/articleshow/35884334.cms published on 22 November 2013, updated on 1 June 2014 and accessed on 11 July 2018

narrowed down a list of disciples who were the closest to him and started to keep a watch on them.

A court in Surat finally issued a non-bailable arrest warrant for Narayan Sai on 28 October 2013. The son of god did not want to be questioned but the arrest warrant meant that anybody aiding him to avoid the police would be termed an abettor.

# 5

# The Answer Is Forty-two

Narayan Sai travelled incognito through various states after hiding for three weeks in Gujarat. En route, he stayed at the farmhouses of his father's devotees. His trusted aide, Hanuman (Kaushal Kumar Thakur), was with him at all times; the driver, Ramesh, joined them later. The police described Ramesh as an ace driver who knew the roads they used to escape like the back of his hand. 'A GPS device may fail, but Ramesh won't,' said a police officer in Delhi who had been part of the team searching for Narayan Sai.

Tracing Sai was not easy and the police spent a brutal fifty-eight days trying to locate him. During that time, they missed him several times. After a point, they started to raid the ashrams where he might have been hiding. They even went down to an ashram in Mumbai's Virar, where Narayan Sai had some business interests in various trusts.

But, Sai was not to be found. They did see[1] a hideaway ready on the grounds, concealed by grass. The team, which included women constables, made a thorough search of the premises and seized several documents stored in cupboards.

The police had put out notices for information that would lead to the capture of Narayan Sai. Shobha Bhutada's phone number had been shared by a TV news station as a point of contact. She started getting around 500 phone calls per day, most of them useless.

'Madam, this man is a traitor, hang him,' said one caller.

'I am a jawan on the border and in your place, I would have shot him down,' said another passionate caller.

One regular caller was an old man from Haryana who would call to offer his blessings and told Bhutada not to get discouraged. 'God is with you,' he said.

There were also threat calls to that phone number. On 16 October 2013, one caller made a death threat.

'If you don't stop searching for Narayan Sai, I will shoot you,' the caller, a man, said.[2]

Bhutada was on her way to Ahmedabad at the time and disconnected the call. He kept calling back and she disconnected it several times. Finally, she picked up the call and the man repeated his threat.

'*Sudhar ja, nahin toh maar dalenge* (Mend your ways, or I will kill you),' he said. On the same day, Narayan Sai's plea for anticipatory bail was being heard in a court and was denied.

---

[1]  https://timesofindia.indiatimes.com/city/surat/Cops-raid-Virar-ashram-for-Narayan-Sai/articleshow/35885534.cms published on 27 October 2013 and accessed on 10 July 2018

[2]  https://www.youtube.com/watch?v=D20xnh2L64A published on 21 October 2013 and accessed on 10 July 2018

When the threat was repeated on 18 October 2013, the Surat police registered a case against the caller, traced his cell phone location and arrested him from Madhya Pradesh. The man later said that he was not directly related to the ashram but the news coverage had inspired him to make the call.

Around 9 or 10 a.m. on 26 October 2013, another call came on Bhutada's phone. The information it gave was so specific that it seemed quite convincing to her, she says.

'Narayan Sai is in Ahmedabad and he has put up at Sevani's flat, who has been Asaram's follower for a long time. He is hiding there,' the caller said.

Prahlad Kishanchand Sevani's flat was located at Shopper's Plaza VI opposite the Municipal Market in Ahmedabad's Navrangpura area. Inquiries revealed that he was indeed a follower of Asaram. The investigating officer, Mukesh Patel, kept busy with paperwork that day.

Bhutada consulted Asthana, quickly put together a team and set off for Ahmedabad. They reached the city around 2 p.m. and headed for Navrangpura, on the west bank of the Sabarmati, barely a couple of kilometres from the riverfront.

Bhutada was the only woman among eight policepersons, all in plain clothes, seated in two sedans, both of which were officers' private vehicles. Bhutada sat with three others in a Swift Dzire. Police personnel had been stationed near the police headquarters in Ahmedabad, waiting for orders, in case they were needed.

The Ahmedabad police had not been informed. The Surat police wanted a quiet entry into the city, without raising any alarms, and a quiet exit, in case they did not find anything. There had already been several disappointments. Shivanand Jha, who at the time of writing this is director general of Gujarat police, was then commissioner of police in Ahmedabad.

Some of the policemen were armed. The plain-clothes constables did not have guns but the officers did. Bhutada had her Glock 9mm on her person. While her role in Gujarat has been of crime detection and maintenance of law and order, the gun was no stranger to her.

Bhutada had been trained in arms at the National Police Academy in 2008, when K. Vijay Kumar was its director. Vijay Kumar has a reputation as a super cop, and had shot to fame when he was placed in charge of the special task force which had a mandate to hunt down the sandalwood bandit, Veerappan. Vijay Kumar ended the fifteen-year-long Operation Cocoon in a short time by engaging in encounters which reduced Veerappan's team till the man himself was traced down and shot dead in an encounter.

The experience in operational commands of the Border Security Force during militancy in Kashmir and the success of Operation Cocoon earned Vijay Kumar recognition as a counter-insurgency expert, since he had dealt with guerrilla soldiers as well. He retired as chief of the Central Reserve Police Force (CRPF) in 2013. I met him last when he had just retired and had been appointed adviser on Naxal management to the ministry of home affairs. Just past sixty, he was fit, maintained a rigorous discipline and continued to advise on counter-insurgency operations in central India and training security personnel for them.

At the police academy, Vijay Kumar insisted on training officers for jungle warfare, so that they could deal with guerrilla fighters. Bhutada remembers firing close to 5,000 rounds from various kinds of weapons—assault rifles such as MP-5, AK-47, sniper rifles and handguns. But it was not general target practice, there were simulations of how to fire blindfolded, with a flashlight blinding the eyes, from moving vehicles, firing from a motorcycle, and so forth.

Bhutada had first been assigned as an officer in Jammu and Kashmir and Vijay Kumar's arms training had been important for her. Her posting was at a police station that supervised the Indo-Pakistan border of the state. During her initial days there, a flash on the police radio announced that someone, presumably a Pakistani national, had set off a fire in a field across the fence but on the Indian side of the border. The moment she went across the fence, she heard police jawans unlatch the safety locks of their assault rifles. A senior officer was not supposed to go across the fence and she was called back by her colleagues, saying the fire department would handle it.

That night, a constable handed her an AK-47 assault rifle.

'What do I do with this? I have a handgun.'

'Ma'am, if we all get shot, what will you do? So, keep this.'

Bhutada lay awake with the assault rifle on the table next to her bed, her heart pounding. Practice rounds had been fine, till she was left alone with the assault rifle. She got up a few times to check if the safety catch was locked, worried that she might suddenly wake up and fire the weapon in her sleep.

The novelty of carrying a gun doesn't wear off easily. It feels good to some but storing it can be a great liability, especially if there are children around. It feels reassuring to many when they are given a tough assignment during which carrying a gun is more than a requirement of the uniform.

The Surat police team parked their vehicles in a crowded area of the market in Navrangpura, next to some street food eateries, where the sedans would not draw anyone's attention. The dark-tinted windows provided them cover.

During the entire stakeout, which lasted fourteen hours, Bhutada did not step out of the vehicle even once. She does not drink water in these situations to avoid washroom breaks. Even if the public would not, she did not want to risk a policeman on duty identifying her. The local police would be curious about why a Surat police team was present there without informing the local police station. After the several failures, Bhutada wanted to avoid any chance of a leak at any level that might have warned their target. Jha was sporting enough not to blow his fuse later.

As they waited, there was not much to do except exchange departmental gossip. During a field assignment, hierarchical lines dissipate and the team opens up with the senior.

But is it difficult being the only woman in such situations and the boss to boot? Bhutada quotes Facebook chief operating officer Sheryl Sandberg's philosophy from her book *Lean In: Women, Work, and the Will to Lead* (Knopf, 2013), '"Coffee time is the real time where you build actual relations which help you in your business." Stakeouts are situation where your team gets to know you. Till that happens, they don't know that you can sit with them in the car for twelve to fifteen hours at a stretch.'

Time passed with such water-cooler gossip and snacks from the fast food eateries. Once in a while, they would drive around the block and choose a different parking spot upon return, to avoid suspicious eyes, even though the area was quite crowded.

The day passed as did the evening. The pav bhaji and vada pav ensured that no dinner was required. Also, they could not overstuff themselves in case they needed to move swiftly. A few times they contemplated going into Sevani's building and raiding the place for Narayan Sai.

At 5.30 a.m., the Surat police team decided to turn back. Shobha Bhutada felt a little uneasy. She thought to herself that they had been at the spot where he was said to be hiding. They had seen no sign of Narayan Sai and discussed if they should probably search the apartment. Bhutada was also mindful of media pressure. There were daily news reports about how Narayan Sai was evading arrest and it had placed the Surat police in an embarrassing position. Most of the state's cops were on the lookout, as were teams in other states. Could she afford to turn back?

Bhutada had discussed this earlier with members of her team. They did not want to disturb the possible hideout. What if Narayan Sai returned? It was premature to rule out the possibility of his coming back another day. The source was reliable and they wanted to nab Narayan Sai. They could come back later.

As these thoughts raced through her head, the two cars drove eastwards and over the Gandhi Bridge across the Sabarmati. It was still dark and the cars got off the bridge and turned left, northwards, towards the IPS mess in Shahibag, on the way to the airport.

Bhutada thought out aloud now. A spark had set off several thoughts in her mind. Narayan Sai could have been locked in the flat all this while and they might not have known it. Else, he could have moved on and left a clue. Someone could come back and ruin any leads they might get if they went in now.

It was her call. She had to take it. And she did.

As they neared the familiar landmark of the IPS mess ahead (7 kilometres away from Sevani's flat), Bhutada told them to turn the car around. Nobody questioned her authoritative tone. They knew it was the boss speaking. An order had been issued; it was no longer a suggestion or a mere thought. The conflict had been resolved.

'*Antaratma* (inner consciousness).' She smiled when I asked her what had inspired the decision. She doesn't have a definition for it. Some may call it an investigator's hunch, a gut feeling that triggered off the adrenalin that was required for what they were in for next.

They returned to the spot and called Sevani to the building. Sevani's son, Sunil, came half an hour later to give them access. Two of the constables remained at the gate, others surrounded the entire building and the stairs before the rest of the team went up with the younger Sevani.

At the apartment, the police found soiled clothes that belonged to Narayan Sai. Sunil Sevani pretended not to know whose clothes these were.

Another apartment, number 205, was also locked and Sevani said he definitely did not have the keys for it in his set. So, the police said they would write a *panchnama* (seizure list) and break the door down. It was opened and inside they found that a single bedroom was locked, unlike in other flats. The police wanted that lock opened as well.

'There is nothing in there, ma'am. I have shown you all the flats and this room is also empty,' Sevani pleaded.

'No problem. We just want to make sure that it is empty,' Bhutada said.

Sevani's heart seemed to sink and his face turned ashen. He unwillingly unlocked it for the police.

In the *Hitchhiker's Guide to the Galaxy* (Pan Books, 1979), Douglas Adams wrote that the answer to the ultimate question of life, the universe and everything else, is forty-two, as developed by the supercomputer, Deep Thought. More than three decades after the book was written, the number would have a different meaning for the police, which was searching for answers about

Narayan Sai and an entirely different one for Asaram, since none
had been able to unravel the deepest secrets of his empire till
then.

Stacked against the wall were forty-two gunny bags. Sevani
went silent and plopped down on the floor outside. The police
asked where they had come from.

'I don't know. Ashramwale have left it here,' he replied.
His father, Prahlad Sevani, later told the investigators that he
had neither sheltered Narayan Sai nor provided storage space
for the forty-two bags. Sevani claimed that his friends at the
Motera ashram had asked him for the key to the apartment
which he had given them. He claimed that Narayan Sai's aides
then stashed the forty-two gunny bags and other items into his
apartment. It sounded much like the poem in Lewis Carroll's
*The Hunting of the Snark: An Agony in Eight Fits* (Adamant
Media Corporation, 1876):

> He had forty-two boxes, all carefully packed,
> With his name painted clearly on each:
> But, since he omitted to mention the fact,
> They were all left behind on the beach

Carroll's use of the number forty-two is speculated to have
been an inspiration for Adams's use of the number forty-two
as an answer to the ultimate question. The police seemed to
have stumbled on the answer too, but in their case, the question
was, what was in these forty-two gunny bags? They started
to pry them open and found them filled with documents of
ownership of land and other assets. There were land deeds from
Rajasthan, Maharashtra, Gujarat, Jammu and Madhya Pradesh.
The property documents would give the police addresses of all

the ashrams and teams could be sent there to trace Narayan Sai. There were boxes of literature published by Asaram's organizations, mostly of his spiritual discourses. There were also several copies of a pamphlet titled '*Sach*' (Truth) with the cover line '*Bapu ko Jail Kyon Bheja* (Why Bapu Was Sent to Jail)'.

As they dug deeper, they found handwritten chits, ledgers, registers with entries in crores, records of investments. Bhutada realized that these were more than just land deeds and made a telephone call to Asthana. They discussed what to do with the stash. By that time, the stakeout team was tired and Asthana knew they would need a fresh pair of eyes for the due diligence required for a panchnama and Mukesh Patel was summoned with another team to conduct the exercise. The room with the forty-two gunny bags was sealed and two policemen from the Navrangpura police station were posted outside with .303 rifles.

The media had learnt about the raid and a few journalists landed up at the market in Navrangpura. They could not recognize the plain-clothes constables but did find out that they were policemen from Surat. The Ahmedabad police was informed and when the media asked for a press briefing, Bhutada called Jha for his permission to address the media. He agreed.

'The room is stacked with documents. So, we are hopeful that there might be detailed accounts of whatever information we need for our investigation,' Bhutada told reporters.

The remaining apartments were also locked and the Ahmedabad police now asked Sevani to open them. They found a suitcase full of twenty-two bottles of Indian manufactured foreign liquor (IMFL) worth around Rs 50,000. For this, Sevani was charged with breaking the prohibition law in Gujarat. The forty-two bags of documents of course led to something entirely different.

The building, which had been developed by Sevani, was found to be promoted by him in a joint venture with a company, believed to be a *benami* (illegal) front for Asaram. The directors and shareholders were close aides of Asaram, whose addresses were in Motera and who were part of his innermost circles.

The police spent a lot of time in Sevani's flat going through the documents. They provided a deep insight into Asaram's empire of murky real estate deals and high-value cash loans at exorbitant interest rates. Since they were still on the trail of Narayan Sai, they looked for clues that might help them track him down. The soiled clothes were not of much use except to note that Narayan Sai was no longer wearing his trademark white clothes. Had he never gone there (or fled for that matter), the police would not have stripped the entire building to search for him or clues to track him down. The forty-two bags would have remained untouched and the question to Douglas Adams's answer would have never been discovered in an Indian detective's context.

The computer's hard drive revealed '*kachchi*' balance sheets—actual accounts of their empire and not the sham documents that were filed to revenue authorities. It showed the undeclared income and undisclosed investments. A detailed look at these documents revealed that taxes had not been paid for these transactions.

It turns out that the godman who spoke of benevolence and spirituality was a loan shark, which explained the goons that passed off as 'close associates' or 'most trusted of devotees'. The devotion was for fat interest rates of Rs 1,635 crore that was given to 500 borrowers, a lot of it in cash. Of this, Rs 1,350 crore was loaned to 350 borrowers. The property was 'benami', that is, it was held in the names of other people, mostly devotees.

But, their own accounts showed that these were owned by the godman. The benami and other investments, including real estate, amounted to around Rs 2,200 crore.

The largest amount of land held by both Asaram and Narayan was in Gujarat. They owned forty-five properties in ten districts of Gujarat; and thirty-three places across eight districts of Rajasthan, Madhya Pradesh, Maharashtra and Andhra Pradesh. These properties were held in the name of Asaram and Narayan Sai, and also as benami (as per the income tax department) in the names of Bhadresh Patel, Ajay Shah, Ajay Sharma, Kailash Dobhi, Sunil Sevani, Ganga, Jamuna and Kaushik Popatlal Vani, the man who managed the financial empire and is credited with suffixing several zeroes to the income generated from the ashrams and other 'godly ventures'.

Ganga and Jamuna were close aides of Narayan Sai, who had changed their names. The younger godman had set up trusts in the names of other associates, including one in Mumbai registered in the name of Mahendra Chawla, who has filed criminal cases against the godman for misusing his trust and fooling him into signing blank sheets of paper that were used to draw up the trust papers.

Narayan Sai invested around Rs 155 crore in two US companies—Soham Inc. and Costas Inc. Undeclared direct investments by Indian residents in foreign companies are illegal. This was widely discussed in the public domain following the 'Panama Papers' leak to the International Consortium of Investigative Journalists (ICIJ) through German reporters, Bastian Obermayer and Frederik Obermaier, who won a Pulitzer Prize for their work. The two exposed how billionaires, including Indians, had used a Panamanian law firm, Mossack Fonseca, to invest in obscure offshore companies in countries with opaque and low-tax jurisdictions. When the story was reported in India, the government tasked a special investigation team (led by Justice M.B. Shah) on black money to probe the allegations. Narayan Sai does not figure in the list reported as the 'Panama Papers' but the regulation became amply clear to the public at large when the Panama Papers were first reported in 2015.

In 2015, when the police had revealed some of Sai's secret financial empire and murky dealings, his lawyer had dismissed the claims as false. 'He is being made a scapegoat,' Kalpesh Desai, one of Narayan Sai's lawyers, told[3] Uday Mahurkar, author and senior journalist with *India Today* magazine. Desai repeated the same to me in June 2018, when I met him at his office across the road from the Surat district court complex.

Asthana's expertise as an investigator of economic offences came in handy. He directed the Surat investigators to scour through the data in the best way possible and compile their findings, which came to 900 pages. Asthana himself wrote a covering letter, forwarding their findings to the income tax authorities and the enforcement directorate, saying that the black money was used for personal and professional gain and should be investigated thoroughly for income tax violations.

'The documents and data show large-scale tax evasion and malpractices by Asaram and Narayan Sai and also a large number of traders, businessmen and real estate dealers,' he wrote.[4]

The Surat police had already started a nationwide manhunt for Narayan Sai. Asthana announced rewards for information leading to the arrest of the absconding godman and also issued

---

[3] https://www.indiatoday.in/magazine/cover-story/story/20150817-asarams-empire-of-deceit-820220-2015-08-06 published on 6 August 2015 and accessed on 14 August 2018

[4] Ibid.

lookout notices at airports, in case he tried to flee. He reached out to police departments across the country and tried to track the mobile phone locations of Narayan Sai and his two trusted aides, Ramesh and Hanuman.

Finally, Narayan Sai's location was tracked to New Delhi. The Delhi police was informed, and they started to track him as well.

# 6

# Many Tragedies and One Happy Ending

During the hunt for Narayan Sai, the police discovered that it was his close aide, Monica Purshottam Agrawal, who allegedly supplied him with SIM cards, provided him with logistical support and coordinated his bail applications while he was on the run.

When the media got wind of the fact that the police were tracking Monica as an abettor in Narayan Sai's escape, they transformed her into Narayan Sai's 'Menaka' after the mythical apsara. She was projected as the chief among his aides, along with allegations that she would recruit women whom he sexually exploited. They blew her up into a superwoman who was directing Narayan Sai's every move and knew every detail of his activities. The police, however, found this to be untrue.

'Monica may have influenced others to join his sect, but there is no such evidence that she was recruiting women for Narayan Sai to exploit them sexually. That is unnecessary exaggeration by the media,' Bhutada told me. Other police officers concurred.

Bhutada and Mukesh Patel thought her to be an idealist who looked upon Narayan Sai as her guru. Even if she had aided him, it was because she gave him the benefit of doubt; as she said later, she had never been sexually assaulted by him.

Ultimately, Narayan Sai's arrest was the result of intelligence, surveillance and a nerve-racking car chase by the Delhi police.

The police had kept all the phones connected to Sai under surveillance but had not managed to hear his voice even once because he was constantly switching mobile SIM cards. They started to look for leads to trace the numbers that Ramesh and Hanuman would call from. Eventually, they managed to trace a number for Ramesh.

Narayan Sai was at the time hiding in a cowshed attached to the farmhouse in Ludhiana of an associate of his father. By the time a Delhi police team reached there, he hoodwinked them and fled.

On 4 December 2013, Sai and his associates left in a Ford EcoSport vehicle, headed for Delhi to sign legal paperwork, presumably for an appeal in the Supreme Court. By now, the Rs 5 lakh in cash that he had begun with from Ahmedabad was depleted by half. Narayan Sai and his aides were not aware that a day prior, the Delhi police had informed its counterpart in Punjab to be on the lookout for Narayan Sai. As the EcoSport drove past the Punjab border into Haryana, along the Grand Trunk Road, a policeman on duty spotted them and alerted officials.

Another Delhi police team[1] left for the Grand Trunk Road, with around thirty policemen in nine police cars, some of them

---

[1]  https://indianexpress.com/article/news-archive/web/58-days-on-run-asarams-son-narayan-sai-arrested/ published on 5 October 2013 and accessed on 11 July 2018

unmarked. A few of the cars were posted along the highway in case he tried to slip into one of the roads off the highway. Somewhere close to Markanda, a Delhi police team spotted the Ford EcoSport on the other side. They immediately took a U-turn and started to follow Narayan Sai's car. One of the unmarked police cars followed the EcoSport closely, while the others stayed at a distance.

Ramesh, who was driving the EcoSport, zipped past the other cars and expertly navigated his way through the highway traffic. Just before they reached Kurukshetra, Ramesh pulled into a petrol pump. The police car trailing them called for backup. As Ramesh got out of the car to fill petrol, the police car casually pulled in behind the EcoSport. The policemen got out of the car and one of them caught hold of Ramesh while another took the keys out of the EcoSport's ignition.

'Ramesh?' asked the policeman who had caught hold of the driver.

'No, my name is Suresh,' he replied.

Narayan Sai, who was sitting in the car, heard this exchange, opened the door and tried to run. His head was covered with a turban and his face sported a light stubble. He was wearing dark, shaded trackpants and a jacket. Hanuman and a minor boy, who worked with them as a cook, were the other passengers. The car was stocked with rations and Sai was left with Rs 2.5 lakh in cash, the bulk of the exhausted money had been used to buy fuel.

The Ford EcoSport belonged to a Meerut-based follower of Asaram. Both him and the Ludhiana businessman were booked on charges of abetting Narayan Sai's escape.

~

The Surat police managed to get a transit remand for Narayan Sai and transported him to the court in Surat which was monitoring the rape probe. It granted the police permission to hold him for fourteen days in their custody. Unlike Asaram who never opened up or accepted the charges made against him in custody, Narayan Sai, it seems, was willing to sing for his supper. The police were curious about him and interrogated him for hours. Just to reiterate, anything said in police custody is not admissible in a court of law, unless specifically and independently restated before a magistrate.

Nevertheless, many of Sai's admissions during interrogation confirmed the charges against him. Once he opened up, he spoke of many other women. At least three police officers who were present at the interrogation told me that he gave the names of more than twenty women that he had raped. Later, they took him to the scene of the crime on a trip that was videotaped, where he provided graphic details of what had happened, where and how objects in the rooms were different now, close to a decade having passed since the events he was describing.

Following the interrogation, of the twenty–twenty-one women Sai had admitted to raping, a sanitized figure of ten was initially reported in the newspapers. When describing the instances of sexual assault, Sai seemed convinced that he was a reincarnation of Krishna and that the women were his '*gopis*'— which corroborated what the younger sister had told the police in October 2013. Three of the investigators told me, 'Sai felt it was his duty as their guru to "satiate the sexual needs of my female devotees. I am their guru, their father, their lover."'

During interrogation, Narayan Sai broke down and told the police that he never wanted this life for himself. 'At one point, I wanted a normal life, especially after I was married,' he confessed. 'My father pushed me into becoming his successor.'

Contrary to what they projected in public, the relationship between the godman and his son was not cordial in private. Vani was the important one for Asaram, along with others in the tier system of bhakts and aides who had more power than Narayan Sai over the empire.

'*Vani ki chalti hai* (Vani runs the show),' Sai had remarked to the police.

The son of god did not have a free hand over the empire and was given an allowance. If he needed money, he would have to ask for it and the specific amount would be handed to him. That definitely limited his own godliness.

When the forty-two bags of documents were seized, Narayan Sai appeared to be convinced this was a larger divine plan in his favour.

'I will get it now. It won't go to Vani.' The thought seemed to make Narayan Sai happy and he smiled after he told the police this. He appeared desperate to get hold of the papers and other data recovered from Sevani's flat.

Sai blamed his father for being a negative role model. Both father and son had their own set of goon-like followers who could turn violent and abusive at a single gesture from their respective leaders. The father was accused of manipulating female devotees into letting him sexually exploit them, as was the son.

In the case of many fake godmen, devotees often may not realize they are being exploited till much later. For instance, Kripalu Maharaj was known to tell his female followers, '*Tu mera premi, aa gale lag ja* (You are my lover, come embrace me),' and devotees would succumb thinking they were being blessed. These devotees in turn would greet fresh victims by saying they had been 'blessed with pure devotion'. Something similar happened at Gurmeet Ram Rahim's ashram where women were groomed to think of his sexual assaults as some kind of blessing.

Witnesses have said and it has been widely reported that Asaram would select the women he wished to be brought to him during sermons. The son adopted a similar practice. On the one hand, they would wax eloquent about dealing with greed—*paap ka baap* (the genesis of all sin)—and on the other, they would be scouting for the next devotee to exploit.

Narayan Sai's wife, Janaki Narayan aka Janaki Devi, confirmed to the police, the court[2] and the media[3] about his sexual relationships with women bhakts. But she clarified that she was not aware whether the sex was consensual or not.

Janaki had filed cases of adultery, divorce, domestic violence and maintenance against Narayan Sai. He had not given[4] her any money for expenses for two or three years till the time she filed the case against him in 2015.

For several years after their marriage, Narayan Sai managed to conceal his sexual antics from her. When she came to know of them, she confronted him only to be met with denial. Sai continued with his liaisons and when Janaki found that he had not changed, further marital discord ensued. The straw that

---

[2]  http://www.newindianexpress.com/nation/2016/apr/20/Narayan-Sais-Wife-Tells-Court-Their-Relations-Werent-Cordial-926863.html published on 20 April 2016 and accessed on 2 July 2018
    https://www.youtube.com/watch?v=UbTwjvaiuBg published on 9 September 2015 and accessed on 2 July 2018

[3]  https://www.youtube.com/watch?v=UbTwjvaiuBg published on 9 September 2015 and accessed on 2 July 2018

[4]  https://www.youtube.com/watch?v=UbTwjvaiuBg published on 9 September 2015 and accessed on 20 June 2018

broke the camel's back was when she discovered that Narayan Sai had allegedly fathered a son with a follower, Jamuna, and wanted to legally adopt him, or that is at least what she told the investigators in Surat.

Jamuna, along with another aide, Ganga, were two of his closest bhakts and were co-accused in the charges of rape against him. Jamuna's real name is Bhavna Patel and Ganga's is Dharmishtha Patel. Their names had been changed when they committed themselves as followers of Narayan Sai, who had rechristened them, just as he had renamed Kaushal Thakur 'Hanuman'. This was a practice at the ashrams and as the younger sister had pointed out in her testimony to the court, nobody knew the real names of most committee volunteers and bhakts. If their families were to search for them, nobody may be able to locate them, unless it was the godmen or one of his functionaries who were aware of the real names.

Despite Janaki putting her foot down, Narayan Sai remained adamant about adopting Jamuna's son. Finally, she agreed, provided Sai would stop his illicit affairs, which is what she thought they were. According to what Janaki told investigators, Narayan Sai responded by saying that she could not limit him since he was Krishna reincarnate, and being with his gopis was part of his *leela*.

Janaki was clear she did not want to be a part of this leela and asked him for a divorce. The scandal that this was likely to cause among their followers was too great to comprehend for the two godmen. Asaram's daughter had already divorced her husband. His son, who was also his heir, could not be reduced to a mere mortal whose wife had divorced him. Asaram's wife had never publicly separated from him and there was no marital discord between them in public.

For two years, Janaki tried to get a divorce but Narayan Sai continued to postpone it on some pretext or the other, saying he was busy with sermons and rituals. Just the usual, mundane duties of the son of god.

The revelation that Sai had fathered a son with a bhakt was additional evidence for the police and they wanted to conduct a DNA analysis on father and son. However, they were unable to trace the child.

It seems that after Janaki refused to adopt him, Narayan Sai reportedly arranged for his legal adoption through another method, though the police are yet to get hold of proof for this. Narayan Sai arranged the wedding of his other close bhakt, Ganga, with a follower so the two could legally adopt the child, who was shifted to study somewhere in Rajasthan.

After Narayan Sai's arrest, Janaki completely dissociated herself from the ashram. She was threatened several times after lodging a case for maintenance in Indore and had to shift between the homes of her sisters and her parents several times.

Once Sai was in custody, Monica herself came to the police. She had been a committed volunteer at the ashram for eight–nine years but when she was faced with legal trouble, the organization refused to help her with the costs, and she was left on her own.

Monica had been the cause of much jealousy amongst the rest of Narayan Sai's female followers, some of whom labelled her 'Radha', a reference to the favourite consort of the god Krishna.

Monica was different from the others. Smarter than the rest the police had interviewed, Bhutada told me, with a certain spark about her. Many women who went to stay at the ashram did so due to personal difficulties; some were poor, some were destitute, some had problems at home and in family life, some were widowed. Monica seems to have been genuinely motivated to lead a spiritual life.

All police officers remain convinced that Narayan Sai is a 'pervert'. He apparently tried to flirt with women police officers even during interrogation. He would say, 'I have a mesmerizing effect on women. There is something in my personality,' and begin to stare at an officer. The expression on Narayan Sai's face, seated on the floor, had been enough to make for a comical scene that sent the officer into peals of laughter.

Though he was quite forthcoming about his lifestyle, he found it difficult to talk in front of a woman officer. So, during a round of questioning, he requested that Bhutada, the only female officer present, leave the room. 'I cannot say certain things in front of ma'am,' he said. So, Bhutada stepped out and the others filled her in on the details afterwards.

Monica point blank denied that she had had a sexual relationship with Narayan Sai, but was shocked to learn that he had said the opposite to the police during his interrogation. The specific charge against her initially was that she was a recruiter for Sai. She was accused of convincing girls that complying with the wishes of the son of god was the surest way to achieve nirvana. She flatly denied any part in this.

Narayan Sai's system was simple, like Asaram's. Once a woman decided to commit to them, she would be worshipped in the ashram and treated as if she were a goddess. It was a big thing for many of the women who came from socio-economically impoverished backgrounds.

'*Ab toh aapki moksha prapti ho gayee hai* (Now you have attained nirvana),' the new recruits would be told once they started to abide by the directions of the son of god.

The girls would look forward to the interactions with Narayan Sai. He was their only male contact, since he had mandated that the women wouldn't be in contact with any other man. When interviewed, many of the women admitted they had had sex with Narayan Sai, under his influence as their guru. But, they refused to register any complaint or lodge an FIR. This included two women with whom he had been at the same time. Till then, there were only rumours of Narayan Sai having sex with multiple women simultaneously. These would remain rumours because though the police were able to interview some of the women, they did not want to lodge complaints.

A detective asked some followers about it. One of the women, from the Gambhoi ashram, had said they would escort Narayan Sai to meet powerful people. Even when he went to meet with a former President of India (while the latter was still in office), they would accompany him and one among them would first spread a cloth (*aasan*) on the chair before he would sit down.

So, when a girl with low literacy levels and without any power or agency sees a man with such influence, she remains in awe of him and his power.

According to the police, many of these women continue to stay in the ashram because they have left their homes and in-laws' homes. They literally have no one else to go to. Disbanding these places would mean relegating them to homelessness. Many cannot hope to get married any more after the disrepute of being attached with the father and son. Perhaps this could explain why many of the ashramites have continued to defend the godmen despite the shocking charges against them and Asaram's conviction in the POCSO case. Just like there is no legal provision to regulate godmen, there is also no legal provision to tend to women inmates once an ashram is disbanded, women who may find themselves at the mercy of the state or a court.

'They are actually trapped,' noted Bhutada.

The women accepted that they had had sexual contact with Narayan Sai. Consent was on the basis of his being their spiritual guru; to them, whatever Narayan Sai was doing or saying must be right.

The guru is in charge of the bhakts who live with him, in his care and under his organization's roof. Based on the 2013 amendment to the law on rape,[5] a guru sexually assaulting his devotees, who are under his charge and care at an establishment run by him, may be interpreted as rape. That was also the interpretation used by the court in Jodhpur in its verdict on the POCSO trial, especially because Asaram was head of the trust which ran the school where the minor girl, Mita, was studying.

Section 376C of the Indian Penal Code reads as:

Sexual intercourse by person in authority 376C. Whoever, being—

a. in a position of authority or in a fiduciary relationship; or
b. a public servant; or
c. superintendent or manager of a jail, remand home or other place of custody established by or under any law for the time being in force, or a women's or children's institution; or
d. on the management of a hospital or being on the staff of a hospital, abuses such position or fiduciary relationship to induce or seduce any woman either in his custody

---

[5]  Explanation (D) to Section 376 read with Section 376(2)(D) of the Indian Penal Code 1860

or under his charge or present in the premises to have sexual intercourse with him, such sexual intercourse not amounting to the offence of rape, shall be punished with rigorous imprisonment of either description for a term which shall not be less than five years, but which may extend to ten years, and shall also be liable to fine.

Narayan Sai was in a position of authority vis-à-vis the women at his ashram. Besides, there are other charges against him such as wrongful confinement, 'unnatural sex' and sexual assault, amongst others. The police have also made a case of conspiracy—of baiting the women by recruiting them under the garb of a spiritual life and influencing them, then exploiting them by misusing the trust they placed in him.

'The investigation has shown that most of the women in the ashram were victims of sexual abuse,' three police officers told me. One of them admitted he had been sceptical at first but several interviews with the women and other witnesses convinced him about the sexual exploitation perpetrated by Sai.

Life after the complaint has not been easy for the two sisters. They have to be under security at all times. Their eldest sister, who continues to be a diehard bhakt of Asaram, has reprimanded her sisters for their allegations against him. Her in-laws are also followers and she was willing to sever her relationship with her younger sisters for the disrepute they had brought to the godman.

The dedicated followers are relentless. As Vikram Singh, superintendent of Jodhpur jail, had told me, some still visit the jail and circumambulate around it. To them, it is a temple where their god is in residence for the moment. Thousands have flocked at any opportunity to get a glimpse of him.

The police found it difficult to believe some of Janaki's statements about Narayan Sai, one of the reasons being that she had also tried to get a divorce from him and could be considered a disgruntled wife. So, they arranged a meeting where Janaki was made to confront Narayan Sai with her accusations.

So, in the room, Bhutada was seated on a chair and had Narayan Sai sit on the floor. Bhutada asked Janaki to sit on a chair. But, Janaki couldn't, with her husband on the floor in front of her.

Bhutada had to give her a lecture on feminism. To the cynic, it might raise a question about how despite being in custody, the woman was still uncomfortable sitting at a physically higher position than her husband. Narayan Sai too may never have imagined that he would have to sit at his wife's feet.

Janaki gave the same statements that she had made earlier and Narayan Sai accepted many of those. In court, Sai's lawyers have hotly contested that he fathered Jamuna's son. In front of Janaki and the police officers, Narayan admitted asking Janaki to adopt Jamuna's son, because he had fathered the child.

~

Monica ended up being charged for harbouring an offender under Section 212 of the Indian Penal Code. But, the police firmly believe that she had a minor role to play and was really disappointed at the way the organization had treated her.

During one of her interactions with the police, Bhutada remarked, 'You are so smart, you could easily have been seated on this side of the table.'

That, Monica had later told the police, was a trigger. She returned to studying and prepared for the civil services examination. In 2017, she passed the Union Public Service Commission's examination and her high score got her a rank of 143[6] and a probationary job with the Indian Foreign Service. She was not yet convicted when she applied for and was recruited to the civil services. A conviction would mean dismissal from the services; otherwise, hers might possibly be the only happy ending in the gory aftermath of the tale of Asaram and his son.

The police think that Monica was deceived at some level. After the results, she came down with her family to meet all the police officers at their new postings and thanked them with tears in her eyes. In July 2018, before I finished writing this, I approached her for an interview to record her version of events and the inspiring narrative of how she had transformed herself. She declined to talk and her brother got in touch with me instead. Their family had faced severe problems because of the controversy around the godman and his son. They did not get in touch with me after that.

Those who have had the chance to observe both father and son say that Asaram comes across as the livelier of the two. There are scores of videos online where the godman breaks into song and dance during his sermons. In one particular video, he takes off his lapel microphone, gets up and grabs a cordless one and starts to sing along with a Punjabi carol. Narayan Sai unfortunately comes across as an inarticulate, underconfident man, leching at women around him. The women followers, who considered him the son of god, did not question his deportment. It is not known whether this was because they

---

[6]  http://www.upsc.gov.in/sites/default/files/CSM16FQ1.pdf accessed on 12 July 2018

considered him to be divine by association or because they were scared of him in some way.

~

The statements made by the complainant and the confessions of Narayan Sai had to be corroborated. The ex-devotees who had turned against their former masters all came in one by one to do so. Mahendra Chawla, who was Narayan Sai's aide for several years, seemed to have coordinated with many of the witnesses over time and it became easy to reach out to the other witnesses through him. Earlier, they had testified before the Justice D.K. Trivedi commission and now some of these testimonies would be used to establish the rape case against Narayan Sai. The same was done in Gandhinagar, where the rape charge levied by the elder sister was being tried.

Chawla's key testimony was a note supposedly in the handwriting of Narayan Sai that had some so-called occult formulae, under the headings:

'*Mrituk vyakti ko jeevit karne ki vidya* (How to resurrect a dead person)'

'*Chori ka maal wapas lene ka vidya* (How to recover stolen goods)'

'*Putraprapti ka tantravidya* (How to give birth to a son)'

Narayan Sai was confronted with these accusations—was he indeed a powerful occultist? Had he mastered a form of magic and used it for the benefit of those who approached him?

The police confronted Narayan Sai with these theories. What about those people who approached them for medical cures?

The people who would go to them would already be under some form of treatment. He would not advise them to stop that treatment but add to it his own little tricks. There would be prescriptions such as, 'Burn a feather, dissolve it in milk and drink it.' This was all in his handwriting, as per Chawla's statement. Narayan Sai's theory was that if 25 per cent get a positive result, that would get them more followers, and of course more money through donations and *bhandaras*.

Where did he learn these supposed occult practices from? Was his father the teacher, since the senior godman had also been charged with indulging in occult practices. To the police, who employ rational deduction in their investigation, the occult seemed like a ruse to lure more followers. So, they never pursued this theory, possibly missing on either unearthing a bizarre story or unmasking sheer lies.

Chawla told me five years ago, and reiterated twice later, that Narayan Sai had a teacher in Jharkhand. Sai had taken Chawla and another one of his aides to the Chhinnamasta (or Chhinnamastika) temple in Rajrappa near Ramgarh in Jharkhand. It is a couple of hours' drive from Ranchi and in my early years as a reporter with the *Hindustan Times*, I have been there a few times.

The deity Chhinnamasta is the Tenth Mahavidya of Tantric Lore and the temple in Jharkhand (like another temple of the goddess in Chintpurni in Himachal Pradesh) is considered an important place for tantric worship. Chawla claimed that Narayan Sai took them there and introduced them to his occult teacher.

Chawla, who at the time had been with Narayan Sai only a few years, was curious about occult practices. Sai wanted them to stay there and train with his teacher. But, the teacher did not agree. Tantra shastra and the occult are powerful tools, the teacher said, and would take a toll on the soul of the one who used them.

'These are innocent, pure souls. I do not want to see their souls ruined,' said the teacher to Narayan Sai and sent them on their way.

Shantilal Vaghela, who lost his boy in 2008, has not accepted any explanation other than an occult ritual to the strange way in which his son's corpse was discovered. The ribcage was split wide open and the organs were missing. The vest was found some feet away. The cousin's body, lying next to Shantilal's son's corpse, was not in that same condition. It was missing a few toes but did not have any other major damage.

When pressed to confirm if these things happened, Narayan Sai merely gave a mischievous smile and told the detectives, '*Aisa hota hai kya* (Does this really happen)?'

~

There is more than one way to look at the content of Narayan Sai's discussions with the police. When a person is held in custody and questioned, no matter how he may appear, he is at a disadvantage and is constantly trying to improve the circumstances he finds himself in. He might say things just to get it over with and there may be exaggerations and things that people want to say. Perhaps, it is out of that desperation that Narayan Sai supposedly offered Asthana a post to come and manage the ashrams. It caused much mirth in the police department for days. The policemen could not imagine the hard-nosed detective replacing Vani to sit in an ashram and run it.

Our lawmakers did understand the mentality of an accused in custody and discussed it when they decided that a person's statement to a magistrate will overrule admissions made to a

policeman. It is up to the policeman to confront him with proof
or theories and question him to get more leads.

From another perspective, police custody is when a person
is at their most vulnerable. This often creates situations in which
they might confess the truth about themselves. There may be
exceptions, when they can keep quiet for the first fourteen and
then another ten days. But, the many police officers I have
met over time have told me that many people surprisingly
start to confess things about themselves which they might have
concealed from the world.

Narayan Sai's life as the 'son of god' did not give him so
many opportunities to open up to people, to really speak. The
only possibility was his wife but they did not enjoy a congenial
relationship. In his interactions with the police, he finally
stopped running and was no longer in the company of people
who were in awe of him or his father.

# 7

# Shylock Comes Undone

There is a point in time, or perhaps a specific action or thought, that cannot be accurately explained. Some like to say that 'the stars were aligned in a certain fashion', some call it fate, others talk about 'a larger plan'. I have no fancy name for it nor can I precisely pinpoint the exact single moment that caused an unexpected-yet-important event. It could be a collection of events, a culmination of multiple die being cast and falling in a particular sequence. Eventually, the initial trigger may be lost, and we are left solely with its outcome.

As far as the crumbling of Asaram's financial edifice was concerned, some might construe that it began when IPS officer Shobha Bhutada decided to turn her vehicle back, against the advice of her tired colleagues, to check whether Narayan Sai was indeed hiding in Prahlad Kishanchand Sevani's flat. Bhutada herself cannot say what exactly prompted her to make that decision, perhaps, because the brain does not record every decision made after a sleepless twenty-four hours spent cramped without water or bathroom breaks, in a car with her

team. But, she feels that such a point may have never come had
Narayan Sai not fled when the police wanted to question him
in the first place.

As a result, the police busted Asaram's criminal empire and
managed the most in-depth look into the inner workings of the
godman's cult, its very foundation, and the kind of financial
clout he had built over four decades.

The documents—58,000 leaves of various books,
ledgers, scraps, loose pages, pinned sheets and digital data
on a computer and digital hard drives—were structured first
by a chartered accountant who worked for close to ten weeks
with then Surat commissioner of police, Rakesh Asthana.
The economic offences specialist put them together, studied
them, undid them and restitched them into a 900-page
summary with a cover letter that was reported in the media,
based on a February 2014 press conference by Asthana in
Surat.

'The documents and data show large-scale tax evasion and
malpractices by Asaram and Narayan Sai and also (names) a
large number of traders, businessmen and real estate dealers.
They used black money thus generated for professional and
personal gains. Since the matter has national and international
ramifications, it should be thoroughly investigated under the
Income Tax Act,' Asthana had written[1] in the letter which,
along with the documents, he passed on to the income tax
department.

---

[1]  http://www.dailymail.co.uk/indiahome/indianews/article-
   3190648/Asaram-s-sordid-network-fraud-money-lending-shady-
   land-deals-Documents-blow-lid-guru-s-greedy-empire.html
   accessed on 30 June 2018

The estimated worth of the godman's empire, excluding his properties, was pegged at Rs 10,000 crore.[2] The income tax department had found a document, dated sometime in 2013, which reportedly said[3] that Asaram had earned Rs 419 crore in a single year as interest alone from the high-value cash loans that he gave. Bhutada told me that this was the one document that stood out in the pile for her when she went through the papers, which were in English, Hindi and Gujarati. There were rumours of huge amounts of cash to the tune of hundreds of crores, kept close at hand, but this was never found. By the time the documents were properly decoded, it was nearly two years since the discovery of the forty-two bags.

There were[4] investments worth Rs 6,000 crore in various instruments such as Kisan Vikas Patra, mutual funds, government bonds, debt funds, securities, fixed deposits, etc. Other details also surfaced over time, which the media reported whenever the godman was in the news. The income tax department, in the meantime, went through the documents with a fine-toothed comb.

The Income Tax Act allows revenue authorities to assess unpaid tax for six years. The investigation wing at Surat conducted the investigation into the documents while the assessment wing in Ahmedabad calculated the amount of tax Asaram owed to the exchequer. They pieced[5] together an account of how the operation was run. The assessment report,

---

[2]  https://www.ibtimes.co.in/asaram-bapus-net-worth-self-styled-godman-his-trove-riches-767674 accessed on 30 June 2018

[3]  Ibid.

[4]  https://indianexpress.com/article/cities/ahmedabad/asaram-sai-have-vast-land-holdings-properties-worth-rs-10000-cr-surat-police/ accessed on 30 June 2018

[5]  Details accessed by author through extensive interviews with sources.

which has been filed with the income tax authorities, runs into 1,914 pages over four volumes, of which one only contains documents annexed to the assessment. The main order itself is around 550 pages, the balance is made up of two elements. One is the annexed documents. The other is an explanation of the methodology used to arrive at the assessment.

The documents in the cache discovered by Shobha Bhutada and the Surat police personnel go back to 1977. The forty-two bags of 58,000 documents were a huge find but none could authoritatively say that these were all the documents pertaining to Asaram's empire. In fact, there is a suspicion that there might be more elsewhere. Even so, this stack definitely allowed more than a sneak peek into how Asaram operated and how much his empire was worth.

The chief source of income was cash donations made by devotees. The umbrella trust was the Sant Shri Asaramji Bapu Ashram Trust; 'everything else is a smokescreen', is how one investigator described it. During his deposition to the Justice (retd) D.K. Trivedi commission, the godman himself said[6] he had more than 400 ashrams. The trust was registered as a religious trust which exempted it from income tax. It was registered under Section 80(g) of the Income Tax Act, which means donations to the trust were exempt from income tax for the payer. At the time of writing this, the income tax department had cancelled these registrations.

The cash donations were collected at the ashrams and at places where satsangs and other events were held. Code words were used for the collection points, for instance, Vyas Peeth or

---

[6] Interview of Subramaniam Iyer, advocate for Shantilal Vaghela, conducted by the author

VP meant the place where the godman himself sat and addressed the public. Vyas is believed to be a reference to the sage Vyas. VPL stood for 'Vyas Peeth-Ladies', meaning where the godman addressed women devotees. BDD was an acronym for 'Buddh Dakshina donation', a direct reference to the bodhi tree under which the Buddha is said to have achieved enlightenment. This was also referred to as 'Bud Peti' in the books. These places were where the highest cash collections were recorded because of the godman's presence.

Most of the donations were not entered in the account books and the cash was transported and stored by a select group of aides—at the highest strata of a four-tier system, detailed below. The ordinary volunteer, or even the motley crew of former aides-turned-witnesses, did not have access to, or responsibility of, the huge amounts of cash. Apart from cash, donations were also made in cheques, demand drafts, jewellery, land and foreign exchange.

A person who studied and scrutinized these documents told me that the collection had always been accounted for in informal books, away from the declared income of the trust. 'It was a practice that seems to have continued from the beginning, though, they could have easily declared this income. Had they employed some corporate accounting firm, they would have set their books straight according to law,' he said.

So, why employ this roundabout way and deliberately suppress income which was not subject to any tax?

'One reason could be that had it been booked in the trust's books, Asaram and his cronies could never have used it for any personal gain. Then, the money could not have been invested in the loan business,' he explained.

Asaram's interest in disbursing loans seems to have begun in 1993–94. Since then, he has given loans to at least

550 people over twenty years. One of the witnesses in the Justice (retd) D.K. Trivedi commission, Raju Chandak, had deposed[7] that the godman would use a team of goons to threaten borrowers who defaulted on interest payments. The seized documents alone revealed that Rs 3,000 crore had been lent by Asaram, while the income tax department assessed that loans worth Rs 1,500 crore remained active, generating an interest of Rs 700 crore between 2007–13. The rates of interest varied from 1 per cent per month to 2.5 per cent per month.

Six builders were loaned high sums of money. These included a Delhi-based builder who was loaned Rs 200 crore, a Jaipur-based builder-cum-chartered accountant who was given Rs 100 crore, while Sevani, at whose flat the forty-two bags were found, owed the godman Rs 100 crore. The flat was located in a building that had been built as a joint venture between Sevani and a company whose owners were the godman's trusted aides. Details of the six builders and the other borrowers of cash have been sent to their respective income tax circles for tax assessment.

At the top of the four-tier hierarchy that ran the financial empire was Asaram, supremo of the organization. The most trusted aide was Kaushik Popatlal Vani, the Nagpur-born former engineer-turned-disciple who was one of the few devotees at the Motera ashram with his own quarters, and who was answerable to none but Asaram himself. It is said that even Narayan Sai had to ask Vani when he needed money for anything—from an enterprise to the most minor of expenses. Financial independence

---

7    Deposition of Raju Chandak, former aide to Asaram, to the Justice D.K. Trivedi commission in 2009

was one of the reasons why Narayan Sai was trying to build his own empire, though his ashram at Himmatnagar in Gujarat is rumoured to have had a more sinister purpose.

Vani was questioned once by the Surat police while they were investigating Narayan Sai, to get a fix on the godman's empire and other details. Vani came but refused to answer any questions and in the absence of any specific proof, the police could not detain him. While he was with the police, he refused to drink a drop of water or touch any of the food offered to him. In his fifties, Vani is short and slightly built with salt and pepper hair cropped close to his scalp.

Later, when some evidence was found against him, Vani vanished off the face of the earth. He has not been located ever since. At the ashram, I casually asked about him and was told that nobody knew where he was. Sureshanand, Asaram's Vedantic understudy who began all his satsangs and, in the godman's absence tended to the flock and delivered the sermons, disappeared too. I had really wanted to meet him to understand the spiritual side of the godman, but Asaram's spokesperson, Neelam Dubey, said that he had left soon after the charges in 2013. 'He has gone into *ekant dhyan* (isolated meditation),' is how she described it.

Not exactly below, but after Vani, and almost on the same tier, was Ajay S. Sharma, a chartered accountant, who also had extensive knowledge of Asaram's empire. At the same level was Gaurav Bajaj, considered a computer expert. The third tier included aides such as Meenaketan Govindpatro, Naresh Bhagurmal, Naval Kishore, Laxmikant Dwivedi, Mani Patel, Umesh Totlani and Shobhraj Thakore, a trained CA. Vani was assisted by Dev Kumar, who otherwise belonged to a lower tier but by being privy to the kind of information that Vani had, could be placed in the third tier. In several of the seized documents, these people are identified by their initials.[8]

The fourth tier included those who lived in the ashrams as committed, surrendered volunteers, many of them acting as couriers and delivery people. They had surrendered their lives and will to their guru, clad themselves in white kurtas and pyjamas, and attended to the miscellaneous chores around the ashram.

One such volunteer gave me a lift on his scooter out of Motera as I was leaving the ashram. This person, who would not give his name, said he went to Jodhpur several times just to get a glimpse of his guru. 'My mother had gone too, as did my sister, and the police baton-charged them, but my mother told them that she would keep coming, as did I. And, I returned every opportunity I could get. We even performed *parikrama* of the Jodhpur jail,' he said.

It is important to know about this fourth tier. Asaram's accounts show that he spent on their clothes, food and other charitable acts while accommodating them at the ashrams. Some had opted to live at the ashram due to poverty, while many came of their own choice. Their surrender to the guru came with a price tag, though.

Of the reams of documents found in the forty-two bags were chequebooks with blank leaves, all duly signed. These belonged to bank accounts opened in the name of volunteer-devotees who stayed at the ashram. Investigations revealed that these accounts had been opened on the basis of proof-of-address certificates issued by the umbrella trust at the Motera ashram. In fact, all the people had given the ashram as their address and rightly so, since

---

[8]   Information based on interviews with income tax officials.

that was where they lived. Scrutiny of the bank accounts revealed that the cheques were used to make miscellaneous payments and many fixed deposits had been made to these accounts. None of them were registered with the income tax department. Spreading small amounts of cash over several accounts helps avoid detection of large-scale financial fraud.

~

As mentioned earlier, the tax demand alone was of Rs 3,100 crore, without penalty, from 2007–13. The total amount was Rs 3,000 crore for donations and other transactions during this period. The 30 per cent penalty meant this figure would go up to Rs 4,030 crore—a hefty recovery amount for revenue authorities.

The IT circle's Surat investigation wing probed the case, which was then transferred to Ahmedabad for the final order.

The final order has been challenged before the CIT Appeal bench no. 11, where it is pending. Once confirmed, the penalty on this would be 30 per cent. After this, it would go to the Income Tax Appellate Tribunal (ITAT).

Since the final order is already given, there is no possibility of it going to the Settlement Commission for a settlement of tax dues. Because they have contested the tax dues, the trust can no longer opt for a settlement of undeclared income or assets.

The status of Asaram's main trust stands cancelled. This is the Motera ashram trust, the main one; the others are a smokescreen. It has been reduced to a mere association of persons (AOP) and will no longer get the benefits of a trust or Section 80(g) benefits, an income tax officer told me, adding that the trust's registration under Section 12AA of the IT Act, which gives taxation relief, stands cancelled, and the only way to restore it is through years of potentially expensive litigation.[9]

Asaram is a trustee of the organization but did not appear as involved in its financial structure—something the income tax department found surprising. A bribery case involving Narayan Sai shows how the financial empire was controlled. When Sai wanted to bribe a Surat policeman, C.M. Kumbhani, he wrote a chit, which 'Rupabhai' or Naresh Mankani read and handed over the money to Uday Sanghani. The handwritten chit had the same value as a bank's demand draft; no cheque could loosen so much cash from a bank in one go without raising eyebrows.

In fact, in his deposition to the enforcement directorate (ED), Mankani's deposition reads, '. . . that he told Uday Sanghani that without any written authority from Narayan Sai he would not be able to give him any money'.

Clearly, disbursing such an amount on his own without express written permission was above Mankani's paygrade but this also shows how the power structure shifted after Asaram was remanded to custody. Previously, Narayan Sai complained that he had to turn to Vani for every bit of cash. Now, he could move Rs 1 crore with two lines and his name scrawled underneath.

The search and seizure took place in seventy locations across the country, on people who had availed of Asaram's cash loans.

Asaram had floated some companies in which he parked the interest earned from loans. The income tax department looked at these companies and found each of them to have served different purposes. They were used as vehicles to park cash that was not booked as cash. Arjun Navnirman Pvt. Ltd was used to

---

[9]   See Notes for explanation on this.

park unaccounted money in real estate. Other companies were used to park money in various places or to route cash.

Several of the companies are Kolkata (Howrah) based and Gopal Das appears as a director common to them, who used to look after the network of suitcase companies in the region.

The amount of interest generated from loans disbursed by Asaram and his cronies in some years went up to Rs 300 crore. Right now, the seized documents show that there was Rs 1,500 crore principal still outstanding to the outfit. The total estimated interest earned but not declared during the six-year period was Rs 700 crore, as per their documents.

There are many loans for which interest could not be collected. There was a collection team that would strong-arm those who defaulted on loans. One such loan recovery agent of Asaram is among his many former aides to have turned into witnesses against him. He has given testimony in some cases but was hesitant about giving further interviews due to safety concerns.

The modus operandi has been shared with other income tax circles and details of foreign exchange transactions sent to the Foreign Contributions Regulations Act (FCRA) department of the Union home ministry, and to the ED and the charity commissioner. The probe did not turn up direct hawala operations but there are some transactions that are in the nature of hawala. For instance, some NRI devotees would avail of cash loans and park shares in their foreign companies with the godman as collateral. These shares were shown as gifts. One US-based devotee, Sailesh Shah, took a loan of Rs 10 crore. He used to live in Ahmedabad's Vastrapuram and now lives in Garden Park Estate, Chino, USA. Inquiries revealed that he had several financial fraud cases in the US.

The empire is run through a network of fifty-two entities that include trusts, foundations and private limited companies. There are reportedly 400 branches, or branch-ashrams, but the number of proper ashrams is actually 250, as discovered by the income tax department. The number of 400 reported by Asaram appears inflated as several of these so-called ashrams are really small huts and temples built by his devotees and the land on which these establishments are constructed has been donated to the trust. The same was the case of Ranjit Deora, at whose house Asaram sexually assaulted Mita.

All the properties of the various trusts, societies and companies have been attached by the income tax department till the assessed tax amount is recovered by the revenue authorities. The list goes up to 175 properties, for which separate notices were sent to district magistrates of the areas where the properties were located. None of these could be disposed of till the tax collection was done. The income tax department is positive of a massive recovery by auctioning these properties, unless Asaram and Narayan Sai miraculously find the money to pay the amount, once the order is confirmed.

The main trust has forty-nine bank accounts and several investments including mutual funds, debts funds, all of which were attached by income tax authorities. Upon confirmation from the ITAT, these properties will be auctioned on failure to pay the tax and penalty amounts.

The individual accounts of Asaram and his family are not hefty and their returns were not more than Rs 10–20 lakh in a year. The properties in the name of Narayan Sai and other family members are few.

If the entire sum of Rs 3,000 crore of unaccounted money is brought into the books, it would be difficult to utilize those funds for personal or individual use. Since the beginning, these funds had been kept out of the accounts. Re-entering them would mean that the trust would control them and they would be under the scrutiny of the authorities. They could not be used for any kind of loans or other shady businesses. The empire of cash stash ran parallel to the legitimate one under Asaram's trust.

The Mahila Utthan Trust, which runs the organization's ashrams for women, was established as a separate entity. When I went to Motera, the signage was being changed to Sati Anusuya Trust, also one of the fifty-two entities scrutinized by the income tax department and whose registration had been cancelled.

The trading activities of Asaram's operations included selling incense sticks, soap, food items, Ayurvedic preparations, among other things, as also the publication and distribution of in-house magazines. Mahendra Chawla started out loading such goods into trucks and later graduated to supervising the trading. He would go to camps and other events where he would set up a mobile trading post to sell the items to devotees, who bought these believing them to be sacred and beneficial because they were branded with Asaram's name. The reality was that the manufacturing was outsourced, as per Mahendra's testimony and the records shown to the income tax department.

A pharmacy in Surat manufactured the Ayurvedic formulations, which the ashram continues to sell. The tax department also noted that the list of Asaram's branded items included some which later Baba Ramdev's Patanjali also started to sell, such as *chyawanprash*, honey, and so forth. In 2013, I bought a large bottle of amla juice extract from the store at the Kota unit. By the time I reached Delhi the next day, the contents of the bottle were putrefying and I had to throw it away. The manufacturers and wholesalers of these items were also given cash loans, while, in many cases, the money used to pay the manufacturers was through cash deposits made to bank accounts of ashramites.

During the assessment, Ajay S. Sharma, the chartered accountant devotee, used to file replies on behalf of the trusts. Later, he was replaced by Rajesh Bharti, who was also made a trustee of the main trust. No personal hearing was granted to them, but notices were sent to the trust at its address in the Motera ashram. Sharma, and later Bharti, would go and file their replies with the income tax department.

Asaram's followers use several videos and photos to showcase his charitable work. This includes donation of clothes, books and miscellaneous items to devotees. Many of these devotees either were or would become residents of Asaram's ashrams. The fact that these residents were made to sign affidavits and given certificates attesting the ashram as their permanent address has been mentioned earlier, as also the bank accounts opened in their names, and the chequebooks with signed blank leaves. The chequebooks would be stored with the financial managers and aides of Asaram's trust. Some devotes were also made directors in the companies, such as Dinesh Bhagchandani, who was attacked in March 2014. None of these account holders had IT PAN and these accounts have been frozen.

The funds from these accounts, which could be defined as benami, were used for purchases required by the trust for its trading activities. The income tax department discovered cash deposits made to the benami accounts as the source of their funds.

The building where the forty-two bags were found is itself the subject of a probe. The income tax probe found that its construction was financed as a joint venture between Sevani and a company in which Asaram's most trusted aides were directors.

At the time of writing this, the income tax department is in the process of trying to get an evaluation of the market value of Asaram's properties. The conservative value is estimated to be between Rs 700 to Rs 1,300 crore.

This valuation may be incorrect on many counts. The actual area of the ashrams has not been considered in many cases. There are several charges of land encroachment and disputes regarding the properties occupied by the ashrams. The income tax department has received land-related complaints from several people who were unable to get relief from courts or the administration. Besides that, the income tax department is yet to hear back from land records offices across the country regarding both the circle rate and the market valuation of the 175 properties they had attached. The figure could take the actual value of Asaram's empire much beyond the initial assessment of Rs 10,000 crore.

~

**Note on income tax assessment following judgment of the Gujarat High Court, accessed by the author.**

DECISION OF THE HIGH COURT OF GUJARAT AT AHMEDABAD IN SPECIAL CIVIL APPLICATION NO. 2705 OF 2017, RE: *SANT ASHARAMJI ASHRAM VS DEPUTY COMMISSIONER OF INCOME TAX*, DELIVERED BY JUSTICE M.R. SHAH AND JUSTICE B.N. KARIA, DECIDED ON 26 APRIL 2017

Asaram's umbrella trust had challenged a show cause notice issued to it by the income tax assessing officer in Ahmedabad to appoint a special auditor. Some of the material from the

forty-two gunny bags and the response of the
trust to it had been discussed in this order.

While the income tax investigation into the
seized documents was pending, the department
wrote to the main trust and asked for its
income tax returns between assessment years
2009–10 and 2014–15, along with the returns
for financial year 2014–15. These encompassed
income tax returns for seven financial years,
between financial year 2008–09 and financial
year 2014–15. This would help clarify the
financial affairs reflected in the reported
revenue of the trust and what was found in the
58,000-document bundle.

Based on the seized documents, the income
tax department sent a detailed questionnaire to
Asaram's trust for clarification and asked them
to submit 'ledger accounts, bank statements,
confirmatory letters from unsecured depositors'
and so forth. The income tax authority told the
Gujarat High Court (GHC) that 'huge donation
in the form of cash was found to be deposited
which was found to be unaccounted'.

The income tax assessor felt that because
of 'the complexity and multiplicity nature of
material', the revenue authorities would have
to appoint a special auditor to make a proper
audit of Asaram's financial affairs. The Income
Tax Act, 1961 provides for a special audit of
this kind under Section 142-2A subject to a
well-reasoned approval from a senior official
of the income tax department of the rank of
chief commissioner of income tax (CCIT) or
principal commissioner of income tax (PCIT).

As required by law, before approaching
higher officials for an approval, the income
tax authorities sent the trust a thirty-one-

page-long, show cause notice dated 18 October 2016, to give them an opportunity to be heard. They were asked to say why a special auditor should not be appointed in their case. On 24 October, the trust's representative requested a week's adjournment. On 1 November, the income tax department extended the adjournment by another week on the request of the trust's representative. This was repeated on 7 November. Finally, on 15 November, the income tax department refused to grant any further extensions and requested the PCIT to grant approval for a special audit.

This timeline also shows that the income tax department had been organizing and studying the data for more than a year and a half, having received it on 9 March 2015, as per their submissions to the GHC, recorded in the judgment dated 24 April 2016.

The income tax department told the GHC, through its lawyer (senior advocate Manish Bhatt), that the revenue officials wanted a special audit to avoid an inaccurate assessment of the trust and its affiliates. On 23 November 2016, the PCIT granted approval to the income tax officials in Ahmedabad to conduct a special audit. The trust felt that a special audit was not required and challenged the decision of the PCIT before the GHC.

The lawyer for Asaram's trust, senior advocate S.N. Soparkar, argued that the order to appoint a special auditor did not have enough supporting reasons. He also said that the income tax department had not granted enough time to the trust to argue its case before the assessing officer. Soparkar presented several relevant judgments to buttress his argument

and also said that he should have scrutinized
the accounts of the trust before directing a
special audit.

Bhatt pointed out to the court that the
thirty-one-page-long, show cause notice was
detailed, and shared its contents. The income
tax department had shared a soft copy of the
documents from the forty-two gunny bags with
the trust on 6 May 2016, and sent questionnaires
based on this material dated 18 July 2016,
regarding the trust's books of accounts. On 21
July, the trust 'feigned ignorance about the
queries raised in the questionnaires'.

The income tax department's lawyer said
following a reminder to Asaram's trust on 1
August 2016, the trust responded on 12 August,
in which it 'admitted that the documents
belonged to it but feigned ignorance as to how
the same reached third parties'.

On 22 August, the income tax department
provided Annual Information Return to the trust
and sought an explanation to this information.
On 26 August, the trust responded by sharing
the regular returns it had filed for income
tax though it had been sent a notice dated 1
February 2016, under Section 153C of the Income
Tax Act to file special returns. Such special
returns under Section 153C are sought after
documents have been requisitioned following a
tax raid.

The income tax department also provided
details of bank accounts of the trust on
5 September. On 6 September, the revenue
authorities asked for the names and details of
the bank accounts of Asaram's devotees (whose
accounts were later suspected to have been
misused to launder cash). On 9 September, the

trust responded saying it could not provide the bank details sought. On 16 September, they again sent the financial statements of several people to the trust and this exercise was repeated after a fortnight of a request dated 12 September, by the trust, which claimed that the soft copy of the documents was not legible.

Following this correspondence and due to a lack of answers, the tax assessing officer finally sent the show cause notice dated 18 October asking why a special auditor should not be appointed. After four opportunities over three weeks, when the trust failed to respond to the show cause notice, the assessing officer sent a request to the PCIT for its sanction to appoint a special auditor. The file noting for this was shared with the GHC. On 23 November, the PCIT passed the order to appoint a special auditor who would audit the 58,000 documents, the digital data and the books and returns of the trust. This order was sent to the trust on 28 November.

In para 6.3 of its judgment, the GHC noted, 'It appears that from 42 gunny bags, cheques, promissory notes, blank allotment letters, purchase sale deeds as security against loans were found. The name of the petitioner [Sant Asharamji Ashram] with others appear in the master ledger. A search and seizure action under Section 132(1) of the IT Act was conducted at various places including Ahmedabad, Surat, Vadodara and other cities across the country on beneficiaries of transactions uncovered from requisitioned material. A huge cash inflow and outflow were prima facie not found in the regular books of account. Large number of existing bank accounts in the name of Sadhaks,

KYC documents of bank accounts and NSCs, KVPs revealed the address is that of Asaram Bapu. Use of 7 companies for laundering of cash and use of 5 proprietary concerns for laundering of cash are detected. Diversion of funds for real estate purpose has been detected. The books of account show receipts from donation and Dan Patra, however the donation receipts as per the books of account are found to be meager whereas the donation receipts as per the requisitioned material are found to be very huge. Therefore, from the requisitioned materials it has been prima facie revealed that the Trust had diverted its funds in making advances of cash loan and interest charged thereon.'

The GHC overruled the objections of the trust and allowed the appointment of the special auditor.

Identical objections were raised by at least three companies in which Asaram's aides were directors. The same bench of the GHC overruled their challenge to the order of the income tax authorities to appoint a special auditor to audit the material. In the case of Ulhas Securities, the order was passed on 13 February 2017. In the case of Pratius Merchants and Dhanpati Marketiers, the orders for both were passed on 26 April 2017. All three orders were written by Justice Mukesh R. Shah, who, at the time of writing this, was the first puisne judge of the Gujarat High Court.

The special audits eventually led to the nearly 2,000-page-long assessment order passed by the income tax department against Asaram's trust.

# 8

# 'One Big'

Asaram seems to have been fairly efficient at managing his empire, aided by a close group. These aides, in turn, had a network of several builders and 'businessmen', who were quick on their feet and resourceful.

Each ashram was self-sufficient, but its functional head was connected with Kaushik Popatlal Vani, Asaram's left-hand man for all financial matters, and reported to him for key matters. Being the successor to this empire was frustrating for Narayan Sai, who was forty-one years of age at the time of his arrest. Father and son would have conflicts in private over control of their empire, to which only a few were privy. An income tax investigator also told me that he found no trail that showed that Narayan Sai had any control over the finances.

Police officers who interrogated the son said that was a common complaint among all of Asaram's family members. He held the reins of his empire tightly, through Vani, and used them to exercise control over the family. The son had to ask Vani for permission to access funds and other resources. Some of Asaram's closest aides told the police that the father seemed to think that the son was not smart enough to handle the empire. A Surat-based journalist for a prominent English daily told me that he had met Narayan Sai several times and found the godman-in-waiting to be neither proficient in scriptures, unlike his father, nor very bright.

'We met with him several times when we had access and he would respond very easily to any question asked of him,' the journalist had told me at his office in Surat.

There was one opportunity that Narayan Sai did have to prove to his father that he could manage matters but he seemed to have bungled it up. This was when Narayan Sai, during his interrogation, almost managed to bribe a police officer in order to recover the documents from the forty-two gunny bags. The recovery of those documents was crucial to Asaram's empire.

Then again, as Shobha Bhutada pointed out to me, had Narayan Sai not made a run for it, the police, income tax officials and the general public would have never found out crucial details about how the godman's empire was run.

Narayan Sai not only bungled up the one opportunity he had to prove to his father that he'd make for a worthy successor, he also managed to land himself and several of Asaram's key aides in yet another case. A bribery charge[1] for Rs 8.1 crore led the ED to swoop down on the godman's son and revealed additional details about how the cash-rich empire worked.

During his interrogation, Narayan Sai had tried to bribe several police officers. When he was on the run, Sai had been informed about the forty-two gunny bags recovered from Sevani's flat. He was questioned about them by Rakesh Asthana

---

[1]  FIR no. I-37/2013 lodged by the DCB police station, Surat.

during one late-night interrogation session. During such
sessions, Sai would be seated on the floor while the officers
would be on chairs. Sai had never been treated like this before.
The year he was born, his father was already preparing to set up
his ashram in Motera. As he grew up, he became accustomed to
being treated as the son of a guru.

That night, Narayan Sai felt he had had enough of being
questioned and treated like a criminal. Earlier, he had tried to
bribe policemen whenever he was alone with one. It had not
worked, but then, he had offered much smaller sums of money.
He had even tried to cast a 'spell' on Shobha Bhutada with the
'hypnotic power of his eyes', but she had managed not to swoon
over his self-imagined primal charm, otherwise invisible to the
human eye.

While Narayan Sai was trying his luck in police custody,
Asaram's aides were growing restless and did not want to leave
the brokering of a deal to the godman's son. Their mission[2]
was simple—replace the incriminating documents in the forty-
two gunny bags with rubbish. With this purpose in mind, they
started to reach out to multiple people.

In 2013, Uday Sanghani had been Asaram's devoted
follower for twenty-one years and was trusted with some of his
darkest secrets. It is not clear how much he knew, but in the
four-tier system, he was somewhere in the third tier. Sanghani
was not one of the faceless bhakts who managed handles on social

---

[2]  Sequence of events based on statements of Hasmukh Upadhya,
    Hitendra Waghela, Reena Waghela, Ketan Patel, Bhavesh Patel,
    Ghanshyam Tank, Kanti Parikh, Raghuvirsinh Zhala, Bipin Bhave
    recorded by the ED on several dates under Section 50 PMLA.
    Statements part of PAO and prosecution complaint filed by ED
    before PMLA court.

media, posting about corruption in the judiciary or about how the Hindu community knew Asaram was blameless. Sanghani was neck-deep in larger operations and was responsible for many of the legal hurdles for the authorities dealing with the material seized from Sevani's apartment in Ahmedabad.

When the forty-two gunny bags were seized by the police, a group of Asaram's closest aides were activated. Sanghani claimed he was sent to Surat to handle Narayan Sai's legal defence, though what transpired next showed that he was also a key person in 'mission gunny bags'. Through an intermediary, he reached out to Sub-Inspector Chandra Mohan Kumbhani, who was part of the team investigating and questioning the godman-in-waiting.

Narayan Sai had two main difficulties—the police wanted to send him for narco-analysis and DNA examination, and also he was unused to the hardships of life in custody. Not only was he being treated as a common criminal, the food was not appealing to him and he complained about it to the police officers many times. The police would get him a Gujarati thali, as sanctioned and paid for by the government. But Narayan Sai was used to the finer things in life and even if he ate simple food, it had to be the best.

Sanghani and Kumbhani struck a deal for the gunny bags, to make life in custody easy for Narayan Sai and to keep him from being subjected to a narco-analysis test. The price for Kumbhani's help was Rs 5 crore. He said he would 'handle' his seniors and dropped a few names, including Jabha, whom Narayan Sai had already approached and failed. Sanghani did not have access to the cash and went back to the ashram to talk to the man-in-charge, Naresh Mankani (aka Rupabhai), and another trusted ashramite, Bhadresh Patel.

Mankani was administrator of the Surat ashram and though he knew Sanghani as a trusted aide, he could not disburse such a large amount of cash without authorization by Asaram or someone extremely close to him. Sanghani, Mankani and Bhadresh Patel explored all avenues of getting hold of the money and spoke to other aides, including a builder, Ketan Patel, who had been an associate of Asaram's. Between 6 and 12 December of 2013, Ketan Patel met with Sanghani and Bhadresh Patel twice to organize Rs 5 crore. Ketan Patel had been briefed by none other than Asaram's main aide—Kaushik Popatlal Vani.

In the meantime, Sanghani conveyed the difficulty of getting the cash to Kumbhani without sanction from Asaram, who was in custody in Jodhpur. Kumbhani arranged a meeting between Sanghani and Narayan Sai, while the latter was still in police custody. Those in police custody are rarely allowed to meet anyone other than their lawyer, unless sanctioned by a court of law.

During their meeting, Sai did not respond but on 12 December 2013, he summoned Sanghani through Kumbhani. Bhadresh Patel deployed Dhiraj Patel, an ashram inmate for more than two decades and a low-level volunteer who drove cars including a Wagon-R. Dhiraj Patel remembers ferrying Sanghani twice in the Wagon-R between the Surat ashram and the Chowk Bazar police station, where Sai was being held at the time.

On the second meeting, Narayan Sai gave Sanghani a handwritten chit for Mankani which showed that he was not convinced about giving Kumbhani the entire amount of Rs 5 crore in one go. Before handing him the note, Sai wanted some confirmation from Sanghani that the deal was genuine. He asked Sanghani if Kumbhani would be able to bribe Shobha Bhutada.

The sub-inspector said he would not be able to 'manage' her. This seemed to satisfy Narayan Sai. The incriminating note that Sai wrote was in Sindhi, the lingua franca of the godman, his son and their close associates. It simply said, 'One big has to be given to Uday bring it here.'

Unaware of the kind of informal demand draft Sanghani was carrying, Dhiraj Patel drove him back to the ashram. Sanghani showed the note to Mankani and Bhadresh and asked for the 'one big', code for Rs 1 crore in cash. No matter how big an ashram, Rs 1 crore is a huge amount to collect and store. A large number of Asaram's followers were economically backward and their donations would not have totalled Rs 1 crore unless the cash was purposely not deposited in the ashram trust's bank account.

Mankani later told detectives that this money was collected from donations and sales of ashram literature and audio CDs of Asaram's satsangs. Let's consider that this Rs 1 crore was collected in a single year and then multiply that with the number of Asaram ashrams which are approximately 175, as per the income tax department, without counting the small plots and temples that take the total to 400. If indeed Asaram's books and audio CDs were fetching close to a crore in revenue from a single ashram, multiplying that with the 175 ashrams would make him a top-billed writer and recording artist who would have no need to loan out cash on interest.

Manhar Patel, an ashramite for more than twenty years, eight of which he had spent as a bookkeeper, was later summoned by the sleuths. He said that the ashram's revenue accounted for Rs 1–2 lakh per month from donations and the sale of farming and dairy products. Most of this, Manhar Patel said, went back into the ashram to pay for food and other living expenses. The

Motera ashram made direct payments for major expenses such as construction costs and so forth.

Manhar Patel's testimony showed that there was unaccounted cash available in the Surat ashram. What was its source? And if it was above board, why was it not in bank accounts, as in many other religious organizations?

These mundane deliberations were immaterial for Sanghani, who stuffed the 'one big' in two bags and got back in the car with Dhiraj Patel, for his third trip to the Chowk Bazar police station in Surat. This time, Sanghani did not go inside the police station and waited for Sub-Inspector Kumbhani to join him in the car. When he did, Dhiraj Patel turned around to see Sanghani open the two bags and show Kumbhani the cash.

In the scheme of things, Kumbhani was a junior officer. Narayan Sai's was a high-profile case. All of Surat knew that the police commissioner, Rakesh Asthana, was handling the investigation himself. What authority could a lowly sub-inspector have except be a broker for senior officers? He needed someone in the commissioner's office and reached out to his leader, Police Inspector S.A. Jabha, with the proposal to make things easy for Narayan Sai and replace the material in the gunny bags. Jabha was affronted but instead of reacting immediately, reported it back to Asthana, who was fed up with some of Narayan Sai's tricks and realized this was a great opportunity to nip any corruption in the bud.

Asthana laid a plan to nab Sanghani red-handed with the bribe. He asked Jabha to accept Kumbhani's offer and plan a sting operation. It was not as if the police were unaware of the plan. They were still listening to phone calls between Asaram's aides in order to round up all those who had abetted Narayan Sai's escape in the face of summons and court-issued warrants.

The police also wanted to trace Vani, who possibly held the key to decoding the contents of the forty-two bags.

There were conversations, mostly in Gujarati, in which the aides, unaware that their phones were tapped, openly discussed the bribe. For instance, Hitendra Waghela was heard telling someone on the phone, 'Madam is not agreeing on Rs 25 lakh, she will need Rs 30 lakh.' Listening to the conversations gave Bhutada sleepless nights because the bags were in her custody, locked in an antechamber in her office.

The transcripts of the recorded conversations were submitted to the Surat court probing the bribery charges.

'They sounded so confident that for a moment, I started to doubt if the bags had been removed. I woke up in the middle of the night one time and went to office to check if the bags were intact,' she told me later.

On 12 December 2013, after Kumbhani got into the car outside the Chowk Bazar police station in Surat, and checked the cash, Dhiraj Patel drove the car a little further to where Jabha was standing. As soon as they handed the cash to Jabha, other policemen appeared and detained Sanghani and Kumbhani along with the 'one big'.

Sanghani, Narayan Sai, Dhiraj Patel, Bhadresh Patel, Ketan Patel, Mankani and Manhar Patel deposed under Section 50 of the Prevention of Money Laundering Act (PMLA), 2002. The interview by ED officials is different from those conducted by the police because the ED is a quasi-judicial authority. Most of the accused retracted their statements in letters to the ED, alleging that they had been coerced.

If these were untrue, where did the Rs 1 crore come from and what was it doing with Sanghani and the policeman Kumbhani in the ashram's car that Dhiraj Patel was driving? The ashram's bookkeeper Manhar Patel's statement to the ED clarified that this was not part of the Rs 1–2 lakh revenue per month that they collected from Surat. So, Mankani had cash in large amounts stored with him and the 'one big' from it was used to allegedly bribe policemen.

~

The trail did not end with the 'one big' because the deal between Sanghani and Kumbhani was for Rs 5 crore in cash. So, after the Surat police detained Sanghani and Kumbhani in the raid, they set about finding out where the rest of the cash was and how the conspiracy had been hatched.

Ketan Patel, another Surat-based associate of Asaram's, was involved in a land deal in Abhwa and Rundh in Surat. For this deal, he was working with two businessmen, Hasmukh Upadhyay and Bhavesh Chatur Patel. In December 2013, when Asaram's men were trying to find a way of recovering the material in the forty-two gunny bags from the police, Ketan Patel met Upadhyay and Bhavesh Patel and discussed the matter with them. Ketan was desperately looking for a solution and had reached out to many people. Upadhyay told him about a tout called Hitendra Waghela who claimed to know many police officers.

Waghela was a small-time BJP party worker and a full-time real estate tout in Ahmedabad. He was caught up in his aspirations of becoming a big builder and a power broker. He liked to boast about his 'links' with several police officers. The truth, of course, has a different version of itself. Waghela had got hold of the public mobile numbers of police officers and would routinely send them greetings, the kind that flood WhatsApp these days.

Every morning, he would send 'good morning' text messages to several IAS and IPS officers. So, after several such good mornings, Waghela had sent a 'Happy Diwali' message to a senior police officer, who had responded with 'same to you', and Waghela had shown it around to some real estate dealers who were working out deals with Ketan Patel—a close aide of Asaram. Once, Waghela even visited the IPS officer to introduce himself as the same Hitendra Waghela who sent the messages. The officer had greeted Waghela, offered him a glass of water and sent him on his way.

'Many people send greetings. Normally I don't answer them. But, say on a festive occasion, you are in a celebratory mood and send back a greeting or respond with a "thank you" without realizing how it is going to be used. Later, we learnt that Waghela had retained that message in his phone and flaunted it to people,' the police officer told me.

One of the people who had heard of Waghela's so-called 'contacts' in the police was Hasmukh Upadhyay, a builder— among the many that the authorities would later learn was connected to Asaram's business investments. Upadhyay and Bhavesh Patel were Ahmedabad-based builders who were working with Ketan Patel to acquire land in Abhwa and Rundh in Gujarat.

Waghela was one of the brokers in the Abhwa–Rundh land deal. Upadhyay reached out to him and told him about 'mission gunny bags'. Waghela had no idea what he was getting into and committed to getting the job done in Rs 30–35 lakh. To Ketan Patel, that was a small price to pay for an empire worth thousands of crores. It was a steal.

Waghela had one condition—he wanted a token sum of Rs 10 lakh in advance. Upadhyay agreed and his partner,

Bhavesh Patel, handed the cash to Waghela at a hotel barely hundred metres from the Surat railway station on 10 December 2013. They later claimed that the cash—strangely enough, the exact same amount they needed to keep Waghela happy—was kept handy for requirements for the land deal.

Waghela transferred the money through a hawala agent in Surat to his wife in Ahmedabad and told her that it was part of a land deal. The next day, Waghela returned to Ahmedabad and deposited Rs 2.2 lakh in his bank account, retained Rs 10,000 at home for expenses and kept Rs 7.7 lakh with some associates. Waghela, his wife and the associates later deposed these facts to the ED.

A few days later, Waghela's friends read of his arrest in the newspaper in a bribery case and realized that the money in their possession could become hot for them. So, they headed over to Waghela's house and handed the money to his wife. Waghela's wife had also realized that her husband was not brokering a land deal but something more sinister. She withdrew the Rs 2.2 lakh deposited in the bank to pay for legal defence. On 20 December 2013, the Surat police seized the Rs 10 lakh from her, bringing the total seizure of cash for bribes to Rs 1.1 crore.

~

Apart from Ketan Patel, Hasmukh Upadhyay had also spoken to other people regarding 'mission gunny bags'. One 'Bansibhai' (Bansi Durlab Patel) had called Upadhyay on 8 December 2013, four days after Narayan Sai was arrested, and offered his assistance.

Later, Upadhyay had several phone conversations with Ketan Patel, who seemed to be coordinating the mission. In one conversation, Upadhyay told Patel that he would require Rs 7 crore to get the work done. In a subsequent conversation, Patel told Upadhyay about Sanghani's deal with Kumbhani for Rs 5 crore, which he said they should handle. In another conversation, Patel told Upadhyay that the entire deal would take around Rs 13 crore.

Patel spoke to Kaushik Vani in Ahmedabad for the Rs 13 crore, but claimed that Vani did not give him the amount. This confusion remains unsolved because Vani refused to cooperate with the police and since there was no reason to place him under arrest at the time, he was released. He has not been found till the time of writing this.

Sanghani and Bhadresh Patel told Ketan Patel that the ashram had arranged Rs 1 crore and in an emergency, they might need him to come up with the balance Rs 4 crore for the bribe. Upadhyay told Ketan Patel that the mission was on track.

After busting Sanghani and Kumbhani, the Surat police interrogated the former and gathered that the remaining amount was with Ketan Patel's accountant, Himanshu Shukla. They then conducted a raid at Shukla's office on 12 December 2013, and found Rs 4 crore in cash. The next day, they raided his home and found Rs 3 crore in cash. This brought the entire seized amount in the bribery case to Rs 8.1 crore.

So, what was the source of the money that was gathered in a bid to extract the godman's financial records from the clutches of the police? Ketan Patel told investigators that the money was from the cash component payment from the sale of flats in a building in Surat's Pal area. But, the flat buyers when questioned by the police and the ED denied giving given him any cash. Even if they had, it was an absurd amount to have been paid in cash. It is well known that most builders operate through both cash and bank transactions, where the ratio is usually 60:40 or 70:30 (white : black) of the purchase price. The cash remains below the taxman's radar and floats around in the economy. The total sale value recorded in the sale deeds of the flats came to Rs 1,34,64,450, paid through bank transactions. That would make the payment ratio 20:80, meaning 80 per cent in cash, which is unheard of. Besides, the payments had been made between October 2011 and January 2013 and it is unlikely that the cash would be lying around for such a long period of time.

Shukla told the investigators that he had got the cash from Ketan Patel, who was called in for questioning again and asked about the Rs 7 crore found with Upadhyay's accountant. In 2015, Ketan Patel had also filed a separate plea before the Surat court to release the amount of Rs 7 crore to him, claiming it was not connected to the bribery charge and he had kept it to pay outstanding amounts for the Abhwa–Rundh land deal.

That brought the focus back to the land deal. The property in question is 'disputed' and the land developers had to pay in the neighbourhood of Rs 60 crore for it. Ketan Patel claimed that the amount of Rs 7 crore was meant to make payments for this land. The ED found that this explanation was not plausible because Ketan Patel had raised Rs 3.5 crore through several loans of small amounts to pay for the Abhwa–Rundh land deal. '. . . In this connection, Ketan Patel had availed loans totalling Rs 3.5 crore for the purpose of the land deal at Abhwa and Rundh even though by his own admission he had Rs 7 crore at his disposal,' the ED noted in its attachment order.

This Rs 7 crore was discovered on 11 and 12 December 2013. As per the schedule of payments for the Rs 60 crore land deal, Ketan Patel had paid only Rs 1.5 crore. The next payment of Rs 9.5 crore had to be made on 30 October 2013, and he had already missed that deadline by a month. If he had Rs 7 crore for that land deal, why would he have defaulted on it by a month? The third instalment of Rs 49 crore was due in January 2014.

'The amount of Rs 7 crore was seized by the police from Ketan Patel as the same was kept by him for the purpose of offering bribe to the police, judiciary, etc. . . .' the ED concluded in its attachment order.

The source of the Rs 7 crore still remains a mystery.

In 2015, Asthana forwarded a 900-page report on the documents in the forty-two gunny bags recovered from Prahlad Sevani's flat to the income tax authorities. The press had already shared some of its contents, starting from Shobha Bhutada's seizure. Legislation makes it a statutory duty to hand over to any competent authority evidence found during investigation by any agency.

Asaram's aides did not want the forty-two gunny bags handed over to the income tax department and having failed at their attempt at bribing police officers, they decided to try their luck in court. Uday Sanghani had challenged[3] the income tax department's move to requisition these documents from the Surat court, in whose custody they were. Sanghani first approached a sessions court in Surat to get certified copies of the documents in the gunny bags, but lost. He then appealed

---

[3]   https://indianexpress.com/article/cities/ahmedabad/asaram-case-hc-upholds-handing-over-42-bagsful-of-documents-to-it-for-probe/ published on 21 January 2015 and accessed on 28 June 2018

to the Gujarat High Court (GHC), where his plea was rejected once again.

In the meantime, income tax department investigators filed a plea before the additional sessions court in Surat where Narayan Sai was being tried on rape charges. On 9 December 2014, the Surat court passed an order handing over the gunny bags and their contents to the income tax investigators. Sanghani approached the GHC with a petition to quash this decision.

The first argument of Sanghani's lawyer was that the seized records would be required in another FIR that had been filed against Narayan Sai and Asaram's aides. He also said that there was no approval recorded by any of the senior income tax officials under Section 132A of the Income Tax Act. Besides, Sanghani's lawyer pointed out, the sessions court in Surat had not allowed the income tax officials to seize the Rs 8.1 crore used by Sanghani to bribe Kumbhani.

The state prosecutor who appeared for the tax department stated in court that the time factor was crucial. Investigation needed to begin before 31 March 2015, otherwise another financial year would be lost to the statute of limitations, which binds tax probes to the six previous financial years.

Sanghani's arguments did not work at the GHC. The prosecutor pointed out that the seizure was made in the rape case in which Sanghani was not an accused. Therefore, he had no cause to approach a court about the fate of the documents in question. For the same reason, Sanghani would not be eligible to receive certified copies of the seized documents or the digital data.

Sevani, from whose house the documents were recovered, did not seem to have any objection to them being handed over to the income tax authorities. His lawyer had said so in the Surat court and he reiterated it before the GHC.

Justice Vipul Pancholi noted in his order[4] that Sanghani was not an accused in the rape case, that the investigators in the rape case did not require the seized documents to prosecute the charges and that Sevani, from whose house it was recovered, had no objection.

Justice Pancholi also noted that Sanghani had not said anywhere (he had filed two petitions earlier before the high court) that without certified copies of the seized documents, he would not be able to defend himself in the bribery case. Justice Pancholi dismissed Sanghani's plea but allowed him three weeks to appeal. Sanghani approached the Supreme Court of India, but a bench of Justice Dipak Misra and Prafulla Pant dismissed it, confirming the Surat court's decision to hand over the documents and the digital data to the income tax department's investigation wing for a thorough probe.

The Surat police lodged an FIR against Sanghani, Sub-Inspector C.M. Kumbhani and seven other accused under Sections 213, 214, 217, 119 and 120(B) of the Indian Penal Code, 1860, and Sections 7, 8, 9, 12, 13(1)(G) and 13(2) of the Prevention of Corruption Act (POCA), 1988.

The police informed the income tax department, which made a preliminary inquiry into the bribery incident and found the Rs 8.1 crore of cash to be undeclared income. So, the income tax investigators decided to recover the tax on the bribe amount and asked the Surat court to hand over the cash to them. Since the Surat court was still trying Sanghani and the others on the

---

[4]    Special Criminal Application 58/2014. Re: *Uday Navinchandra Sangani vs Vikrant Pal Singh and Two Others* before the high court of Gujarat at Ahmedabad. Justice Vipul M. Pancholi decided on 20 January 2015.

bribery charge, it refused to do so, as it was required for the trial under the POCA law.

The GHC, however, ruled[5] in favour of the revenue investigators, since the income tax probe was bound by a statutory timeline. Justice Sonia Gokani maintained that the cash should not have been left lying with the police but put in a bank locker after recording its serial number. Besides, the judge said, the cash itself need not be produced for the trial but a video record, or a written record in the panchnama, would be enough for the bribery trial. The cash was to be kept in a fixed deposit with the State Bank of India till the income tax department completed its proceedings.

~

The perseverance with which Sanghani and other aides of Asaram pursued the contents of the forty-two gunny bags—bribing cops and going to court—shows the importance of the documents and digital data to Asaram and co., including those who were now emerging as businessmen with easy access to large amounts of unaccounted cash for their operations. These businessmen were also willing to risk their necks to help the godman, though not all of them were his devotees.

What will be revealed in the coming pages is how Asaram's enterprise included high-value cash loans to several businessmen, most of them builders, at high rates of interest. Were these then collections of outstanding interest amounts? For those who

---

[5]  In the high court of Gujarat at Ahmedabad; Criminal Revision Application (against order passed by subordinate court) No. 77 of 2015; Justice Sonia Gokani on 31 July 2015

were devotees, this episode leaves a question mark over their willingness to employ dishonest methods to help Asaram, a spiritual leader who preached against greed and vice. Did the guru give his sanction? Going by the testimonies and records of various probes, Asaram's close aides and successor certainly seemed to have his approval.

# 9

# The Real Asset

Acommon characteristic of religious organizations in India seems to be their fondness for land. It is difficult to go to any town or city in India without coming across a few common names of religious organizations with a massive following. Some of this land may have been acquired or granted years ago, and as cities have expanded, parts of it may have come to be in prime locations.

For instance, in north and central India, ashrams of the Radha Soami Satsang Beas are spread across cities and towns. Baba Ramdev traipses a thin line between a corporate brand and his identity as a spiritual leader. His acquisition of some tracts of land, including at throwaway prices, from the government has been questioned.

The voracious appetite of religious organizations for real estate is somewhat akin to the hunger of large corporations in India—when they set up industrial units, they want land in thousands of acres not just for a plant but to 'develop a township' and 'develop the surrounding areas'. This can be broken down in simple language as amassing land banks which will later be used as real estate banks in the name of rehabilitating those whose livelihoods they have upset.

In 2012, while assisting the author Sudeep Chakravarti for a part of his book, *Clear Hold Build: Hard Lessons of Business and Human Rights in India*, published by HarperCollins in 2014, we came across the story of 5,000 acres of prime agricultural land that a large steel corporation wanted to acquire. The land was so fertile, the farmers claimed, that it did not require any chemical fertilizers and so they did not want to let it go. But, that did not stop the steel corporation's officers from trying. Eventually, the landowners drive SUVs and the luckier of the landless peasants become nightwatchmen (the security and maintenance requirements are largely outsourced to professional agencies).

In Brahmapur, Odisha, I saw 'rehabilitated' peasants living in small, boxy apartments as part of their compensation packages. The factory for which their land had been acquired, had been cancelled but the land still remained with the corporation.

The land taken up by godmen is usually used to construct 'ashrams'. However, several of them including tainted ones such as Asaram, Gurmeet Ram Rahim, Rampal, among others, use the land to create a kingdom of their own. Some may argue against referring to corporate townships in the same breath, though these can also be run like mini-fiefdoms. For instance, at one such township in eastern India, they not only do not allow a municipality citing a lease deed of the colonial era, but also run a parallel security and intelligence apparatus.

Many news reports about tainted godmen refer to ashrams as 'small townships'. This term may be erroneous in many cases. The ashrams are presented as romantic communes to outsiders, but for the inmates, they can often be virtual prisons managed according to the diktat of the person who runs the organization. This is also one of the first indicators that the organization may be a cult. Throw in some religious philosophy and a few rituals, and you have a religious cult, which is quite different from what religious philosophers and academics might describe as a 'sect' of Hinduism.

An extreme example is a commune established by Ram Vriksh Yadav at a government-owned garden in the heart of Mathura city. In 2016, I travelled[1] to Mathura after the police had stormed the garden to evict the settlers, who, forgotten by the rest of the world, had been camping there for around two years and had built their own mini-country in the heart of India.

Ram Vriksh Yadav was a follower of the godman known as 'Jai Gurudev' aka Tulsidas Malhar, famous for having posed as an incognito Netaji Subhash Chandra in the late 1960s. Malhar had invited Gumnami Baba, another godman who enjoyed the myth of being Netaji Bose, to address a rally in Kanpur. Prior to the rally, Malhar had widely publicized that Netaji was alive and had agreed to finally surface. When Gumnami Baba did not arrive, Malhar went on to address the rally, which created an impression that he was in fact the long-lost Netaji. Malhar built his following among the Dalits and tribals of Uttar Pradesh, Bihar and Madhya Pradesh.

Malhar's hardcore followers were supposed to wear clothes and Gandhi caps made of jute. Many destitute followers who were unable to afford the jute-textile clothes instead restitched jute gunny bags into clothes, wearing them even during the

---

[1] https://www.outlookindia.com/magazine/story/netaji-didnt-start-this-fire/297286 published on 20 June 2016 and accessed on 28 June 2018

extreme summers of central and north India. His followers who were doctors attended to patients while wearing jute clothes. Lawyer followers attended court in a jute-fabric version of the lawyer's customary uniform.

After Malhar died in 2012, there was a tussle between his three most powerful followers. The chosen successor, some say, was Umakant Tiwari, supposedly the one who was more spiritually evolved. Malhar's driver-cum-aide, a young man called Pankaj Yadav, was the son of a lawyer and senior functionary of Malhar's trust. Yadav took over as the successor and became close to the senior Samajwadi Party leader Shivpal Yadav.

Tiwari was banished from the main ashram in Mathura to one in Ujjain. Several trustees sued both Tiwari and Yadav to remove them from the ashrams they had occupied as self-styled successors. The third 'successor', Ram Vriksh Yadav, fought with everyone else and departed to another ashram in Madhya Pradesh but was not satisfied there. Ram Vriksh was interested in politics and had even contested the Uttar Pradesh state assembly elections on a ticket of the 'Doordarshi' party launched by Jai Gurudev. He launched a coup to take control of Malhar's Mathura ashram after the godman's death in 2012, but was unceremoniously ejected after a brief skirmish with Pankaj Yadav's men. Ram Vriksh culled his own following out of Malhar's followers, weaving a myth around Netaji's unrealized dreams for India.

In 2014, Ram Vriksh along with a small band of followers set off for New Delhi for an indefinite protest till the government implemented his demands, which included launching Netaji's currency notes. For one rupee, a citizen should be able to buy 40 litres of petrol, 60 litres of diesel and 12 tolas (around 140 grams) of gold. When the motley crew reached Mathura, the Uttar Pradesh state government put him and his followers in the 200-acre horticultural garden, guided by Ram Vriksh's political sponsors. They were plied with food and rations, which they sold to unsuspecting neighbours at throwaway prices. The whole charade lasted for two years till the Allahabad High Court, acting on a petition of the Mathura Bar Association, finally told the police to throw the godman and his followers out, ending in a fierce gun battle which left a few policemen and twenty-three of Ram Vriksh's followers dead and scores injured.

Ram Vriksh was charred to death in the violence, which also razed to the ground the structures they had built in the garden, where many poor people had come to take shelter. Once these people entered the illegal ashram, they could not leave without keeping a family member as collateral to ensure their return. There was a strict regimen in place that included prayers, timed meals, schooling for children and chores for others. The garden became a small country with a system of governance, controlled by Ram Vriksh and his closest followers, many of whom carried firearms. Guards patrolled the periphery and kept prying eyes out, except on visits chaperoned by community guardians or when the neighbours were invited to purchase vegetables and groceries from the 'discount mart', a fraudulent resale of government rations. There was a court which decided disputes and conflicts. The politburo also decided lyrics for the prayers and had made an anthem for the community.

~

Asaram's model was different and definitely not as extreme in the way it treated its residents. In his personal life, some have described Asaram as being prone to fits of violence. Narayan Sai said so during his interrogation, as have others such as Prakash, the aide who remained with him to take care of him despite being granted bail. Even after his acquittal, Prakash remains to take care of the godman, who uses him as a punching bag. The reason, say former close aides, was his fondness for wielding control over those around him. Therefore, he was the one who set most of the rules for his ashram, which he treated as his own kingdom.

At each ashram, there was a throne on which Asaram would sit and deliver his sermons. Anybody delivering sermons in his absence would not sit on it, but next to it. Shortly after the minor girl lodged a rape complaint against him, the ABP News journalist Abhisar Sharma had conducted an interview of Asaram, which is available on the broadcaster's social media channel. While Sharma is seen standing on the ground and conducting his interview, the baba is seated on a throne saying that the charges are bogus. In many pictures, Asaram is seen wearing a crown, as was Narayan Sai on a few occasions, including in his wedding photographs. These are no paper or plastic crowns but appear ornate, made of a yellow metal. I never got close enough to one to see if it was actually made of gold, as it appeared to be.

To establish a kingdom, one must have land to build upon and feudal lords do not entrust such tasks to others. Much of the land that Asaram owns has been under the scanner. When his influence and follower base grew, many started to pledge their own lands as 'gurudakshina', a token to one's guru that they said was a Vedic prescription. It can be safely assumed that this prescription came from their guru. Literature from Asaram's trusts enjoins the ashramite to obey the guru. Asaram has himself told followers not to disagree with his commands. For example, Narayan Sai's wife told the police in a videotaped deposition that she was told she would have to marry Narayan Sai; the consent was the result of the guru's diktat.

Many of Asaram's ashrams have been mired in controversy with allegations of land-grabbing. Asaram's spokesperson Neelam Dubey told me how, one day, he had wandered to a spot on the banks of the Sabarmati in Motera village where bootleggers used to brew illicit liquor. Others, including former aides, will tell you that Asaram himself used to sell illicit liquor till he saw an ashram that was already there and realized what a great business opportunity it presented. However, these allegations remain unproven. The only witness to come forward was one 'Kalaji' during the Justice Trivedi commission, who said he used to manufacture the brew and supply it to Asaram, who would retail it in Motera.

As his follower base grew, the ashram at Motera started to physically expand too, till some villagers wondered whether the godman had conjured souls into the walls and barbed wire fences that seemed to keep moving forward of their own accord to swallow up more land. Ever so often, volunteers would appear from the ashram and be seen doing some work outside the premises. Even on the day I visited, they were tearing holes into the tarred approach road to the Mahila Utthan Ashram in Motera to erect a sign to rename it as Sati Anusuya ashram. Some villagers eventually complained to the then Narendra Modi–led government in Gujarat about the automatic barbed wire fences and walls of the Motera ashram.

Anandiben Patel, who later became CM of the state, was Gujarat's revenue minister in Modi's Cabinet. Responding to a question in the Gujarat Vidhan Sabha, she said[2] that the Motera ashram had encroached on 67,059 square metres of land. The government had earmarked this land for the Metro Rail project in Ahmedabad and took it back.

~

In the 1970s, Hindu spirituality found many seekers in the West, popularized through the Beatles and their association with Maharshi Mahesh Yogi whose ashram the Fab Four also visited in India. The image of Satchidananda Saraswati inaugurating the 1969 Woodstock festival is an iconic one. Hippies began to wander into India either looking for oneness with Krishna through ISKCON or a direct connection to Shiva through the chillum.

In the 1990s, it was yoga that revived an interest in Indian spirituality in the West. Those such as Satchidananda Saraswati had established evangelical cults and communes in the US. The interest, as has been observed, was largely directed towards pop Hindu spirituality, sold through words that roll nicely off the tongue—moksha and nirvana. Handy yoga gurus prescribed meditation, aum and calmness of mind, which quickly became consumables across yoga studios. Controversial yoga guru Bikram Choudhury had launched studios across the US in the 1970s but started to train yoga teachers only in the 1990s, as the demand for them skyrocketed.

Through the 1980s and 1990s, some NRIs and those returning from foreign lands visited Asaram. A golden opportunity presented

---

[2]    https://indianexpress.com/article/news-archive/web/exclusive-the-rise-and-fall-of-the-guru/ accessed on 23 June 2018

itself and the godman started to visit the US and Canada with his son. But, they did not have any organization or land there. During their visits to the west coast of the US, they would stay at the house of Jayanti Patel, an NRI who had left India many years ago but had found a guru in Asaram during his visits home.

I met Zubin Patel in Surat, the son of a childhood friend of Jayanti Patel's. He told me the story of Jayanti Patel and Asaram Bapu and of another devotee, Kanti Prasada. In New Jersey, when Asaram would stay at Jayanti Patel's place, he started conducting satsangs and met many people who eventually became his devotees. As his flock grew, Asaram proposed that they form a non-charitable trust called the International Yog Vedanta Society, a name which bore a strong resemblance to its desi cousin, Asaram's Yog Vedanta Sewa Samiti.

Asaram became the president of this society, Narayan Sai its vice president and Jayanti Patel secretary, since they required a local name and address to register it officially. The plan was to spread bases in the US and later in Canada too. As the secretary and a US citizen, all legal documents bore Patel's signature.

Patel claimed not to have questioned the documents he was asked to sign, since it had to do with his guru's work. Besides, he had a successful pharmaceutical business and did not have much time for the society other than as an avenue for spiritual expression.

What Jayanti Patel did not know at the time was that in the early 1990s, a married couple who were Canadian nationals of Indian origin, Kanti Prasada and his wife, had gifted the land for an ashram in Indore to Asaram. They passed away together at the ashram in 1993. Prasada's family later claimed that they had not been told of their parents' death.

Kanti Prasada also owned property in Toronto, and in his will dated June 1992, he had chosen his daughter, Usha Prasada-Kole, as the administrator of his estate. But after his death, Asaram produced a will dated August 1993, according to which the godman claimed that Prasada had willed the property in Toronto to him as well.

The heirs of Kanti Prasada did not travel to India to challenge the 'gift' of land in Indore. But, they drew a firm line when it came to the property in Toronto and challenged it. The will that Asaram had produced was filed through the International Yog Vedanta Society and bore the signature of Jayanti Patel.

While Asaram and Narayan Sai were in Canada, they were served summons to appear before the General Division Court in Ontario, Toronto, which they did not heed. Jayanti Patel, who had sponsored the International Yog Vedanta Society, was made a party in the civil dispute of which he had neither any idea nor would have suspected the origins of.

The court in Toronto examined both the wills and decided the one produced by Asaram's trust to be fake. 'This court adjudges and declares that the signature on the 3 August 1993 will is not the signature of Kanti Prasada, deceased, and that the will was not duly executed by him,' wrote the judge in her 9 September 1997 order.

Canadian law would have required forensic examination by handwriting experts at the time. It is not known if that was done. Whatever the court's reasoning may have been, it imposed the cost of 321,593.41 Canadian dollars on Jayanti Patel, recoverable with interest at the rate of 5 per cent per annum from March 1998. Applying the approximate currency exchange rate of 1998, this amount came to around Rs 9 crore at the time.

In 2000, the Prasada heirs moved a court in New Jersey to have the Canadian court's judgment executed and recover the amount owed to them. The New Jersey court froze Jayanti Patel's assets and attached his properties in November that year. He called his guru and asked for the money. At first, Asaram told him that he would arrange the money but after a few calls, changed track. Money and materialism were '*moh maya*', the godman told Patel. Thereafter, he stopped taking Patel's calls and instead, his aides would respond with threats.

So, Jayanti Patel filed an affidavit at the court in New Jersey and cried his heart out, claiming his was a vicarious liability. 'Not only are the plaintiffs undeserving victims but so am I,' he wrote and suggested that the court find a way to drag Asaram to the US.

Patel said he had no idea that of the many papers that he had signed as 'secretary' of the International Yog Vedanta Society, one would be a forged will, which, he wrote, Asaram's aide Jagdish Vyas had asked him to sign. He did not know Prasada, nor of the plan to take over his property in Canada.

Asaram had attempted to replicate the Indian model of running his organization in North America. While he had used the International Yog Vedanta Society for one set of activities, he had also set up another trust called Shri Yoga Vedanta Ashram, which allowed him to purchase a property in New Jersey worth far more than the 3,21,594 Canadian dollars that he owed the Prasada heirs. It also enabled him to evade liability in the Canadian court's decree.

Jayanti Patel had no option but to beg for fairness. He had worked hard all his life, only to find his savings taken away rudely from him, all because of his faith in a godman. He also counter-sued Asaram for fraud. However, he ultimately had no option but to liquidate some of his assets to pay the amount to the Prasada heirs. So, Patel made a trip to India.

Before Jayanti Patel's pockets became lighter by Rs 9 crore, he used to stay for at least a month at the ashram during each trip to India. His North American credentials had bought him a ticket into the godman's inner circle. On his trip to recover his money from the godman, Jayanti Patel found himself barred not only from the godman's core group but also from entering the ashram.

'Eventually, he (Jayanti Patel) was disheartened and stopped coming to India for quite some time,' Zubin Patel told me. 'He gave up hope of recovering the money and would not speak of it. That was till 2013; the arrest of the two godmen in rape cases gave him some confidence and I was asked to approach the police and register a criminal complaint.'

Jayanti Patel's complaint to the Surat police is still pending. In it, he charged Asaram of swindling him in the name of faith and exploiting his trust in him. He said that till 2014, he had been unable to file a criminal complaint because Asaram was a 'very heavy-headed influential personality who claimed to have many political and mafia connections, had extorted me and put me in fear of injury . . .' Patel claimed that 'the forged will was prepared by both the accused [Asaram and Narayan Sai] in criminal connivance'.

Had the Canadian court's decided interest rate (of 5 per cent per annum) been applied, Asaram would owe him Rs 24 crore today. If you apply exchange rates and inflation surges, the amount would be higher still.

~

The income tax department attached Asaram's ashrams after its investigation to collect tax dues. The documents recovered from the gunny bags showed that the ownership documents of the various properties were not in order. In Sabarkantha district in Gujarat, for instance, the godman and his family posed as farmers to buy agricultural land. In other cases, pieces of land were still in the names of original owners and had not been transferred, raising suspicion as to how they had been acquired.

Besides, there is the perennial question of the total worth of Asaram's empire. It is difficult to answer because many of his ashrams occupy more land than the trusts actually own. Simply, some of the ashrams are bigger on the ground than on paper because they have been built by encroaching on other people's land. In some cases, the government managed to get back its land but in many cases, government officials allegedly facilitated the land-grab.

The Motera ashram, too, extended far beyond its legal limits and had taken over government land through illegal fencing. The Ahmedabad collectorate forcibly took back these lands when the Ahmedabad metro railway project was being planned. Many other ashrams have controversial histories of land-grab, and at the time of writing this, their land has not been recovered despite orders from all courts in the land including the Supreme Court.

One such case pertained to land in Ratlam, Madhya Pradesh, where Asaram built a large ashram. Paras Saklecha, a former MLA, said that in 1997 Jayant Vitamins Ltd was declared a sick company. In 1999, Asaram walked in with permission to conduct a three-day camp on this company's land. Till 2018, his organization had not left. Eventually, the locals lost interest after the company's pending labour dues were paid up. But, the serious fraud investigation office (SFIO) decided to probe how the godman came into possession of the company's property—200 acres that was worth a whopping Rs 700 crore in 2013.

The Surat ashram of Asaram is another glorious example of how the godman and his henchmen grabbed private and government land with the help of a state minister, despite objections from government officials, including those from the minister's own department.

Sometime in the mid-1980s, a farmer who was a disciple of Asaram's donated his agricultural plot to the godman in Surat's Jahangirpura area, along the northern bank of the river Tapi in the city. Asaram built his ashram there around 1985. Mukesh Sailor, a local politician, claimed that the donor of the land later became a gatekeeper at the ashram and is still seen at the gate from time to time.

Sailor, a BJP member and a former municipal councillor, was a trustee of a fishermen's trust in Surat in 1992. The trust owns twenty-six bighas of land in Jahangirpura, which it leases out to landless farmers to cultivate. The ashram was built on an area adjoining this trust's land. In 1989, the ashramites started to use the fishermen's land to enter and exit the ashram because it gave them direct access to the main road. They even changed their main gate to this side of the ashram.

Initially, it was not a cause for concern because Asaram's followers would cross the trust's land on foot. But, when they started to ply vehicles on it, those who had leased the land from the trust objected and it led to a clash in which Asaram's followers opened fire at the protesters. An FIR was lodged and Asaram's followers are being tried on those charges.

The number of visitors and ashram residents increased with time, and consequently so did the size of the ashram. Once again, vehicles started to ply through the land owned by the trust. In 1994, the trust decided against any confrontation and erected a boundary fence but not on the periphery of the land. They constructed the boundary wall in such a manner that it left a ten-foot-wide patch running parallel to the land. It became a pathway that gave the ashramites better access.

According to Mukesh Sailor, the ashramites tore down this fence too, even though it was within the trust's land. This angered the trust, which would not succumb to the bullying. An ugly war of words broke out. 'Then it came to blows and then stones were pelted by both sides. Today, people can go to the police to fight with Asaram. Back then, you had to do it yourself and the police would not always help,' claimed Sailor.

While a camp was being held at the ashram, the fishermen went on a fast which was covered by the media. The next day, Asaram came out and apologized to the fishermen, asking them to end their protest. Since then, the ashramites have not tried to encroach on any part of the fishermen trust's land but not without regular mediation between them. Other neighbours were not so lucky, including a reputed literary figure of Gujarat whom Asaram's followers roughed up and who eventually sold his property and left.

Some farmers in lands adjoining Asaram's ashram faced the worst of it. In 1972, the Gujarat government planned to build an embankment on the Tapi. The plan was firmed up in 1976 and the irrigation department acquired the land in 1977. The government took notional, viz. on paper, possession of the land and physically it remained with the farmers, who continued to cultivate it on a lease for an annual rent. After the embankment was built, excess land was left over. In 1986, the Chimanbhai Patel–led government in Gujarat decided to return the excess land to the original owners, who were already tilling it, over a period of time. Later, the Surat Municipal Corporation decided to acquire this land for a waterworks project to meet the demands stemming from the rapid growth of Surat city.

Under a scheme called Ganotdhara, the government had allotted these lands on the bank of the Tapi to farmers. Harishchandra, Gajanand and Laxmanrao Vyas were three farmers who had been allotted land in 1967. In 1977 they had also won a national agriculture award from the government for a variety of large watermelon they had grown on their land. This land was adjacent to Asaram's ashram and was a part of the land acquired by the Gujarat government for the embankment project. Around 80 per cent of their land was not utilized in the embankment project and the Vyas family tried, unsuccessfully, to get it back.

In 1996, Asaram's followers assaulted the farmers cultivating the Vyas's land over a tiff regarding the boundaries of their respective lands. 'It took us around two to three hours to get to the spot, and within that time Asaram's followers erected a wire fence and took over our land. We went to the ashram to talk to them and solve it peacefully. The ashramites told us that we could take it back if it was ours. So, we removed the fence and asked them where they wanted to keep it. They told us to keep it wherever we wanted and so, we just left it on the land. They took photographs of the scene, submitted it to the police and lodged an FIR claiming that we had tried to take forceful possession of their land illegally,' said a member of the Vyas family. The possession of the land continued to be with Asaram's ashram thereafter.

Once they had possession of the land, the ashram expanded rapidly and over time built a permanent cowshed, an Ayurvedic centre, shops selling Asaram's branded merchandise, residential quarters, a refractory, offices, and so forth.

The Vyas family made futile attempts to negotiate with Asaram. A man who worked as a labourer and drove a tractor on the Vyas's agricultural land had become a disciple of Asaram and shifted into the ashram. He became the intermediary between the Vyas family and Asaram's aides. Incidentally, says the Vyas family member, that man was murdered some years later and his corpse was discovered at the crossing near the ashram.

The municipal corporation learnt of the encroachment by Asaram's ashram and tried to remove it. Asaram's men attacked the municipal functionaries as well as the policemen who accompanied them and the government officials had to retreat. This took place in 1996, when Shankarsinh Vaghela was the chief minister of Gujarat with Congress support.

Asaram's ashram applied to the government claiming they had possession of the land acquired by the government and since it was not being used, it should be granted to the ashram. In 1997, Vaghela's government obliged them, for which the ashram was asked to pay around Rs 30 lakh. Congress MLA Atmaram Patel was the minister in charge of the land and revenue department. In effect, the Vaghela government legalized the ashram's land-grab. The actual process was completed within twenty days. Patel overruled objections by the commissioner of Surat, the mayor of the city and the deputy secretary of his own department.

In 1998, the Vaghela government told Surat city authorities to acquire other lands in Rander village for the proposed waterworks for the city. Not only was the godman given land illegally but the waterworks project was also shifted elsewhere by acquiring more land from other farmers.

Now, the Vyas family had two problems. One, they had to retrieve their land from Asaram's ashram, which had illegally grabbed it. Second, the land was still under the legal ownership of the government.

So, they went to the high court in 1999. In 2006, the judge called the secretary, revenue department, Government of Gujarat, to be personally present with the records. He wanted to scrutinize the documents to see how Atmaram Patel had regularized 'the encroachment in favour of the respondent No. 4 [Asaram's ashram]'.

The revenue secretary turned up in court two days later with two files. One file was on the possession of the land and the second was on the regularization of the encroachment by Asaram's ashram. The court took the files from him and let him make photocopies so that he could seek instructions from the 'highest authority' who, in 1997, was the then chief minister, Shankarsinh Vaghela, and his minister in charge of the revenue department, Atmaram Patel, whose role in the matter was discussed and criticized in court.

In 2006, the 'highest authority' had changed to Narendra Modi, who was chief minister of the state. In court, Asaram's ashram admitted to encroaching upon the land in Surat. They made no bones about the fact that they had taken possession illegally. The ashram claimed that since the land had already been acquired by the state, the farmers had no right to reclaim it and the state could deal with the land however it pleased.

Asaram's ashram—the land-grabbers—claimed to have a greater right over the land than the original landowners. They also claimed that their ashram was fulfilling a 'public purpose' through its socio-religious work. Never mind that the 'public' it seemed to serve was limited to those who paid obeisance to the godman.

The state government admitted in court that the decision to hand over the land to Asaram's ashram was illegal but refused to rectify the mistake. The records revealed that the decision to legalize the ashram's encroachment was made by the Vaghela government's revenue minister, Atmaram Patel, despite the fact that the Surat authorities needed the land for the waterworks project.

In 1996, both the commissioner and the mayor of Surat had also objected to this illegal regularization in favour of Asaram. Atmaram Patel was not deterred by the objections of these two authorities and instead proposed that additional land should be given to Asaram's ashram.

The deputy secretary of the revenue department noted in the file that the farmers had requested their land back since it was not used in the land embankment project. Revenue Minister Atmaram Patel wrote on the file 'that the concerned land owners have given their consent that they do not want the land and the land be given to the Ashram'.

The farmers objected and said that Asaram's ashram had forged their signatures and they had not given any such consent. The entire process of granting the land to Asaram's ashram was done within a mere twenty days.

Atmaram Patel also pardoned a substantial chunk of the penalty to regularize the encroachment. The amount for legalizing the land-grab as decided by the revenue minister was what he stated to be the market value of the land, viz. Rs 14 lakh. The penalty should have been calculated as an additional two and a half times the market value, which would make it a total regularization fee of Rs 42 lakh. Atmaram Patel put the penalty amount at only one time the market value and came up with the amount of Rs 30 lakh for 34,400 square metres of land that had both prime agricultural and real estate value. The high court itself said that the value of the land would have actually been Rs 3–4 crore at the time.

The icing on this land-grab cake was that Asaram did not even pay the reduced amount to regularize his encroachment. The valuation was done by the department only in 2006—the year the Gujarat High Court took it up—and then too Asaram paid the match just before the final judgment.

The high court directed the state government to pay back this amount for the illegal regularization to Asaram's ashram and asked the state government to recover a fine for the illegal encroachment instead.

In December 2006, the high court wrote, 'At every stage, there is illegality committed on behalf of the State Government and as stated above as such the State Government has conceded that there is an illegality committed by them.'

The high court summed it up in some excellent observations that may hold true for several other tainted godmen.

'Before parting with this judgment, it is to be observed that the of late tendency to encroach upon the Government land has been increased day by day and that too by the trust/ religious institutions like the respondent No. 4 [Asaram's ashram]. First they encroach upon the Government land under the guise of some religious activities and/or alleged public purpose thereafter, the applications are moved to regularize the said encroachment under the guise of religious activities and pressurize the Government to regularize the said encroachment even by threatening that the religious feelings are likely to be hurt,' the high court wrote[3] in its judgment.

---

[3]  Judgment of Justice M.R. Shah in Special Civil Application No. 8955 of 1999, Gujarat High Court delivered on 8 December 2006

'The Government should not hesitate in taking harsh steps for removing the encroachment made by the trust/ religious institutions like the respondent No. 4 [Asaram's ashram] as it is the duty of the State Government to see that the rule of law is maintained. When a poor landless homeless person put up a hut and/or a small kachchha cabin, the Government authorities and/or the local authorities acts promptly, however, it is found that whenever an encroachment is made by some religious institutions/trust and/or others like the respondent No.4 [Asaram's ashram], in spite of opinions against regularizing the encroachment, a decision is taken like in the present case by the highest authorities in the Government like Ministers and/or M.L.As. and the encroachments are regularized.'

The single bench of the high court directed Asaram's ashram to return the encroached land to the state government within three months, which would have been by March 2007. If Asaram did not give back the land himself, the Surat collector would have to claim it by force. Then, they could either use it for public purpose or return it to its original owners after considering their application.

Asaram's ashram appealed to a larger bench of the high court but lost in 2009. Asaram lied in court that they had had possession since 1986. The high court caught this lie.

The bench said,[4] 'The claim that the Ashram was in occupation of the land since the year 1985 is not believable. To us, it appears that it was in or around the year 1995 or 1996 that

---

[4] Judgment of Justices R.M. Doshit and Sharad D. Dave in Letters Patent Appeal No. 182 of 2007 in Special Civil Application No. 8955 of 1999, Gujarat High Court delivered on 25 August 2008

the Ashram forcibly took over possession of the subject lands from the grantees of annual lease.'

The ashram's lawyer also cited an old 'policy' of the Gujarat government that regularized encroachments upon government land.

The high court noted that the policy spoke of 'economical condition of trust, purpose of encroachment and the tendency of the encroaching institution. The impugned order dated 3rd January, 1997 does not reflect consideration of these aspects by the State Government. On the contrary, it appears that the Ashram was already in possession of large stretch of land contiguous to the subject lands. The encroachment had been made with a view to augmenting its own land. The public functions that the Ashram claims to perform could be performed by the Ashram on the lands which were already in possession of the Ashram. Certainly, the Ashram did not encroach upon the subject lands out of necessity.'

The court made an additional direction that Asaram's ashram should deposit Rs 70,000 per month for its continued possession. The ashram appealed to the Supreme Court but was turned down.[5] So, Asaram should have returned the 34,400 square metres of encroached land latest by July 2009, in keeping with the four-month time period allowed by the high court's division bench.

Instead, Asaram built residential quarters for his followers on the Vyas's land as well as a temple. On paper, the government now owns this land but has not taken possession of it and

---

[5] Disposal order dated 30 January 2009 passed by Justices B.N. Agrawal and G.S. Singhvi in Special Leave to Appeal (Civil) No(s).1134/2009; Supreme Court

Asaram's followers continue to use it, until the time of writing. In 2013, shortly after the rape cases, a member of the Vyas family had gone to the plot along with a police inspector. The inspector stopped a short distance away to load his service revolver before proceeding. 'They will not say anything to you but they won't spare me,' he had said, the Vyas family member told me.

In 2013, the Surat collector issued a notice of Rs 18 crore to Asaram's ashram in Jahangirpura for his continued illegal occupation of the land since 1996.

# PART THREE

# 10

# The Dark Arts

Ten-year-old Deepesh had asked his uncle, Shantilal Vaghela, to get him a pair of roller skates. Shantilal's son, nine-year-old Abhishek's wish list included batteries for his synthesizer. Abhishek had begun to take lessons on how to play the musical instrument and wanted to practise. It had to be plugged into an electric socket but the switchboard in Asaram's residential 'gurukul' in Ahmedabad was too high on the wall for the electric cord of the adapter. Since it could be played with batteries, he'd asked his father to get some.

Shantilal was carrying home-cooked food for his and his brother Praful's son. His daughter, Abhishek's elder sister, Kajal, had accompanied him to visit the two cousins who had just transferred to Asaram's gurukul—next to the godman's headquarters in Motera—from the small private school in their neighbourhood in Ahmedabad.

The gurukul would be an instrument of upward mobility for them, because the family was convinced it was a good school. According to the gurukul's website, http://gurukul.ashram.org:[1]

All Gurukuls are built with utmost care. Gurukuls are not just buildings of education but a place of worship for students, a place to perform their Karma Yoga. We believe that a place a student spends almost 6–8 hours that too where his concentration has to be highest, must be comfortable and conducive to learning. Keeping this in mind, all buildings are tried to be kept in compliance with Vastu-shashtra. The surroundings are kept rich in Oxygen by planting Tulsi, Amla, Neem and Peepal around the premises. Inside the premises, well maintained class rooms are filled with positive aura by use of Gou chandan and phenyl. Ample space is available for sports facility in Gurukuls with required equipments and coaches. This clubbed with Vedic techniques of Yoga provide students a very healthy environment for physical development as well.

Shantilal Vaghela was a man of faith and was attracted to the concept of spiritual guidance through a guru. He began to meditate regularly after attending a ten-day Vipassana course at a centre in Dholka (40 km away from Ahmedabad), which requires a vow of silence, cutting off ties with the outside world for the duration of the course, among other restrictions. Nobody in his family was a follower of Asaram but he had heard of the godman. He attended a few events with acquaintances, heard

---

[1]   Extract from homepage of http://gurukul.ashram.org/ accessed on 13 July 2018

his sermons and went back occasionally after taking *deeksha* (initiation) in 2004, but was not close to the other followers. On one such occasion, in the summer of 2008, Abhishek, while on a summer break from school, accompanied his father to an event at the Motera ashram.

At the gate, a volunteer saw the father and son and approached them to admit Abhishek to the gurukul in Motera, where children of several followers studied. Shantilal told me that though he was never a dedicated follower of the godman, the residential school seemed like a good idea at the time.

Abhishek had studied at the Swaminarayan school in their neighbourhood and his parents had contemplated shifting him to a bigger school. The gurukul was residential but inside the city. Alongside academics it stressed on a values-based curriculum. Shantilal came back home, discussed it with his family and organized the admission fee of Rs 20,000. He could not recall if this was for the annual tuition and residency fees alone or included a capitation fee as well.

At the Bal Sanskar Kendra, he met an ashramite called Sanjay. After depositing the fees with him, Shantilal had just stepped out of the office when he experienced unease. 'I felt a sense of panic. I went back inside and told Sanjay-bhai about my discomfort and wanted a refund. But, Sanjay-bhai convinced me that the place was pure, under the influence of the saint and the boy would be fine there. The feeling persisted and I told my wife about it when I returned home. She said that since I had already paid for a year, we could take a decision once it was over.' It is difficult to say if he had a premonition of things to come or parental panic at the prospect of detachment from his child.

When his brother, Praful, heard that Abhishek was going to a better school, he wanted to admit his son, Deepesh, at the gurukul as well. Shantilal tried to discourage his brother and suggested that it would be better to wait until Abhishek completed a year there. But Praful was adamant and Shantilal did not press the matter.

It was past noon on 3 July 2008 when Shantilal arrived to meet with Abhishek and Deepesh. He was headed for another Vipassana meditation course and it would be close to two weeks before he would be able to visit his son again.

'It was amaavas [the day of a new moon], a light day at work and I had to leave the next day for Dholka. I noted their wish list and said I would have it sent,' Shantilal told me. Around 2.30 p.m., he and Kajal bid goodbye to the two children and went back home.

Around 9.00 p.m., Praful received a telephone call.

'Have the children gone home?' the caller asked Praful.

'Who is this?' Praful asked.

'I am calling from the gurukul, your children are not here,' the caller said.

Praful called Shantilal over to his house and told him of the call. The two immediately went to Motera. Pankaj Saxena, the gurupati (head), met them at the stairs of the gurukul.

'The call had come around 9 p.m. and it took us around fifteen minutes to get there. By the time we had reached, all the lights were off. When we went to the children's dormitory, we found them to be already asleep,' said Shantilal.

Saxena took them around inside the building to look for the children. Shantilal observed that all the residents of the gurukul, including the in-house staff, were already fast asleep.

'They serve dinner at 8 p.m. and they couldn't be asleep before it was 9.30 p.m. Later, this led to a doubt in my mind if a sedative was mixed with the food,' Shantilal said.

The Vaghela brothers checked the premises, including the garden, but could not find the children. 'Then Saxena told us to circumambulate (parikrama) the podium eleven or twenty-one times, from where Asaram delivered his sermons in Motera and come back the next morning. The children, Saxena told us, would be back by the next morning,' said Vaghela. It was nearly midnight by the time the two completed the parikrama.

They returned to the gurukul at 6 a.m. after a sleepless night and searched again, fruitlessly. The two fathers wanted the school authorities to lodge a complaint with the police. The authorities said they would speak with the director. At around noon of 4 July, Shantilal and Praful Vaghela went to the police station in a car provided by the ashram accompanied by four people—Pankaj Saxena, Meenaketan Govind Patro, Vikas Khemka and Uday Sanghani. (Sanghani and Patro are key aides of Asaram and are directors of companies that were probed by authorities, nearly a decade after the events described here.)

They reached the Chandkheda police outpost, where Sanghani and Khemka went in to speak with the police. After a while they returned and asked the Vaghelas to come into the station with them. There, instead of the gurukul authorities, the Vaghelas had to make an oral complaint to the policeman-in-charge, who asked them to wait till the evening.

Asaram's aides took them to another police station, where again the aides went in to speak with the policemen before taking the Vaghela brothers in. The policeman sent them back to Chandkheda and said that he would tell the policeman there to accept their complaint. Back in the car, the Vaghelas were told by Sanghani, 'We have to talk to Bapu [Asaram].' Despite their protests, they were taken back to the ashram instead of the police station.

The Vaghelas were made to wait even as Asaram, who was in Pune according to the aides, remained unavailable for phone calls. Around 2.30 p.m., Praful lost his patience and got up to leave. The aides stopped him and went to try Asaram's number again. Asaram himself never carried a phone and usually received calls on the phone of an aide-cum-servant travelling with him.

'Bapu has sent a message that you get hold of the clothes of the children, dip them in water, turn them inside-out and hang them up to dry. Get seven stones from a crossing and put them in water. Then heat the water and cool it down and repeat the process,' the Vaghelas were told. Shantilal would later make an entry in his diary, noting this instruction.

Praful said he did not believe in this hocus-pocus and left. Shantilal requested him to come back. They called their respective wives and asked them to perform this rite, even though it sounded bizarre to them. Around 5 p.m., the aides told them that a student of the gurukul had seen Deepesh and Abhishek on his fingernail. They claimed the boy had seen the two crying somewhere in a garden in Kalol (around 20 km from the ashram). Khemka, Patro and Shantilal again boarded the car.

When they reached the highway, en route to Kalol, Khemka called someone.

'From what I could overhear, I am convinced that Khemka was speaking to a tantric,' Shantilal told me.

They returned to the ashram and by now, Shantilal was also quite upset. He took a walk to cool off and headed to the back (east side) of the ashram. A ten to fifteen minute walk along the riverbed got him close to the water. The Sabarmati had shrunk to a rivulet, the rest of the riverbed was dry.

Around 8–9 p.m. that night, the Vaghelas were finally able to lodge a complaint with the Chandkheda police station.

The next day, they returned and invited journalists to the ashram. The Vaghelas' relatives also joined them. The group accused the ashram authorities of having kidnapped the children and demanded that they be handed over immediately. The protests continued through the day. When they were leaving in the evening, Shantilal saw two police vehicles draw up to the ashram.

Later, they found that an Asaram follower called Sunil Banerjee from Madhya Pradesh, who had come to the ashram for *ekant sadhana* (isolated mediation), had gone to the riverbed for a walk at around 5 p.m. There, he had seen the corpses of the two children. He informed the ashram director, who, in turn, called up the police.

'I feel that this Sunil Banerjee had a role to play in this whole episode. When he went for his walk to the riverbed, he had gone through the ashram and exited the premises from the rear towards the riverbed. Later, at night, he escorted the police through a circuitous route from the outside, past the Motera stadium, which is outside the ashram. That route is slippery and he took the police through that route instead of through the ashram and out of its rear to the riverbed, which is the route he took the first time. I suspect that he knows how the bodies came to be there,' Vaghela told me.

'The information was given between 5 p.m. and 6 p.m., when protesters, including us, and the media were there. But, we did not hear a word about it till the police turned up close to 8 p.m. On 4 July 2008, I had also gone to the riverbed, as I told you earlier. I had crossed that spot where the corpses were discovered later, but I had not seen the bodies there. If the children had drowned in water, the two bodies would have been far apart, but Abhishek and Deepesh were found within ten feet of each other. Besides, the river was more or less dry those days and there was no water in the river that could have washed them to the dry riverbed. So, how could the bodies have reached that spot unless someone placed them there, that too after 4 July, the day I had gone for a walk that side to clear my head?' Vaghela said.

We were talking in Shantilal Vaghela's house in Ahmedabad, in the heart of a middle-class colony. He is a labour contractor and has lived in that area for at least thirty-odd years. With a trustworthy reference, he invited me over to his house and spent half a day with me, reminiscing about the loss of his son and his pursuit for justice, which was yet to reach a conclusive end.

Past the gate and the yard, the drawing room of the Vaghelas' home leads to the kitchen, from where his wife and daughter filled in the details he had forgotten. They helped drag out plastic bags in which the files were neatly packed. Vaghela opened them, pored over them and passed on the ones in English to me. The ones in Gujarati he read and translated out aloud for my benefit.

In the drawing room, an almost life-size framed photograph of Abhishek hung on a wall, close to the entrance. A bright, red rakhi was glued to the frame, right above his right wrist in the photograph.

To illustrate the point about the corpses, Shantilal pulled out a photograph from 6 July 2008, that showed them lying on separate gurneys.

In it, their skin appeared a dark purple to black. Abhishek was lying spreadeagled on his back, naked from the waist down. According to one account he had been discovered fully clothed. The entire body was swollen, the legs were spread apart, the head faced upwards with the eyes shut and the mouth agape to form an 'o'.

The photograph was taken from an angle that was to the body's left. The right hand is not visible in the photograph, the left palm is cropped out of the photo's frame. Apart from the big toe, the rest of the toes from the right foot seem to be missing from the angle in which the photograph was taken.

References to Deepesh's corpse mentioned 'internal organs missing', a tame description at best. There was no skin covering the ribs in front. The ribcage was split open, with the sternum (breastbone) missing. Inside the ribcage, the torso had no organs. The entire spinal column was visible while there was skin on the back of the corpse. The T-shirt was lying a few feet away from where the corpse was discovered.

In the photograph, Deepesh's head is turned towards his left (in the direction of the camera). The eyes seem shut, the nose is missing and the mouth cannot be seen because of a steel pipe in the room blocking the view.

The difference in the state of the two corpses is stark. The post-mortem report[2] showed that Deepesh's body had been received at the hospital around 2.30 a.m. on 6 July 2008, and the post-mortem conducted between 11 a.m. and 1.30 p.m. on that day. It was dressed in a light yellow T-shirt that had a label bearing his name. One sleeve had the legend 'Yoga and Meditation', the other said 'www.ashram.org' and on its chest was written: 'Shri Yog Vedant Ashram'. There were four tears on the T-shirt, three of which were on the left sleeve. The clothes were stained with mud, sand, a brownish fluid and covered in maggots.

---

[2]   Post-mortem no. 1838/08 dated 06/07/2008

The skin had started peeling away and was missing, along with soft tissue, in a few places, which the report suggested was a sign of post-mortem decomposition. The toes of the left foot were missing, which the report referred to as 'nibbling due to animals appreciated'. The ears were also described as nibbled by animals. Missing from inside Deepesh's body were the small and large intestines, liver, stomach, spleen, kidneys and bladder.

The skin and tissue were missing from below the chin to the pubic region. In several places where the skin and tissue were not there, the margins from where they disappeared were irregular, the cause which the report described as 'nibbled by animals'. This means that the report shows that an animal had nibbled at pieces of the exposed skin and tissue. The report did not specify if it was 'nibbled by animals' before or after death.

'Ribs and vertebrae column exposed. All the internal organs missing except heart, part of both lungs, trachea, part of the oesophagus and part of the stomach,' the post-mortem report noted.

The cartilage which join the ribs to the sternum in front was missing. The ears were missing too but the report did not mention nibbling by animals. The right foot had toes missing, again with 'nibbling appreciated', but the missing toes in the left foot did not draw the same observation.

In Abhishek's case, the report[3] mentioned a yellow T-shirt, white shorts and red underwear found 'beside the body'. The T-shirt bore the same inscriptions as Deepesh's T-shirt. There were tears on the sleeves and the neck, described as irregular; and a 12-cm-long tear descending from below the button line towards the right bottom. This cut is not described as irregular.

---

[3]  Post-mortem no. 1839/08 dated 06/07/2008

The toes from his right foot, except the big toe, and ears were missing; 'eaten by animals' as per the post-mortem report.

'How come the entire ribcage is sprung open and the clothes lying nearby, if Abhishek drowned to death? Pandya had told me that many children had gone missing from the ashram and I deposed this before the commission. He was never called to depose,' Vaghela told me. 'One theory suggested that wild animals ate up parts of Abhishek's corpse. Do animals pick and choose? Why would Deepesh's body, found within feet of Abhishek's, remain intact in that case?'

'The parents protested that animals wouldn't pick and choose. Why would one body be found with the thorax open and organs missing, while the other was not, though both bodies were swollen (distended)? How could animals systematically open the ribs?' S.H. Iyer, the Vaghela lawyer told me.

When the bodies were discovered, Asaram's aides seemed to be in charge. They stripped a key hanging from Deepesh's neck to check if it was the key to his locker. This angered Praful, who lost his patience, and assaulted Pankaj Saxena, the gurupati. Saxena called people at the ashram and they came in cycle-carts with batons. 'The police said that we should leave because they would assault us. If the people from the ashram could attack us, what was the police's role? How can the police be scared of them? They also stopped our well-wishers from photographing or documenting the spot where the corpses were found,' said Vaghela.

Later that night, while it was still dark, the corpses were shifted to the hospital. The incident and the lack of police action prompted protests and the Vaghelas sat on a fast to demand a CBI probe. During the fast, several BJP workers came to ask them to break the fast but the Vaghelas did not relent. Amongst them, Vaghela recalls a BJP worker who was later inducted to the board of the Ahmedabad District Cooperative Bank.

Ten days into the fast, which had been widely covered by the media, Narendra Modi, then chief minister of the state, called them for a meeting. As they sat down on the couch in the CM's office in Gandhinagar, with a television news camera recording the meeting, they were offered what appeared to be glasses of water. As soon as the Vaghelas drank it they realized it was lemonade.

'He tricked us, we thought it was water offered since we had just sat down and did not know that it was lemonade. Modi then told us that since we had ended our fast, we should not worry and that he would ensure we got justice. The government will leave no avenue unexplored for us, Modi said,' Vaghela said.

By the time they came back, the news flashed that Narendra Modi had succeeded in ending their fast. Modi, with Amit Shah present, addressed the media and said that he had promised an investigation into the deaths and that the truth would be revealed.

'I had requested Gujarat High Court—that high court order a judicial inquiry and if there is any fault in the investigation or it is being diverted, then the chief justice of the Gujarat HC should look into it and there should be transparency. This government will not let any culprit go. Citizens of Gujarat know this government very well and I am confident that we will find the truth. And, this truth will not allow anyone else, ever, to commit any misdeed in Gujarat,' Modi had said.[4]

---

[4]　https://www.youtube.com/watch?v=aZRF-I2jW8o published on 21 September 2011 and accessed on 2 July 2018
https://www.youtube.com/watch?v=12REfBjPEJ8 published on 13 November 2015 and accessed on 2 July 2018

Simultaneous to the news flash, a local BJP worker in the Vagehlas' neighbourhood disrupted the activists sitting with the Vaghelas and dismantled the small podium built for the fast. 'You have already made an arrangement with the CM,' he claimed.

The tussle between the government and the protesters continued and during a clash, the protesters were detained. Vaghela went to the secretariat to talk to the then home minister of Gujarat, Amit Shah, and asked him to release the detainees. 'He told me that the men had damaged public property. I asked him what he had done to arrest the murderers,' Shantilal said.

During the protests, a volunteer with the Jan Sangharsh Manch (JSM), Amrish Patel, had met Shantilal. He offered free legal aid through JSM. Shantilal hung on to his visiting card and discussed it with Praful, who did not want to be associated with the organization because of its anti-establishmentarian image. The JSM was founded by the late Mukul Sinha and his wife, Nirjhari Sinha, both trade unionists who had fought many a battle in Gujarat. The forum attracted several activists and the JSM's efforts are well known in appealing to courts for special probes into Gujarat's mysterious encounters and other high-profile probes.

Shantilal told his brother that it was a good thing that the JSM was anti-establishmentarian because the police had not probed the case. Nevertheless, Praful approached a famous criminal lawyer, who refused to take on their case. Shantilal convinced Praful to go to the JSM, which had offered to give them pro bono support. They met Amrish Patel, Mukul Sinha and S.H. Iyer, whom they appointed as their lawyer.

The protests against Asaram drew the support of many people, including the volunteers of the JSM. One such volunteer was Jignesh Mevani, who was elected to the Gujarat

Vidhan Sabha in 2017 on an independent ticket, who recalled how Ahmedabad had been shut down for a day because of the strike called by the protesters against the non-action of the government. He would play a further role, much later.

National media also took a deep interest in the godman. Till then, there had been wisps of fleeting news about him, he having built sufficient political capital. The anti-conversion activism under Asaram, the challenging of the popularity of 'Western pop' practices in India, and so forth had played well with a majority of the Hindus in Gujarat and elsewhere. It had brought political support and the administration had overlooked the organization's land encroachment and other charges, as outlined earlier. By that time, the case of the land-grab by the Surat ashram was already in the high court. It had been reported but there had not been anything as sensational as the twin murder case.

The protesters camped outside Asaram's Motera ashram and the media followed. People started digging into Asaram's past, beyond the biographical pamphlet which his trust had published. Stories started spilling out and investigative reporters reached out to former devotees and aides who had parted ways with the godman. The mainstream media started to report about the godman. The former aides started to make claims about how the godman was involved in occult practices and some provided graphic details of their experiences to journalists.

The next full moon (that of July 2008) was Guru Purnima, which, as per Hindu tradition, is a day when devotees and followers pay obeisance to their gurus. Asaram had planned an event at his Motera ashram to accommodate as many of his devotees as possible. That day, 18 July 2008, the ashram would be filled with several people: lay followers, residents of other ashrams, the ashramites themselves and others who would come to listen to the godman and spend time at the Motera ashram.

Since the disappearance of the children, Asaram had not made any public statement and Shantilal Vaghela and others felt that he was shielding the accused and not cooperating with them. The protesters decided to camp outside the ashram and force the hand of the godman or the administration.

On the day of Guru Purnima, police were deployed at the ashram for both the event as well as to maintain law and order during protests. Till then, there had only been sporadic incidents where people had complained of having been beaten up and since there was enough security, the event was expected to pass peacefully.

But, the protests turned violent that day, for which each party blamed the other. The media was present to cover the protests and to see whether Asaram would come out to address the protesters. The ashramites had invited some journalists to attend the Guru Purnima event, to counter some of the bad press they had been getting since the death of the Vaghela cousins.

Gopi Maniar, Gujarat bureau chief of the Hindi news channel Aaj Tak (part of the India Today Group), was one of several mediapersons who were at the ashram that day.[5] By that time, charges of occult practices and witchcraft had started to surface and there were directions to cover it on a daily basis.

'There were thousands of attendees of the event and several police personnel were posted there. While we were inside, the clash between the protesters and the ashramites turned violent. Stones were pelted and the clashing mob had set fire to some

---

[5] Interview conducted by author on 3 July 2018 at Ahmedabad.

things. The police also deployed water cannons and had begun a baton charge,' she recalled.

Maniar was standing with the camerapersons of her channel and Times Now. The Aaj Tak cameraperson went to another location to cover the clash while the Times Now cameraperson remained with her. The two of them saw a truck full of people armed with rods, sticks and farming tools on their way towards the site of the clash.

'We thought they would spread the violence to the residential area in the vicinity of the ashram and decided to follow them to witness what they were up to,' said Maniar. 'Unfortunately, they realized that we were following them.'

The armed crew stopped the vehicle, got off it and charged towards them, though the policemen were just a short distance away and headed towards this armed mob of Asaram's followers. One of them caught Maniar by the hair, another by the arm and dragged her to the middle of the road. Yet another one of Asaram's followers hit her on the back with a rod.

'I am a journalist,' Maniar screamed, hoping it would stop them.

'You are the ones who have spoilt the image of our guru, a saint, and of the ashram,' they retorted, while the assault continued.

Another set of Asaram's followers caught hold of the Times Now cameraperson and threw away his camera, damaging it. They continued to assault him on the head and body, causing several injuries.

They were not the only mediapersons to be attacked. A mob also headed to where the outdoor broadcast (OB) vans were parked with the intention to set them on fire. Some of the OB vans had small generator sets and the reporters pointed at these generator sets and shouted at the mob that these would explode if the vans were set on fire. That stopped them but they did not retreat.

Maniar tried to hold off her attackers with one hand and free her hair with the other, but she was repeatedly hit on the head and arms. When policemen rushed in to help her, they were assaulted as well. A camera was clicking from a few feet away.

The visuals streamed from television sets for days. All the newspapers carried photos and detailed stories of the violence unleashed by Asaram's followers. Maniar became a story herself and the assault on her was covered extensively. Photographers had caught Asaram's goons in the act of assaulting the reporter, the police and others.

After this skirmish on 18 July 2008, the government finally notified the Justice (retd) D.K. Trivedi commission.

Maniar and the others were hospitalized. The doctors diagnosed her with internal injuries and extensive tissue damage and discharged her later that night after tests and a medico-legal certificate that recorded the extent of the injuries. An FIR was lodged for the assaults on multiple people and the case is being prosecuted at a court in Gujarat. Since then, Maniar has encountered Asaram and been to the ashram at least five times in the course of her work. She has identified twelve of her attackers in court.

This episode of violence served to alert the administration about the kind of brutishness that the godman's goons and brawling followers could unleash upon the public and became a subject of discussion in the bureaucracy and the police department. But the threat of violence remained till another incident was reported a year and a half later.

~

S.H. Iyer told me that the Justice (retd) D.K. Trivedi commission worked for nearly five years, till 2013. Around 200 witnesses, including several journalists, students, gurukul authorities and ex-inmates of the ashram deposed before it. The report was submitted on 31 July 2013, barely three weeks before the minor girl, Mita, made her complaint to the police.

The Vaghelas did not want to be a part of the commission; they wanted an independent probe into the unnatural death of their children. For a month, they did not attend the proceedings because they believed that it would not lead to legal action against the accused and that it was nothing more than a forum to defuse their anger.

'I think that the diversion did not work and the commission actually resulted in the truth of Asaram spilling out into the open. The media covered it day by day and reported all that the former aides of Asaram deposed to the commission,' said Shantilal.

Ex-aides Raju Chandak, Rahul Sachan, Mahendra Chawla disclosed several details hitherto unknown in the public domain. 'But, all the things that were disclosed about Asaram and his operations did not lead to any action by Modi, though things were being revealed on a regular basis. Five years later also, they did not do anything,' said Shantilal.

Shantilal considers Mahendra Chawla's and Amrut Prajapati's testimonies to the commission to be the most important. Chawla claimed to have seen Narayan Sai perform a tantric ritual over a child's body and Prajapati had given testimony about Asaram. Another former devotee mentioned exorcism, which is the excuse that Shilpi used to send Mita to the godman five years after the mysterious deaths of Abhishek and Deepesh. Shantilal also questioned the prescriptions that Asaram had supposedly issued over the telephone at the ashram on 4 July 2008.

The police continued with its investigation, which had been handed over to the crime investigation department (CID). The line of questioning showed that the police were following a theory of death by drowning, as it had been hinted in the post-mortem. It wrote to the department of forensic medicine of the B.J. Medical College in Ahmedabad for an opinion on 19 July 2008, with twelve queries based on the post-mortem.

The doctors responded to the queries, notable amongst which were:

— The scalps had not been shaved.
— The clothes had not been removed by cutting them off.
— Deepesh's internal organs were missing and they couldn't rule out that they had been eaten by animals.
— There were no marks left by any weapons on the clothes or the bodies.
— The missing portions were due to animal bites.
— They did not comment on the missing organs.
— The death had taken place between 48–72 hours before the post-mortem.

The time of death was thus placed anywhere between noon of 3 July to around noon of 4 July, since the post-mortem was conducted between 11 a.m. and 1.30 p.m. for Deepesh and between 1.30 p.m. and 4 p.m. for Abhishek. They were last seen by Shantilal Vaghela around 2.30 p.m. (or earlier) on 3 July 2008. The roll call after dinner found them missing.

On 30 July 2008, the department of forensic medicine of the B.J. Medical College in Ahmedabad presented its opinion to the Gujarat CID on the cause of the deaths of Abhishek and Deepesh. The medical evidence was also presented to the Justice Trivedi commission. The opinion was identical in the case of both the boys and noted[6] that the respective bodies were decomposed, there was no detection of 'ante-mortem' (prior to death) injuries on the bodies, that 'no chemical poison was detected', and the forensic science laboratory (FSL) report showed that the 'presence of diatoms could not [be] detected'.

Traces of diatoms (microorganisms found in water) in a corpse show up when a body has been drowned or submerged in water. Diatoms not being found might mean that the cause of death may not be drowning. However, the expert's opinion said: 'Considering above FSL report and postmortem findings possibility of death due to drowning cannot be ruled out, however "no definite opinion regarding cause of death can be given".'

The police were not satisfied by the report and sent in five more questions on 31 July 2008. Three of these questions dealt with death by drowning, one on the possible time of death, and one on 'any marks of murder in both these children found?' The letter noted that 'the case is controversial and it is also Suo Motu filed before the High Court' and that the next date of hearing was on 4 August 2008.

The doctors wrote back on 1 August 2008 that they could not conclude that the children died due to drowning because of

---

[6]  Letter no. FMD/Outward No. 182/08 & 183/08 from department of forensic medicine, B.J. Medical College, Ahmedabad, to the crime investigation department, Ahmedabad

the absence of diatoms. The doctors said that there were three possibilities for the absence of diatoms:

— dry drowning
— death due to vagal inhibition in drowning
— the water which caused drowning did not contain diatoms, which means piped water supply

'Dry drowning' is a controversial subject and has been challenged by academics and experts the world over. In this case, the identical dry drowning of two human beings is not just remote but virtually impossible. 'Dry drowning' refers to death long after contact with water. The theory had been prominently dispelled by a World Health Organization bulletin in 2005, much before the doctors in Ahmedabad responded to the police in August 2008. Vagal inhibition is also a questionable theory since again it happened to both the children at the same time.

The doctors mentioned five reasons for Deepesh and six for Abhishek that favoured the drowning theory. The reasons included sand and mud found on their organs, bodies and clothes.

There are two arguments to be made here apart from many others that experts can raise. First, the mud and sand could have easily been present if the bodies had been dragged or rolled in it. Second, if the boys drowned in water from a piped supply or a purified or treated source, then diatoms would not be present.

While the doctors and the police were exchanging letters, a boy, Vedant Manmode, from Maharashtra, drowned[7] in

---

[7] https://www.hindustantimes.com/india/another-ashram-schoolboy-dead/story-wBuwGevyGf5YuoFnUZdzNI.html published on 31 July 2008 and accessed on 15 July 2018

Asaram's Chhindwara gurukul. He was discovered with his head in a bucket of water in the hostel's washroom. Another boy had been found dead near the same washroom earlier in July 2008. According to news reports[8] both the children's parents said that they did not hold the gurukul responsible for the deaths. However, the two deaths led to outrage amongst the parents of other children and some wanted to take their wards home. Later, the Madhya Pradesh police arrested an older boy, deemed 'mentally unstable' after his supposed confession to the crimes. They said his motive was to cause the school to shut down so that he could go back home as he didn't want to remain in the hostel. His father hotly contested the claim and the story disappeared soon afterwards.

In the cousins' case, the police also asked how long after their last meal did the children die. The doctors responded that, in Deepesh's case, they could not give any conclusive opinion. Though they did not give a reason, it can be safely assumed that it was because his internal organs were missing. In Abhishek's case, 200 grams of partly digested rice suggest the death to have occurred 2–4 hours after a meal. If the boys had dinner that night, then that would place the time of death at midnight, which would mean after the parents had been informed. If it was lunch, then it would be any time on the evening of 3 July 2008, shortly after Shantilal met them for the last time.

A missing part of the evidence, which Shantilal told me, was a peculiar cut on one of the T-shirts, made by a weapon, which was noticed and recorded by the Gujarat FSL. This incensed the

---

8   https://www.hindustantimes.com/india/ashram-row-parents-take-kids-home/story-mGb2lLTWDmO8hzh8ZhsxdK.html published on 2 August 2008 and accessed on 15 July 2008

CID investigator, who demanded an explanation as to why he had recorded this without being asked. The FSL wrote back saying it was part of the procedure and so the samples had been sent.

The letter from the police is curious. Any investigator will want to explore as many leads as possible. The correspondence between the police and the experts they consulted shows that the police were trying to direct the investigation towards drowning and not explore any other possibilities though there was scientific evidence to show that they should have chased other leads.

The able inspector did not give up. He wrote to the doctors who had performed the post-mortem with six queries through an angry letter dated 1 September 2008, the subject line of which said: 'Clear Opinion'. He now wanted explanations about the tears on the clothes and whether there was anything to suggest that blood had been drained from the children's bodies or that organs had been removed in order to know if there were '. . . any marks of death due to Black Magic'.

The response clearly did not satisfy Detective Inspector H.B. Rajput, who sent another letter on 5 September 2008, this time with the subject line: 'Give clear opinions on the questions asked'. Through their reply dated 9 September 2008, the doctors said that there were no such injuries in the case of Abhishek, whose body was found mostly intact. In Deepesh's case, they said that they could not give a conclusive opinion if the organs had been removed after death for 'tantric vidhi'.

Inspector Rajput again picked up the missing organs theory after two months, on 29 November 2008. He said that Deepesh was eleven at the time of his death and 'thus till which age the organs are delicate such that if any animal or dog pulls then there are possibilities of losing? Also, regarding the organs lost what could be the definite reason?' The doctors finally relented and said that it was possible that the organs were lost because of an animal pulling away the organs or eating them.

There is no record of any parts of the organs being found at the spot where the bodies were discovered. It may sound crude and disrespectful to the dead, but in India, most crime scenes are treated with the same level of sanctity as any other public place. The Aarushi–Hemraj double murder happened the same year, in May 2008, and is a fit case to illustrate this. Even if there was any such evidence, it was lost when the police decided not to contain the area and seal it off till a forensics team was available to procure more evidence to pursue lines of inquiry. The police were busy batting for the godman and no FIR was lodged for more than two weeks. There is a case to be made here in favour of ensuring the sanctity of crime scenes as well as videotaping post-mortem examinations. The only examination conducted by a forensics team was two and a half days after the bodies were found, which filed a description of the geographical terrain of the riverbed.

The DIG of police supervising the CID's investigation forwarded this batch of correspondence between Inspector Rajput, the FSL and the doctors who conducted the post-mortem to the head of forensic medicine in Ahmedabad's medical college and civil hospital. He wanted a clear opinion on the cause of death. If it was not by drowning, was black magic involved?

The question may have been put to a tantric because how does a scientist or medical doctor explain black magic practices? The forensic department's head relied on the report of the doctors who had conducted the post-mortem to say that there was no black magic involved. He also sent the same response, that drowning could not be ruled out but a definite cause of death could not be established either. This was followed by a round of queries raised by the DIG of the CID and responses from the forensic laboratory, but without opening any new avenues.

A year after this round of correspondence and queries, the police finally lodged an FIR on 7 November 2009. There seemed to be reluctance to even accuse the ashram and gurukul authorities of negligence. So, Shantilal and Praful approached the high court for a CBI probe. It was after they had filed that writ petition that the police finally lodged an FIR under Section 304 of the IPC. The GHC did not allow a CBI probe into the mysterious death of the two children.

The GHC also said that there was no offence under Section 304, which is the penalty for 'culpable homicide not amounting to murder' and carries a sentence of ten years upon conviction. The high court instead directed investigation under Section 304A of the IPC for 'causing death by negligence' which carries a sentence of only two years.

The Vaghelas appealed to the Supreme Court, where a bench of Justice Sathasivam and Justice Gogoi noted, 'The specific stand taken in the FIR is that had a prompt search been carried out, possibly, the children could have been found alive or, at least, the dead bodies could have been recovered earlier so as to enable an effective post-mortem of the bodies to determine the precise cause of death.'

'It is also alleged that the Ashram authorities had advised the parents of the children to resort to various tantric practices to find out about the whereabouts of the children instead of promptly approaching the police. The failure of the said authorities to effectively man the gates behind the ashram adjoining the river bed have also been highlighted in the FIR as another omission on the part of the ashram authorities so as to give rise to the commission of the offence of culpable homicide.'

But, the Supreme Court did not find it reason enough to probe the deaths as culpable homicide. It relied on the inconclusive medical reports and subsequent opinions that were made to pursue a particular line of inquiry. The discussions between the police and the scientific experts focused on the animal attack theory to explain the missing organs from Deepesh's body. The Sabarmati runs through the middle of Ahmedabad and there are no known quadrupeds in the vicinity which are capable of breaking open a human chest, detaching the sternum, pulling apart the skin and chewing up the organs. The skin may have peeled off due to decomposition, but that still would not explain the ribcage being cracked open in that manner.

It noted, 'The relevant part of the post-mortem report, as extracted, indicates presence of mud in the trachea of the children which fact also point to the possibility of death by drowning. The absence of any injuries on the body of the deceased; the attack on the bodies by wild animals and the possibility of the taking away of the missing organs of the deceased Deepesh by wild animals are all mentioned in the post-mortem report. The said facts cannot be excluded or ignored while construing the prima facie liability of the accused named in the FIR. The absence of any positive material to show the practice of black magic in connection with the incident is another significant fact that has to be taken note of.'

The police made a token arrest of Saxena, Bhati and Patro on 7 February 2011 and Vani, Sanghani and Ajay Shah the following day. All of them had procured anticipatory bail less than a week before the arrests and were released immediately on personal bail bonds of Rs 5,000. The CID filed a charge sheet on 31 October 2012, days before the Supreme Court's decision, alleging death caused by negligence.

The Justice Trivedi commission continued with its sensational hearings for some more months after the charge sheet. Witness after witness deposed about the conduct of Asaram, much of which was reiterated later in the trial of Asaram and that of his son, Narayan Sai. There were tales about sexual exploitation of female devotees at the ashram, the ambience of fear that was used to contain dissent, the misuse of religious doctrine to perpetrate the myth of Asaram as the supreme being in the ashram's ecology and the inviolability of his word. The son was projected as an extension of the guru and was given the same status and responded with the same conduct as his father.

Raju Chandak, a former aide, disclosed many secrets beyond the black magic and was attacked for his troubles. Much later, the police said that Kartick Halder—who had attacked and killed some of the other witnesses after the cases lodged in 2013—was responsible for that shooting as well. Chandak, who survived the attempt on his life, wanted to lodge an FIR against Asaram to probe if he had ordered a hit on him.

I spoke with Chandak during my research but he was reluctant to meet me. 'Journalists come and take statements from us. While it may help some, it exposes us to many dangers, so I would rather not speak,' he had told me.

Raju Chandak's grandfather had been a follower of Asaram's since 1972 and Chandak had been a committed disciple from 1984 till he quit in 2004. 'Narayan Sai was deeply interested in learning tantra vidya from a young age and travelled to many places to learn about it and he would come back from these trips

and tell me about them. The interest in this study increased as
he grew older,' Chandak told the D.K. Trivedi commission.

Chandak said that Asaram had purportedly exorcized
people of ghostly possession in front of him by sprinkling them
with water and by performing some rites. This would go on for
2–3 hours and would end with Asaram declaring, '*Abhi tumhara
bhoot nikal gaya* (The ghost/demon has left your body).' In some
cases, Asaram would get tantrics to perform the exorcism with
him. There were occasions when he would take people into his
hut alone for an exorcism.

In 1997, Chandak told the commission that he saw Asaram
sexually assault a woman devotee in Jaipur. At the time, the
ashram in Jaipur was being built and the door to Asaram's hut
was covered only with a curtain, so Chandak had been able to
look inside and see what was going on. Chandak also testified
that Asaram loaned money on interest and used a gang of goons
to recover loans from defaulters.

Many devotees and others have questioned Chandak's role in
Asaram's organization and whether his testimony absolved him
of what he had been a part of while he was serving the godman.
Since the godman was now at the receiving end, speaking out
against him could be a get-out-of-jail-free card. An FIR was
lodged in Jammu against former devotees, including those who
had testified against him both in court and to the media, and a
prominent journalist, who had covered the allegations against
Asaram. The complainant alleged that there was a conspiracy
afoot to target the godman. There was an accusation[9] that
another former disciple at the Jammu ashram had tried to bribe

---

[9]  https://www.youtube.com/watch?v=YYFHppFoDQ4 accessed on
2 July 2018

an Asaram follower to lie about bodies having been buried in the ashram.

Chandak did not mention Asaram's past as a bootlegger, even though his grandfather had known Asaram during his earliest years. Newspapers interviewed a man named Kalaji Thakore of Gandhinagar, who claimed to have supplied Asaram alcohol in cans. According to Kala and some others, Asaram would peddle the illicit liquor to businessmen on the banks of the Sabarmati near Motera. Later, that is where Asaram built his first hut and then the ashram around it.

When the commission had just started, a tantric called Oghad (Aghori) Sukhram surfaced in Indore. He was well known in the Devas region of Madhya Pradesh. He alleged that Asaram had given him a supari (contract) to fix his enemies for Rs 1.5 lakh using tantric practices. Sukhram made[10] these declarations to a local daily in MP and said that he had prepared an affidavit with all these details including a CD with call recordings as proof.

According to him, Asaram's targets were former associates such as Chandak, former secretary Kaushik Patel, former driver Dinesh Bhagchandani, former Ayurvedic physician Amrut Prajapati and two journalists—Shreyans Shah of *Gujarat Samachar* and Parth Patel of *Desh*, the paper in which Sukhram made these allegations.[11] Sukhram had also deposed before

[10] https://timesofindia.indiatimes.com/city/ahmedabad/ Aghori-sadhu-alleges-Asaram-asked-him-to-kill-6-persons/ articleshow/3405352.cms published on 26 August 2008 and accessed on 1 July 2018

[11] https://www.indiatoday.in/magazine/indiascope/story/20080908- problems-aplenty-737427-2008-08-29 published on 29 August 2008 and accessed on 1 July 2018

the commission and said that both he and Asaram should be subjected to narco-analysis tests to ascertain the truth. This skewed Shantilal's narrative slightly because if Asaram or his son were themselves tantrics, why would they need another tantric to target their enemies using black magic? Why not do it themselves?

One of the longest depositions, which lasted three days, was of Ishwar Naik, an NRI who was based in Canada till he became a follower of Asaram in 1986 and moved back to India. Naik used to live in Canada when his wife's family members died in a car crash. Asaram helped console Naik and asked him to pay Rs 2 lakh for rites to be conducted for the souls of the departed. He also told Naik to surrender to the guru and commit himself to the ashram.

Naik's son, Anang, was also a former follower and had told Naik that on the day of Kali Chaudas Narayan Sai would perform tantric rites in a cemetery.

Naik fell ill and consulted a tantric called Rabbari, who told them that someone in the ashram where they lived had cast an occult charm on his son, Anang, and advised them to leave the ashram. Narayan Sai had arranged[12] Anang's marriage with a female NRI devotee that he had himself had an affair with.

At the time, Ishwar Naik had been given the charge of handling accounts at the Chhindwara ashram while Anang looked after the IT needs of the ashram in Ahmedabad. After their marriage, the woman refused a conjugal relationship with

---

[12] http://www.epaper.timesofindia.com/Repository/getFiles.asp?Style= OliveXLib:LowLevelEntityToPrint_MIRRORNEW&Type=text/ht ml&Path=AMIR/2010/04/21&ID=Ar00601 published on 21 April 2010 and accessed on 28 June 2018

Anang saying, 'I belong to Narayan Sai.' Naik had given a CD with proof of the marriage ceremony, which was conducted by Narayan Sai. After the wedding, Anang was dispatched to the ashram in Delhi to instal computers but his wife was retained in the ashram. On Rabbari's advise, they parted ways with the godman as did Anang's wife, who, Naik told the commission, had tried to commit suicide but failed and was sent back to her family in England.

As per Asaram's website, Ishwar Naik had said during his deposition that he had found solace in the ashram and that chanting mantras helped him. The website also says that when he had been ill in Canada, his wife had chanted the Mahamrityunjay mantra on Asaram's advice, and it had cured him.

The trust also mentions a miracle that he deposed about. Asaram had organized an event near Ratlam, attended by tribals. After lunch, Asaram had given Naik a bundle of currency notes to distribute to the tribals. Naik kept distributing the money but, magically, the bundle was not depleted till the last person had been given money from it. Asaram's organization also accused Naik of defrauding people and creating conflict between ashramites.

Asaram's followers have maintained throughout that the way of their guru is Vedantic Hinduism, the philosophy is based on the Vedas, and neither Asaram nor they believe in tantra or practise any dark magic.

After evading several summons for six months, Asaram finally deposed before the commission for a full day that stretched well into the night on 1 December 2012. During his deposition, Asaram denied all allegations of black magic and stated that he followed Vedantic philosophy. Before the hearing, several of his followers thronged Judges Bungalow, where the commission was holding its hearings.

At the hearing, Asaram relied on the laboratory findings that no black magic had been performed on Abhishek or Deepesh. He made a sensational disclosure that two weeks after the boys' disappearance, Saxena had told him that someone called Gossai had tried to abduct the two boys. Besides, there was no evidence that any such abduction attempt had ever taken place. The gurukul or the ashram had not filed any complaint with the police either.

Shantilal recalled the time when he would attend Asaram's programmes. Even then, he was unable to connect with the godman at a spiritual level. He felt conflicted because he did not feel a bond with the godman within. 'Why am I unable to feel devotion for my guru?' he would question himself.

Once, when standing in queue for prasad at the ashram, Shantilal noticed that there was a different queue for those who gave money and for those who didn't. The conflict within him inflated and Shantilal decided he wanted to meet Asaram. So, he approached an ashramite and expressed his desire to meet the godman. The ashramite, Shantilal alleged, said it would require some money, around Rs 5,000. This, naturally, deepened the inner conflict he was already grappling with.

~

'After Asaram's arrest, we told the media that there had been no action in the murder case or a decision. The rape case was solved in five years. So, the media questioned the government and they keep giving assurances, but nothing has happened,' said Shantilal Vaghela.

The conviction of Asaram on charges of violating the POCSO law has given some sense of closure and justice to many. Many are reassured that both father and son are confined behind bars. But, in at least this case, the door to justice seems to have been half-shut for a long time.

In 2017, Jignesh Mevani, who had protested along with the Vaghelas in 2008 as a volunteer with the Jan Sangharsh Manch, launched himself into electoral politics following his successful leadership of a Dalit movement from Una in Gujarat. In the 2017 Gujarat state assembly elections, he was elected from the Vadgam electoral constituency to the Gujarat assembly on an independent ticket. In the first assembly session that he attended, Mevani asked a starred question that created a ruckus in the house on 14 March 2018.

Mevani wanted to know when the Justice (retd) D.K. Trivedi commission report would be tabled in the house and what was the reason behind the delay in tabling it. The answer that came later said that it was under consideration. During the session, BJP legislators were angered by this question and threw slurs at Mevani. The Congress supported Mevani's questions and demanded an answer. The BJP legislators blamed the Congress government of having supported Asaram.

The Commissions of Inquiry Act requires a submitted report to be tabled in the house within six months, but the government had withheld it for nearly five years, when Mevani asked the question. Pradeepsinh Jadeja, the Gujarat minister of state for home affairs, differed and said it was not mandatory.

'The decision to table the report is still under consideration. As per a court order, it is not mandatory to table such reports in six months. That provision is directory, not mandatory in nature,' Jadeja said in the assembly.

A Congress legislator, Shailesh Parmar, alleged that the BJP was trying to protect the godman. Jadeja in turn pointed out that the land for the Motera ashram had been granted to Asaram during the Congress rule in Gujarat.

Jadeja eventually responded to the leader of the Opposition that the government would release the report after considering some aspects of it. But, he did not commit a timeline for it.

During the discussion over the question, the Congress and BJP MLAs blamed each other for supporting the godman. The Congress wanted a discussion on the deaths of the Vaghela cousins. The case was still sub judice before a court of law at the time. A BJP MLA, Jagdish Panchal, took a dig at Congress MLA Pratap Dudhat, who rushed out of his seat, grabbed a microphone off a desk and flung it at Panchal. Thankfully, the microphone missed Panchal by inches and the story missed the front pages the next day. The assembly had to take a break because of the violence[13] among the legislators.

Some people claim that certain 'sins are unpardonable', that 'there is always divine retribution', while atheists mutter 'what goes around comes around'. I don't know if harm to children falls within the range of these eventualities. Objectivity and rationality transcend viewing events as 'sins' or stating them in terms of binaries of good and evil. Therefore, we are not able to understand or prove occult practices in the absence of actual evidence for we are usually concerned with crime and the rule

---

[13] https://ahmedabadmirror.indiatimes.com/ahmedabad/others/watch-ruckus-in-gujarat-assembly-as-bjp-congress-mlas-exchange-blows/articleshow/63299311.cms published on 14 March 2018 and accessed on 10 July 2018

of law in society. Thus, we have no other way of pinpointing certain events in a narrative except by marking their importance.

August 31 is the birth anniversary of Abhishek Vaghela, whose death along with that of his cousin's, as per their families, did not get the justice it was due. On that same date in 2012, the police filed a charge sheet against Pankaj Saxena, Yogesh Manohar, Minketan Govind Patro, Vikas Khemka, Uday Sanghani, Ajay Shah and Kaushik Popatlal Vani.

The importance of Kaushik Vani to Asaram has been clearly mentioned in this book, as has been that of Minketan Govind Patro, both of whose role in the godman's empire was discovered by the income tax investigation. Uday Sanghani has been charged for bribing the police and by the ED for using proceeds of crime for the bribe. Ajay Shah is mentioned as being a benami property holder for Asaram.

It was also on the night of Abhishek's birth anniversary in 2013, that is, 31 August, a year after the police filed a charge sheet against Asaram's closest aides, that Asaram himself was arrested by the Jodhpur police team. The evening that Chanchal Mishra and her colleagues in Jodhpur police were in Indore to arrest the godman, Abhishek would have turned fifteen.

# 11

# A Godman versus the Nation

Jantar Mantar road was the popular venue for protests in the capital for years before Ramlila Maidan was accorded that position. For quite some time, you could see two groups of otherwise dissimilar people occupying the space for similar causes. The east pavement of Jantar Mantar road was occupied by the followers of Asaram Bapu shortly after his arrest in 2013. Across the road from them, on the west pavement, were followers of another godman who took up residence there a year or so later.

The hoardings cried for justice against the tyranny of the government and demanded that it withdraw its case of sedition. It was the first time that I had heard of a saint or godman being accused of sedition. The incidents that led to the charge can only be described as bizarre. The police establishment of an entire state, Haryana, had failed to control the followers of a godman and it had been closely followed by two incidents of mass violence in the state.

On 18 November 2014, several thousand police personnel had to be deployed to arrest one man—Rampal. As they approached the godman's ashram in Hisar district in the morning, the police were prepared but did not expect the standoff to last for so long or that it would end up killing six people and injuring close to 200 and lead to extensive damage of public property. It is necessary to study the violence that was unleashed by Rampal's followers against the orders of a court because it shows the extreme lengths to which a cult's followers can be mobilized or used to act against authority and the rule of law.

Rampal's following was not as big as Asaram's and he did not have the kind of influence that Gurmeet Ram Rahim did in north India. He had adorned himself with the mantle of being both the successor to, and a reincarnation of, the fifteenth-century mystic, Kabir. In 1995, at age forty-three, he quit his job with the irrigation department of Haryana state government to become a full-time preacher of the Kabir panth (sect) in Rohtak. In four years, he had established[1] quite a following and set up the first 'Satlok' ashram on three acres of land in Karauntha village of Rohtak with money from a devotee.[2] The purchase of this property also became the subject of a dispute but Rampal was later cleared of charges.

Kabir had challenged the Brahminical, caste-based hierarchy of Hinduism; his egalitarian philosophy influenced many over the centuries. Rampal embraced this philosophy and rejected

---

[1] https://www.hindustantimes.com/india/rampal-and-his-religious-engineering/story-09ljHfG1JnU02A6lriuMUK.html published on 14 May 2013 and accessed on 5 June 2018

[2] https://indianexpress.com/article/india/india-others/big-picture-the-man-god/ published on 26 November 2014 and accessed on 13 June 2018

the Vedas, influenced by a preacher of the Kabir panth. Before that, he followed the Vedic path and would perform daily rituals such as reading the Hanuman Chalisa seven times a day. In the 1990s, he used a public address system attached to his motorcycle to preach in villages and towns in Haryana. While his influence grew during the early 2000s, he developed a scorn for a popular Hindu sect, the Arya Samaj, which taught the supremacy of the Vedas.

In 2006, Rampal preached[3] against some of the writings of Dayanand Saraswati, the founder of the Arya Samaj. According to several sources, Rampal criticized portions of Dayanand Saraswati's book, *Satyarth Prakash* (The Light of Truth), which the Arya Samajis consider their core code. Rampal stated it to be against society and also impractical.

The website of the Satlok ashram has a webpage called 'What is controversial about Sant Rampal Ji Maharaj'.[4] It contains controversial statements on *Satyarth Prakash*:

> Sant Rampal Ji Exposed Swami Dayanand & his book Satyarth Prakash—Swami Dayanand has made caddish commentaries on topics of women, marriage, sex, widows etc in his book Satyarth Prakash. It contains recommendations about immoral activities and having illicit sex. Chapter 4 (Samullas 4) of Satyarth Prakash is a living proof of the same. Moreover the book contains undignified commentaries on various major religions like Sikhism, Christianity and Islam

---

[3]   https://timesofindia.indiatimes.com/india/Rohtak-clash-Sant-Rampal-triggered-it/articleshow/20021686.cms published on 13 May 2013 and accessed on 5 June 2018

[4]   https://www.satlokashram.org/what-is-controversial-about-sant-rampal-ji-maharaj/ accessed on 5 July 2018

and their patron saints. Arya Samaj (followers of Swami Dayanand) could not tolerate the fact that someone has exposed all the wrong doings of their maharishi and brought them out in the open. No wonder the Arya Samaj will be up in arms and that is exactly what they did in 2006 and attacked Sant Rampal Ji's Ashram.

The Arya Samajis did not appreciate the criticism of the philosophy that they lived by. The sect has a large presence in Haryana and Rampal's expansion overlapped several of their areas. There have been suggestions[5] that the Arya Samajis were threatened by Rampal's rapid expansion. Gurmeet Ram Rahim was already a force to reckon with in Haryana, but Rampal directly opposed them by criticizing the founder of their sect.

Two well-known and prominent Arya Samajis in colonial India were Chaudhary Matu Ram Hooda (also referred to as Matu Ram Arya as many Arya Samajis use Arya as a surname), and his brother, Ramji Lal Hooda. Matu Ram had even adopted[6] the janeyu (sacred thread) and helped spread the sect's philosophy in Haryana in early twentieth century. Matu Ram Arya's grandson, Bhupinder Singh Hooda, was chief minister of Haryana (2005 to 2014) when Rampal publicly criticized Dayanand Saraswati's book. It is not known whether Bhupinder Singh Hooda himself was a practising member of the Arya Samaj sect but his son and three-time Rohtak MP, Deepender Singh Hooda, had said that he was an Arya Samaji. It is worthwhile to note that though D.S. Hooda had links to the Arya Samaj, there

---

[5]  Ibid.
[6]  https://www.tribuneindia.com/2011/20110123/spectrum/book7. htm published on 23 January 2011 and accessed on 6 June 2018

are no claims that he unduly favoured the sect. Functionaries of the Arya Samaj, in fact, later blamed[7] Bhupinder Hooda for non-action.

The enforcement of law took place only because of the intervention of the Punjab and Haryana High Court (P&H HC). It was the same in the case of the violence seen in the aftermath of the conviction of Gurmeet Ram Rahim as also the violence unleashed during the 2016 Jat agitation. All of these happened under the chief ministership of Manohar Lal Khattar.

Anupam Gupta, a senior advocate, is well known for his role in the Justice Manmohan Singh Liberhan commission that probed the demolition of the Babri Masjid. Gupta has also been amicus curiae in several cases of public importance and is well respected as a public intellectual and has emerged as one of the finest jurists in the country. He was a spectator to the Rampal case till he was appointed as amicus curiae in the proceedings before the P&H HC.

'He was the baba before the baba [Ram Rahim] and had attacked a number of judges, who had either refused him bail or issued summons against him. This included magistrates, sessions judges to even high court judges. He published pamphlets against them,' Gupta said.

Rampal's first tussle was with a Kabir panthi ashram of the 200-year-old Garib Das order in Chhudani village in Jhajjar. This was the very ashram where he had taken deeksha in Kabir's

---

[7] https://www.hindustantimes.com/punjab/barwala-episode-could-have-been-avoided-had-hooda-govt-acted-in-2013/story-gP9KYPYw2C52ObY7aA3UoK.html published on 28 November 2014 and accessed on 7 June 2018

teachings. Yet, he did not agree with their version of Kabir's teachings[8] (which he kept harping upon even afterwards) and said so publicly. The Garib Dasis clashed with Rampal's followers who had gone to the ashram and attacked it. When the police rounded them up and took them to a police outpost, it was set on fire.

Rampal's followers blocked[9] the road from Jhajjar to Rohtak for six days when their brethren were arrested. They claimed that the godman was himself away in Maharashtra at the time of the clashes. Around this time, Rampal also spoke against Dayanand Saraswati's writings and these were published as a pamphlet.

Representatives of twenty-seven villages held a panchayat and decided to approach Rampal to supposedly settle the dispute. As per an FIR lodged in the case, on 12 July 2006, the representatives went to the Satlok ashram in Rohtak to meet with Rampal.

The panchayat members accused Rampal of climbing on to the roof of the ashram with his brother, Mahender, and others to pelt stones and shoot at them. The panchayat members and villagers also retaliated, and soon the police arrived at the scene. The police tried to calm the situation and told both sides to cease fighting. The police claimed that despite the warnings, the attack from inside the ashram continued, killing one of the villagers and injuring fifty-nine others.

---

[8] https://www.youtube.com/watch?v=2xa-Q_6xXCE published on 3 March 2013 and accessed on 13 June 2018

[9] Judgment dated 20 November 2014 delivered by Justice M. Jeyapaul and Darshan Singh in CROCP No. 12/2014, in re: *Court on Its Own Motion vs Ram Pal*

The police accused Rampal and thirty-seven others of murder, assault and conspiracy and arrested them, shut down the Karauntha ashram and seized it. The sessions court refused Rampal bail but the high court granted it in April 2008 after keeping him in custody for twenty-two months. The ashram was handed back to him the following year.

In the meantime, the trial proceeded and Rampal denied any role in the murder. His website said[10] that the firearm that was recovered was planted on him and a ballistics report had supposedly showed that the weapon had not been used and it could not even establish when the weapon had been fired last.

The court trying the case had granted Rampal exemption from personal appearance forty-two times and he appeared only thrice.[11] After an appearance in April 2010, he did not show up at all till the judge hearing the case was transferred. The additional sessions judge who replaced him summoned the godman to court. That is when all hell broke loose.

Rampal's followers took over the town and the court premises where the godman was to appear. They turned up wearing some sort of uniform and carried batons. They managed traffic on the road for Rampal's convoy of vehicles and manned the gates of the court complex and the doors into the courtroom where Rampal was to appear. Even lawyers were not allowed into the courtroom. The district lawyers bar association complained to the court and the district judge forwarded the case to the P&H HC.

---

[10] https://www.jagatgururampalji.org/sant-rampal-ji-maharaj/saint-rampal-ji-the-karontha-episode/ accessed on 16 June 2018
[11] Rohtak district judge's report to P&H HC dated 21 July 2014

'He openly and avowedly overawed the judicial system in a manner of organized and wilful anarchy. It was not mayhem let loose in the conventional sense but wilful disobedience and defiance. It is replacement of the secular state and the conventional state apparatus by voluntary, self-styled squads. This was while the police played second fiddle and the political and administrative classes did not take any action and the judiciary came under huge strain. He was the first baba who really took on the Indian judiciary,' said Gupta.

Asaram had refused to appear before the Justice (retd) D.K. Trivedi commission several times till he finally appeared on 1 December 2012. That commission was a quasi-judicial authority created for a specific purpose. In Rampal's case, it was a court of law, a part of the criminal justice system of India. There are similarities in the way both godmen made their respective court/ commission appearances. In Asaram's case, thousands of his followers flocked to the place where the commission's hearing was taking place. In Jodhpur, where the godman was to appear, his followers turned up in large numbers, their prime motive seemingly to get a glimpse of their godman. But, in Rampal's case, witnesses have testified to a simultaneous takeover of parts of two towns and their respective court complexes.

In 2008, after he came out of jail, Rampal found himself locked out of Karauntha and moved to a 12-acre ashram in Barwala, Haryana. That is where he trained his Raksha Vahini (defence force) and constructed a fortified ashram, designed to withstand armed attacks. He shut out the media, which he had earlier used as an ally while preaching.

On 14 July 2014, the Hisar District Bar Association passed a resolution which best describes what happened when Rampal was to appear in court. Relevant extract of the resolution:

It was very much surprising that approximately 50,000 followers of accused Rampal were gathered surrounding the Court complex and later on approximately 10,000 commandos, wearing black clothes, of accused Rampal created a human chain surrounding the court complex and did not allow the litigants and advocates to enter in the court complex at Hisar. It was very much surprising that they demanded the identity card from the advocates who tried to enter the courts and if any advocate did not show the identity card, they were declined entry into the court complex and if any advocate objected, they were manhandled.

Further, it has also come to notice that these followers started to gather from midnight to hijack the area of the court complex which they succeeded and the police was standing like statues without taking any action. All these activities have also been recorded in the CCTV cameras of the court complex which is the evidence of this occurrence.

These followers created a traffic jam on the road and the advocates could not park their vehicles in the [court's] parking [lot] and they parked in the nearby residential area and came [to court] by foot. Some judicial officers also faced these hurdles. The followers raised slogans against the judges and held banners with slogans against judges. The followers entered with arms openly in the court complex and the police did not take any action against these people. Some self-styled commandos/followers along with arms entered into the video-conferencing room without any permission where even police officials are not allowed to enter with arms.

The Bar Association condemns the Haryana government being handicapped in maintaining the law and order in high-profile zones in the court complex and also condemns the bad activities of the followers of accused Rampal.

The Hisar bar went on a 'cease work' till Rampal's bail was cancelled. They resolved to get hold of CCTV footage and send it along with the resolution to the chief justice of the P&H HC.

The district judge of Rohtak sent a comprehensive report to the P&H HC on 21 July 2014 on the status of the case. Rampal's followers published a pamphlet called *Sach Banam Jhoot* in which they defamed the judges hearing their cases as well as HC judges. They also filed complaints against them in court. Soon after the district judge had taken charge, Rampal's followers sent copies of the pamphlets and the complaints in order to intimidate him. In the meantime, there had been no material proceedings and even evidence had not been taken. Since there were so many accused, they would take turns to skip hearings so that the statements of witnesses could not be recorded.

The judge cancelled Rampal's exemption from personal appearance in the hope that those accused amongst his followers would also turn up and the evidence could be recorded in the trial. Rampal agreed to be present in person in Hisar and through videoconference in Rohtak from the court in Hisar. It turns out that Rampal's followers laid siege to both Hisar and Rohtak.

The judge notes, 'On July 14, 2014, accused Rampal appeared through video conferencing. On that day, his followers who were thousands in numbers seized the towns of Hisar and Rohtak. Processions, carrying placards and banners, were held in both towns. The banners had derogatory remarks against judicial officers, in general, and particularly against the undersigned [the Rohtak district judge]. The hooliganism by the supporters of accused Rampal was covered by the media.' The Rohtak district judge also noted that the followers of Rampal had made death threats to him.

Rampal's followers were not deterred by any procedure or discussion of their activities and instead took aggressive steps. They formed an NGO called National Social Service Committee (NSSC) and lodged complaints wherever possible, including to the chief justice of the P&H HC, who is the highest judicial authority of the state and in charge of the administration of subordinate courts.

On 21 July 2014, this organization wrote a letter to the chief justice of the high court giving their version of the events. They claimed to have a membership of 10 lakh and appended what appeared to be signatures of several thousands of people. They claimed that lawyers had barged into the videoconferencing room and flung caste-based slurs at Rampal's followers. The letter, in a way, admitted that Rampal's followers had actually taken over the court complex, as the district bar association of Hisar had already pointed out. Relevant extract of the letter:

> . . . Then they misbehaved with a sister who was wearing a locket of Shri Ramapal Ji Maharaj around her neck and was doing service outside in the premises of the court to maintain order. The complaint about which was given to the S.P. Hisar by the Trustee of the Satlok Ashram Barwala on that very day.

The NSSC accused the lawyers of not wearing the lawyer's garb and claimed that plain-clothes policemen had asked for their identity cards. When the lawyers did not show their identity cards, 'they were sent out by their devotees'.

They said that the court premises were not for lawyers alone but also for the public and that the accused may be accompanied by some people. 'It is natural for 5–6 people to accompany a person who has a court case. If 100–200 people come, then also what's the problem; the remaining will stand outside. They do not stand there for fun. They stand out of devotion. No one can stop them. We are also citizens of India. If in future there is a court hearing of our Satgurudevji, then there is a possibility of arrival of ten times more devotees than 14 July 2014.'

They threatened that they would strongly oppose any move by the courts to cancel Rampal's bail. 'We will take bullets in our chest and die. Even if one child will remain, until then this opposition will continue in a legal way,' the letter said.

'. . . We have lawfully demonstrated against the honourable corrupt judges, which will continue. It will stop only when we get justice.'

The high court did not take these incidents or the threats lightly and on 22 July 2014 took suo motu notice of the failure of the state to maintain law and order in the district court complex and the Rampal followers' 'attempt to subvert the process of law' and issued notice for contempt of court to the accused (including Rampal) in the cases.

A month after this, Rampal filed an affidavit denying that he had organized the chaos in the courts but said that it was done by the NSSC. Ram Kanwar Dhaka, a disciple of Rampal who had formed the NSSC, filed an affidavit before the P&H HC claiming credit for the ruckus. He confirmed that Rampal had not arranged any of it nor asked anyone to attend the proceedings; the devotees had attended on their own. Dhaka deposed[12] that the arrangements had been undertaken by the NSSC.

---

[12] Order dated 24 September 2014 in CROCP No. 12/2014, in re: *Court on Its Own Motion vs Ram Pal*

Rampal did not attend the contempt proceedings in the high court and, strangely, asked for personal exemption, just as he had in the trial court. His lawyer filed a medical certificate by a former top government doctor that said Rampal had fever, diarrhoea and lower backache. The HC saw through the medical certificate and issued a show-cause notice to the doctor, a former district civil surgeon. The doctor was to appear and explain to the HC why it should not get the certificate investigated. In case the medical certificate was found to be false, 'consequences in fact as well as in law shall ensue for Dr O.P. Hooda as well as for Rampal Dass', the high court warned, while directing Rampal to be present for the next hearing.

In the meantime, Dhaka wrote a letter to the Chandigarh administration to provide facilities, including water and sanitation, and provisions for around a lakh of the godman's followers who would flood Chandigarh from 2 November 2014 for the godman's appearance on 5 November 2014. In effect, the godman's followers threatened to take over the union territory for four days. The Chandigarh administration approached the P&H HC to issue directions because they could not make the kind of arrangements required to maintain law and order for one lakh followers of a godman already accused of violent crimes. The episodes in Rohtak and Hisar were an example of what could be unleashed in Chandigarh.

The high court's patience had worn thin by now, between Rampal, his followers and the Haryana state, which was unable to handle them. It asked Dhaka to come to court and explain what he meant by his letter, which was seen as an intimidating gesture, and appointed Anupam Gupta as amicus curiae to assist the court. The Chandigarh government also protested and said that Rampal's appearance in the high court would lead to utter chaos and asked for support from the state governments of both Haryana and Punjab.

Dhaka went underground and his lawyer, who had also been summoned, did not turn up in court. His representative told the court that he was undergoing medical treatment for cancer. Rampal's lawyer said that his client, the godman, had no control over his followers and the NSSC. The high court did not believe this because Dhaka himself had said that the NSSC members had been personally indoctrinated by Rampal into his sect.

The high court made special arrangements for Rampal to first come to a designated guest house in Panchkula, a town bordering Chandigarh. 'The above order is passed by us as we feel that there would virtually be a havoc, in case about one lakh people assemble in [the High] Court to attend contempt proceedings,' wrote the high court directing Rampal and the others, including the doctor who certified his illness, to answer to the contempt notice on 5 November 2014.

Till then, there had been several discussions in the public domain about Hooda's continued inefficacy in controlling Rampal and his followers, who had seemingly declared themselves above or outside the law. On 26 October 2014, Manohar Lal Khattar took oath as chief minister of the newly formed BJP government in Haryana. Khattar was a man from the Rashtriya Swayamsevak Sangh (RSS) and had no prior experience in handling a state even as a minister. Before being made the CM, he had been an organizational leader of the BJP's Haryana unit for close to fourteen years. The focus turned on him to see what he would do as far as Rampal was concerned.

On 5 November 2014, around 40,000 followers of Rampal descended upon Chandigarh and broke through the police barrier placed outside the railway station. Neither Rampal nor his aides turned up except the doctor, whose medical certificate was under question. It turned out that the medical certificate was for conjunctivitis, which the court declared to be a 'lame excuse' to not turn up in court. Rampal continued to claim he was unwell. Dhaka claimed that the NSSC members at the railway station had prevented him from coming to court.

The high court issued a fresh non-bailable warrant for Rampal and Dhaka to face the contempt proceedings on 10 November 2014, since they had failed to appear the several times they had been summoned. The court again warned Rampal and Dhaka to prevent the godman's followers from disrupting Chandigarh.

What happened next is unheard of, but, to be fair, Rampal's continuing reluctance to come to court was also unheard of. The Haryana DGP claimed he did not have adequate police force to arrest Rampal. Besides, the district magistrate (administrative head) of Hisar had appointed a team of doctors. Rampal had admitted himself to a local hospital and the medical team of three doctors examined the godman on 8 November 2014, escorted by the police. It said that he was suffering from hypertension and had been admitted to a nearby hospital after complaining of chest pain and palpitation.

The Hisar district magistrate had no instructions to form such a team but the state's lawyer claimed in court that a follower of the godman had told him of Rampal's illness. The high court understood and recorded its observation that the administration had done so in order to save the police from facing the ignominy of being unable to arrest Rampal. Dhaka was arrested and brought to the high court, which cancelled Rampal's bail.

Rampal's non-appearance in the high court was not just a matter of contempt of court any more. Over a period of time, his followers had bullied the police and judicial officers into submission. They threatened law and order and reduced state authorities to meek participants in a situation which the latter should have been in control of. Faced with the threat of violent resistance, the administration resorted to control the optics by appointing a medical team of its own volition.

Anupam Gupta drew a beautiful analogy in court. He referred to the situation in 1960s' America when the government had directed that there would be no racial segregation of students. The act had been met with aggressive resistance from white supremacists who were in a majority and had to be dealt with by force, even in places of learning. 'The violent resistance to law cannot be made a legal reason for the non-execution of the directions flowed from the court,' Gupta told the court.

'Not only the top brass of the police force and the top bureaucrat of the home department, but also the chief minister of Haryana cannot be spared as there has been withdrawal of police force stationed near the Satlok ashram premises from 7.30 p.m. on 16 November 2014. Unless some instruction had flowed from the plenary authority of the government, the security forces would not have withdrawn from Satlok ashram,' Gupta informed the court on 17 November 2014.

This was a red flag for Khattar, the rookie political head of Haryana, and his top bureaucrats because Gupta's submissions in court in effect pointed a finger at the CM, the DGP and the additional chief secretary of Haryana's home department as having aided in the contempt of court. Both these top officers of the state government were in court, while Rampal continued to claim he was ill.

The plan to nab Rampal began to resemble a small counter-insurgency operation. Rampal was holed up in his ashram with a human shield. The police wanted to avoid bloodshed, as much as possible. There were intelligence inputs that some of the followers were armed and more arms and ammunition had been smuggled into the ashram. The police filed its operation plan in a sealed envelope with the high court, which was convinced that Rampal would soon be arrested. 'The court wanted him smoked out even if he was hiding in a bunker,' Gupta told me later.

Till here, the narration primarily through the high court's orders, was necessary to show the extent to which Rampal had hijacked the situation. Before that, there were two major incidents of violence. Once, when the Garib Dasis clashed with Rampal's followers at Rohtak in 2006, that led to the drama that unfolded in the high court. The second was on 12 May 2013, when the Arya Samajis clashed with Rampal's followers, also at the Karauntha ashram in Rohtak.

Rampal's followers had cautioned the police a week earlier that they expected a confrontation with the Arya Samajis. Hooda, whose links with this sect have been mentioned earlier, was still the chief minister at the time and Rohtak was his constituency. On the morning of 12 May 2013, the mob of Arya Samajis proceeded to the ashram, where police stood guard. Local villagers were upset with Rampal's followers for creating a nuisance around the ashram and also joined the mob that supposedly comprised the Arya Samajis.

The clash left three people dead and more than 100 injured.[13] The mob flung petrol bombs and set vehicles afire

---

[13] https://www.hindustantimes.com/india/3-killed-in-violence-over-ashram-at-rohtak-village/story-0ZB8YVrkOc9b369rnOy5NO.html published on 12 May 2013 and accessed on 16 July 2018

during the clash. The Haryana police tried to stop the mob but failed. There were allegations of shots being fired from inside the ashram, especially because the police too had been shot at. However, that has been questioned because the police were in the middle and could have been fired at from either side. Two of those killed in the violence were Arya Samaj followers. After a two-day deadlock, the Haryana government carted[14] out around 3,000 of Rampal's followers from Karauntha.

This incident is important in the narration of events because Rampal's followers were already seething from this attack and the unceremonious eviction from their godman's first ashram, though Rampal had shifted his headquarters to Barwala after being released from jail in 2008. That too had happened because the Haryana government had seized and sealed his ashram at the time.

The events that took place on 18 November 2014 outside Rampal's ashram in Barwala in Hisar were reported widely by the media. Many journalists present there were injured in the mini war. They have written eyewitness accounts of what transpired.

Rampal's followers had formed a human chain, which the media estimated to have between 50,000 and 70,000 men, women and children. The police reported[15] that it was a human chain of 20,000 of Rampal's followers, including women, children, toddlers and old people. A chunk of women and children (around 2,000) were seated outside the ashram, at the

---

[14] https://www.indiatoday.in/india/north/story/rohtak-clashes-karontha-as-satlok-ashram-eviction-starts-163033-2013-05-14 published on 15 May 2013 and accessed on 16 July 2018

[15] Affidavit dated 27 November 2014 deposed by Shrinawas Vashisht, director general of Haryana police.

gate. Some of the followers later claimed that although they wanted to leave, their children were still inside the ashram and some were held hostage by armed ashramites.

The followers had been told to save their god and they had been told that the police would not attack women and children. They seemed unaware of their godman's repeated contempt towards the trial, what had gone on in the high court as a result and the kind of pressure that the authorities were under.

The police found that 1,000 of Rampal's 'commandos' had stacked rifles, pistols, batons, petrol bombs, acid pouches and stacks of bricks on the terrace of the ashram. The police had come with a force of more than 5,000 including CRPF personnel led by thirteen officers of the rank of superintendent of police. They arrived in 104 Haryana roadways buses and eleven bulletproof jeeps. There were cops from the anti-riot squads and tear-gas squads wearing bulletproof vests and armed with firearms and batons. The police also deployed twenty ambulances, eleven earth-moving/demolition vehicles, nine anti-riot vehicles, eight water cannons, nine cranes, thirteen tractors, eleven fire-brigade vehicles, twelve trucks, sixty-one police heavy vehicles and forty motorcycles. In short, a mini army which cost Haryana alone Rs 15 crore.

The operation began with asking Rampal to surrender using megaphones. When he did not emerge, the police demanded entry into the ashram. They attempted entry several times and failed. First, they tried to remove the women and children at the gate. Ashramites on the terrace threw brickbats, acid pouches and petrol bombs at the police personnel. They were also shot at and nine of the 110 injured security personnel had firearm injuries. The clash left seventy followers injured. The police did manage to evacuate some of the followers and transported them out of Barwala in the requisitioned government buses. The demolition crew tried to break down the walls of the ashram but they were also attacked and had to escape, leaving four of the machines behind which were destroyed.

The *Mail Today* reporter, Ajay Kumar, wrote, 'It was 30,000 police against one man. And while the former lost the battle, the latter lived to fight another day.'

While the number of policemen may be exaggerated, the fact of the event is not. The police beat a retreat in the evening after hours of a standoff following the clashes. They returned the next day and applied enough force to quell the remaining disruptors and eventually managed to arrest Rampal along with some of his key aides. Around 909 people in seven FIRs were accused of rioting, murder, assault, unlawful assembly and a host of other charges. Amongst the followers, a woman died of injuries in hospital and the police found corpses of four women and a child at the ashram. Rampal's spokesperson blamed[16] former chief minister Hooda for trumping up 'false cases' against Rampal and his followers on behalf of the Arya Samaj that led to the violence.

The list of weapons recovered from the ashram is bizarre and shows that the ashramites were either aware of what would be enough to combat the police force or they were ready to face the police with whatever they had. Unless of course they had somehow managed to dispose of other weapons before the police arrived. The recovered weapons included eight 12-bore

---

[16] http://www.dailymail.co.uk/indiahome/indianews/ article-2839983/Rampal-Vs-State-200-injured-Barwala-30-000-security-personnel-fail-break-godman-s-human-shield.html published on 19 November 2014 and accessed on 17 July 2018

shotguns, five .315-bore rifles, one .32-bore pistol, nineteen airguns, sixty-seven spray guns and 130 rounds of ammunition for the firearms apart from blank shells and gunpowder for the blank shells in sealed packs. The weapons list also included one switchblade, sixty-one petrol bombs and nine chemical (acid) pouches. The reserves were depleted since some of these had already been used during the pitched battle. The ashramites had their own riot gear of 5,632 wooden batons, 285 motorcycling helmets, thirty-five fibre shields, two bulletproof vests, slingshots and 1,932 glass marbles for the slingshots.

This was what was pitted against the police of two states, one union territory and central forces at a total cost of Rs 26 crore to arrest a man for continued contempt of court. In August 2017, a court in Hisar acquitted[17] Rampal in two out of the five cases registered against him for this episode.

The direct involvement of Rampal in attacking a police force executing the order of a high court is not the sole issue. It is also about the cult he had created and the extremes to which they were prepared to go for him. There were—as per accounts of both the media and the police, women, children and old people—mostly from economically backward sections of society in the ashram and as part of the human chain at the gate. Either all of them had such blind faith in Rampal that they were willing to face bullets for him, or they were directed to do so by a select few who were running the show. Their sentiment for the cult was so strong that they were willing to take on the government, in its full might, on behalf of their spiritual leader.

---

[17] https://www.thehindu.com/news/national/self-styled-godman-rampal-acquitted-in-two-criminal-cases/article19580543.ece published on 29 August 2017 and accessed on 18 July 2018

Anupam Gupta pointed out to the high court that Rampal had formed a committee (NSSC) for the purpose of taming the judiciary and the bureaucratic administration. 'Rampal will appear, if at all he is compelled to appear, for the hearing of trial only with thousands and thousands of followers. The judicial system will be at peril if such a defiant attitude of an accused who has got the privilege of bail in his favour brazenly exhibits his unruly might through his so-called followers and the private army formed by him,' he told[18] the high court.

The high court noted[19] that '. . . they have even prepared to sacrifice their lives in order to protect Rampal'. The court acknowledged the threat issued by Rampal's followers to the Chandigarh administration and the judiciary. 'We also take judicial notice of the subsequent development in which his followers/disciples/private commandos have waged war against the state which just endeavoured to execute the warrant of arrest pending for long,' the court noted while cancelling the bail it had earlier granted to Rampal.

Since the only record of the court is the formal order or judgment passed by it, we often lose the comments made during these proceedings which are key to understanding the court's mood. In this case, the court's observations indicated that it believed that the state colluded with Rampal's cult. The court also wanted to recover the Rs 26 crore in expenses from the cult that had been expended on the forces sent to arrest Rampal.

---

[18] Order dated 20 November 2014 delivered by Justice M. Jeyapaul and Darshan Singh in CROCP No. 12/2014, in re: *Court on Its Own Motion vs Ram Pal*

[19] Ibid.

After this episode, it was discovered that aiding Rampal and training his army were three ex-soldiers, one dismissed head constable of the Haryana police, a serving soldier and a serving head constable of the Haryana police. This came, to put it plainly, as a shocker that serving and retired soldiers and policemen were aiding a man who was accused of warring against the state. The godman would not submit himself to legal processes— instruments of the state—aided by people employed in service of the state. Gupta told me that at one point, Rampal was himself a government servant, but later, the equation was reversed as he became larger than life and the government was afraid to take action against him.

The law caught up with this warring saint and, on 11 October 2018, a court in Hisar, Haryana, convicted[20] Rampal and twenty-eight of his devotees for the murder of six of his followers, based on circumstantial evidence. Five women and a child had been killed in the two-day skirmish between the devotees and the police, which tried to arrest the godman from the ashram in November 2014. The court also found them guilty of wrongful confinement and criminal conspiracy in the two cases that had been registered.

In preparation for the verdict, the Haryana government deployed[21] around 4,000 additional police personnel in various places in the state, including near his abandoned ashrams.

---

[20] Deepender Deswal, 'Rampal Convicted of Killing Six at Ashram', *Tribune*, 12 October 2018.

[21] https://www.hindustantimes.com/india-news/self-styled-godman-rampal-found-guilty-in-2-murder-cases/story-3shQxxtX8zWEkz8xkmJ9uI.html published on 12 October 2018 and accessed on 14 October 2018

Rampal was tried in a temporary courtroom in the jail where he was being held since his arrest on 19 November 2014 following the mini-war between the police and his followers. The verdict was also pronounced at the makeshift court.

It was not only Rampal that was larger than life, or larger than the government. There were two more incidents in Haryana which saw massive failure on the part of the administration. The first was the February 2016 Jat agitation which witnessed large-scale violence. The high court took it up suo motu after observing the failure of the police to rein in the violent agitators, along with accusations of mass rape. The violent mob attacked police stations, policemen and the offices and homes of senior police officers. The failure of the law enforcers was well recorded in the Prakash Singh report that documented the violence after it had happened.

The third incident, which unfolded in Khattar's first stint as CM, was following the conviction in a rape case of another godman, whom many have called the 'baba of bling'. Gurmeet Ram Rahim gained notoriety for being probably one of the first Indian godmen to be convicted for raping his followers. The conviction by a CBI court in Panchkula led to violent protests by his followers, which is discussed later. The state did have a warning, because on 28 November 2014, Gupta had filed a secret military intelligence input from 2011 (also published in the *Tribune*) that showed what was brewing in Ram Rahim's Dera Sacha Sauda. Before Rampal and his crude commandos took on the might of the state, Ram Rahim had been building an army within his ashrams.

Former army personnel were training Dera Sacha Sauda followers in using weapons. At the time, the rape trial had not concluded and Ram Rahim was also being tried for two cases of murder, including that of a journalist who had first published the rape complaint made against the godman. Ram Rahim had also turned up for his deposition with thousands of followers and it is believed that his aides provided logistical support for the thousands of followers that landed up in Panchkula.

'The religious places are meant only to impart religious discourses and not for giving training to private commandos to protect head of Dera/ashram. At any rate, it cannot be used as a dumping ground of arms and ammunition. We are of the considered view that the training of private commandos and arming them with illegal weapons to protect some individuals would definitely pose a challenge not only to the judiciary, but also to the state at large. Search of Dera to unearth illegal arms and ammunitions and monitoring the activities of Dera on a periodical basis is the absolute need of the hour to avoid future bloody confrontation and also to safeguard the interest of the public at large and the state. Unless illegal activities are monitored by top level bureaucrats and police force, the situation would slip out of hand. Casualty will be more in dimension compared to the one we had faced while executing warrant of arrest against contemnor Rampal,' Justice Jeyapaul noted in his order of 28 November 2014, and directed that it may be taken up as a public interest litigation (PIL).

This means that the high court had actually forewarned the administration of things to come, not just in terms of what cult leaders were capable of, but of what could happen when the state administration responded meekly.

'In both cases—Ram Rahim and Rampal—it was the court which was instrumental in enforcing the law. Without such judicial intervention by the court, that was brave, forceful and candid, there would have been a colossal failure and miscarriage, perhaps collapse, of law enforcement. First, Baba Rampal and secondly, Ram Rahim. The Jat agitation, in between, represents the collapse of law enforcement at the hands of the executive but the court is only conducting a sort of post mortem. All three—Rampal in 2014, Jat agitation in 2016 and Ram Rahim in 2017—show the continuous pattern of the collapse of the state in law enforcement. This includes the political, the executive and the police—hence, the collapse of the state in the most comprehensive sense of the term. Whatever deterrent action was taken in the case of Ram Rahim was the direct implementation and execution of the court's orders. In Rampal's case, the entire operation took place for the execution of the court's non-bailable arrest warrant. The court made it clear that it would take contempt against the DGP and the home secretary and also contempt action against the chief minister,' Gupta told me later.

It was only when Gupta threatened action against the chief minister, citing legal precedents, that the police girded itself to execute the non-bailable warrant. This created a direct genetic link between judicial intervention in the Ram Rahim case where the political executive had to execute the court's order, tragically, under the implicit threat of contempt action. Closet anarchists might find the plight of the police amusing, but the humiliation suffered across the ranks is no fun for the people in uniform. The political influence and capital of godmen and the dependence of politicians on their vote banks may have been responsible for the pathetic situation that the security personnel found themselves in.

'I have always opposed the court taking over law enforcement, but the realities of life brought me face-to-face with the realization that there was no other option. As an amicus in both cases, I have been helping the court to make up its mind to step in where the state fails the will and the courage to act,' Gupta said.

Politicians tried to take credit for Gurmeet Ram Rahim's conviction but it must be clarified, with emphasis, that both the conviction and the action against the aftermath was a result of the P&H HC's direct intervention, as in the case of Rampal.

# 12

# 'Love Charger' Doctrine

The conviction of the Dera Sacha Sauda head, Gurmeet Ram Rahim Singh, has become a legal precedent and will go down in history as a case where a godman was pulled down from his self-installed pedestal. It may be a tragedy as far as his followers are concerned. The godman had built his base amongst the Dalit Sikhs in Punjab and Haryana and his incarceration has left a socio-religious vacuum. Dera followers have started replacing the name of Ram Rahim with that of his predecessor Shah Satnam in some of their merchandise. There are many who still refuse to let go, convinced of their guru's infallibility, like Asaram's followers.

Much has been written about Gurmeet Ram Rahim including a recent book which went deep into his early life and also the empire of crime and violence that he had built. The one aspect that is not spoken about much is his crime against art and culture, the extension of his grotesqueness to music and some films. While I managed to stay away from the temptation of watching him playing an imitation of himself, I could not

263

(thanks to sadistic friends) save my ears from the trauma caused by the tone-deafening experience called 'Love Charger'.

The videos of the song boast millions of views, suspiciously like the millions of social media followers that he had till Twitter and Facebook shut down his accounts. The song's refrain 'I am the Love Charzer' (not charger) is followed by some sort of a yodel, for which the Swiss or the Austrians could have perhaps sued him for distortion of their folk music.

The controversy around this godman began in the 2000s for the criminal cases as well as the act of sacrilege of representing himself in the image of Guru Gobind Singh that the Sikhs accused him of. Ram Rahim stumbled across the media but later seemed to have learnt how to deflect attention through his grotesque fashion sense, appearance and foray into pop culture. After a point, few journalists had the drive or the luxury to chase a story and search for evidence. Most people gave up and as newer batches of reporters were unleashed into the media, they seemed to have no clue about what had gone on hardly a decade ago. There was more interest in mocking him for his sartorial decisions than write about the rape and murder cases that quietly went on in the background.

The real stars of these cases were, of course, the judge at the CBI court, Jagdeep Singh, and the special CBI prosecutor, Harinder Pal Singh Verma. The tremendous pressure created by the followers of the Dera did not deter these two from doing their job. It took years but Gurmeet Ram Rahim was brought to book.

On 21 August 2017, people in Panchkula saw thousands of followers of Dera Sacha Sauda flock to their city. These were not the followers who appeared on television or acted in Ram Rahim's opulent films. These were dirt-poor people who had travelled to see their god. Some newspapers reported that many had travelled on foot to Panchkula. They could not afford hotels and camped by the roadside in large numbers so that they could catch a glimpse of the Dera head. It was not the first time that Ram Rahim was to appear and the P&H HC had noted his followers came in large numbers to support him. The administration and the police in Panchkula knew what was in store. Yet, they were allowed to come into the city and camp[1] there, much to the distress of its residents. The administration seemed to take no concrete action to disperse them. The ripples of this inaction would later be felt as far as the National Capital Region.

The P&H HC took it up suo motu to organize the enforcement of law and order yet again. There were last-minute court proceedings where strong warnings were issued to the Dera chief and he was forced to ask his followers not to worry. The army was deployed and the police brought in additional forces. They could not have a repeat performance of the violence during Rampal's arrest nor of the February 2016 Jat agitation. Ram Rahim made[2] a midnight appeal to his followers to return home before he went to face the verdict of his rape trial.[3]

The followers did not recede and that ultimately led to a violent clash that spilled into the residential colonies of

[1] https://www.outlookindia.com/website/story/dera-sacha-sauda-cult-followers-issue-threats-against-india-on-eve-of-cbi-court-/300654 published on 21 August 2017 and accessed on 20 July 2018

[2] https://www.ndtv.com/india-news/for-ram-rahim-verdict-tension-and-followers-build-in-panchkula-10-facts-1741713 published on 25 August 2017 and accessed on 20 July 2018

[3] https://www.outlookindia.com/website/story/rape-trial-that-has-north-india-on-high-alert/300656 published on 22 August 2017 and accessed on 20 July 2018

Panchkula as well. The city, which was under curfew, saw blood spill on the streets, with more than thirty killed and hundreds injured. The gory video of one Dera follower being shot down after advancing menacingly at security personnel, armed with only a baton, is proof of the kind of fanaticism that seemed to have possessed followers who placed cult above law and personal safety.

Following that, I wrote a cover story for *Outlook* magazine on godmen, trying to decode them as well as their following. Titled 'Goddamn', it was published[4] on 31 August 2017 in the following week's issue (dated 11 September 2017) along with a package of stories from across the country, including one on Chandraswami, who brought the word 'godman' into mainstream media. The story on Ram Rahim and others is reproduced below, with permission:

Goddamn!

He is the man with all the answers, who has the masses and the 'classes' eating out of his hands. He pushes the envelope of profit and power that piety and fealty draw like nothing else. But this heady combo of cult and clout also makes the godman's fall as a common criminal just as spectacular.

God and sometimes the voice of God. He plays stress-buster, therapist, family and business advisor, and the man with all the answers: marketing, yoga, TM, world peace, FMCG goodies, miracle healing, salvation from existential dilemmas. He (it's mostly a he) is also often the object of

---

[4]  https://www.outlookindia.com/magazine/story/goddamn/299260 published on 31 August 2017 and accessed on 20 July 2018

secret envy. Though claiming a touch of other-worldliness, he's so blatantly of this world and totes all the toys that boys like—and in such abundance that it fits most common fantasies. And if there's a whiff of cultic fanaticism at one end, at the other he also possesses that ultimate aphrodisiac: political clout. So, it's always a TRP-booster when a bad boy of babadom bites the dust as a common criminal.

Viewers had their fill of exclamations and schadenfreude last week after the judicial gavel came down on a baba who looks straight out of a comic-strip but has deathly serious aspects to him: on his way to jail, he left a wake of corpses, injured followers, damaged property and a fistful of real heroes. Eyes remained glued to television and mobile screens as the 'baba of bling', Gurmeet Ram Rahim Singh 'Insaan', leader of Dera Sacha Sauda (DSS), was first convicted and then sentenced to 20 years, along with fines, for the rape of two of his former devotees. The anonymous letter that finally led to the conviction described the rape scene as out of a Bollywood B-film, with a pistol on the bed and a pornographic film playing on a TV screen.

A full accounting of what went on at DSS may not be possible—the tales are legion. One case that has resurfaced is that of a man from Jaipur whose wife was escorted out of their room at the Sirsa dera one night and never returned. After futile attempts to lodge an FIR at a Sirsa police station, he tried from Jaipur. The Rajasthan police eventually filed a closure report with the court and the court was about to rule on the closure, when the rape trial concluded and led to the conviction.

Possibly the first conviction by Indian courts of a godman for raping his followers, 'Insaan' is in fairly quasi-divine territory. Babas of all hues and religious persuasions have been branded with sleaze and worse. The common thread is the bouquet of spirituality on offer for the seeker, criminality to lace his pockets, a lust for real estate, a protective entourage, fanatic followers and politicians bidding for their boroughs of influence.

A similar media blitz was last seen exactly four years ago when rape allegations were levelled against Asaram Bapu (real name: Asumal Sirumalani). It's difficult to erase the imagery piqued by news reports of the godman being administered a 'feather test' to rule out any chance of erectile dysfunction before proceeding with a rape trial. Asaram would allegedly throw a fruit at a female follower to mark her for his women apostles to deliver to his ashram for an 'anushthan'. His son Narayan Sai (also later arrested) had an overactive libido too.

The rape allegations against Kripalu Maharaj, a godman from Allahabad, portrayed a scene no less cheesy, with dialogues like 'Tu mera premi, aa gale lag ja' apparently sending female devotees into a hypnotic trance. Later, older female disciples would tell them they had been 'blessed with pure devotion'. The accounts started flowing only when a case was filed in Trinidad and eventually dropped for want of evidence.

In 2011, Kripalu Maharaj's successor, Prakashanand Saraswati, too was accused of molesting a minor. He jumped bail and tampered with the evidence, but was later convicted in absentia with a 280-year sentence. It's believed he made it back to India with a fake passport. In a later account, the survivor described the cultist mentality of her mother, who had told her that she should 'just enjoy it'.

Why do people flock to the garish Ram Rahim, with his put-on ghetto gangsta vibe, superhero flicks and pop ditties like Love Charger that claim an anthem-like appeal among devouts? There are social reasons—the dera movement's origin in Punjab's Dalit matrix, as an alternative to elite-controlled panthic Sikhism, is now well attested (The Dera Sultanates).[5] There are also, of course, spiritual reasons. Says Jyotirmaya Sharma, author of several books on Hinduism, 'The basic charisma that draws followers to cults is that they can have a two-way communication with God, who otherwise doesn't answer directly to their prayers. Within the ascetic tradition, the godmen are seen as an incarnation of a God.'

The social genesis fades into the background as the gurus attain at a stratospheric level of popularity and enter the pop-cult world where new seekers of truth need merely to flip out their smartphone and access social media apps to see posts from their gurus. But a retrospective glance is illuminating. Ram Rahim inherited DSS in 1990 from his guru under a cloud of controversy. Some say DSS's popularity is an index of a government push against the waning Khalistan influence. 'He targeted Mazhabi Sikhs and then broadened his base. Gurus know what to offer a consumer and have a cafeteria-like approach with a variety of products from which you can select. Some sell yoga, some meditation and so forth,' says Bhavdeep Kang, author of a book on godmen, *Gurus*.

The Sikh radicals describe him as the government's Frankenstein. 'Following the green revolution, landless people felt neglected and the SGPC did not evolve any mechanism

---

[5]   https://www.outlookindia.com/magazine/story/the-dera-sultanates/299270 published on 11 September 2017 and accessed on 15 August 2018

to include them in mainstream Sikhism. The Dalits found solace, fulfilment of basic needs and a way out of social evils at the deras,' says Kanwarpal Singh, spokesperson for the pro-Khalistan group Dal Khalsa. Ram Rahim claimed to have set up 'orphanages' within his ashram, but without any official clearance. The dera had hitherto barred Haryana's women and child department from inspecting these 'orphanages'. Only when he landed in custody did the department finally write to district authorities who transferred the orphans to state-run institutions. Amongst them were around 20 minor girls. The dera also ran residential schools and colleges within its borders. Police sources claim there was a direct passage from the godman's residence to a girls' hostel.

Latter-day godmen are of course a kind of genetic mutant emerging out of the old sects and reformist movements. Having lost touch with their social context, they soon forfeit the spiritual one too. Flip the pages and there is evidence that every corner of India has recorded tales of babas exploiting their flock, committing crimes with self-proclaimed divine indemnity and political quid pro quos. This last aspect particularly attracts notice, because it challenges the construct that a godman only feeds the spiritual void or social alienation.

And yet the connection between the spiritual and temporal may be nothing new. 'The general foundational assumption is that a godman of whatever variety must be above worldly considerations and politics and must dispense spiritual solace. But since ancient times, godmen have always competed with each other for lay members, donors, benefactors and royal patronage. Many godmen couldn't have formed their cults without royal patronage,' says

Sharma. 'From 19th century on, the modern nation state that developed needed an alignment with spirituality but that cannot be done explicitly. If spirituality becomes a threat to the state, the state will not tolerate it.'

But what one gets now is increasingly caricaturish versions—often you can trace the arc even within one entity. A godman named Sat Saidata had set up an ashram at Charkhari in Mahoba, Uttar Pradesh, circa 1900. In this village of Dalits, he offered them his name and they took it on as a surname. The village revered both him and his successors. The fourth successor was more ambitious. In 1999, he convinced a devout old woman to commit sati. 'A sati memorial would have drawn more followers. So, the godman was upfront about telling me that he convinced the old woman, whose alternative was to live at the mercy of daughters-in-law and relatives. He was later arrested,' says Sharma.

Or take 'Freezer Baba' Ashutosh Maharaj. Born Mahesh Kumar Jha, he had left his home and became an ascetic in 1973. A decade later, he set up an ashram in Noor Mahal near Jalandhar that soon started attracting migrant labourers from Bihar. In January 2014, the godman died, but his trust claimed he had only gone into 'deep meditation' and would eventually come out of it. They brought in a commercial freezer and kept him in it. In mid-2014, when this reporter ventured into the ashram, it took four rounds of frisking and security checks (the last by the Punjab Police). Approaching 'Freezer Baba' or his abode was impossible, the trust's functionaries said. The son, Dilip Jha, eventually approached the courts to cremate the corpse so as to claim succession. But the Divya Jyoti Jagran Sansthan would not let go of the corpse. At stake was an estate worth hundreds of millions of dollars.

The followers of Balak Brahmachari in Calcutta were not as lucky. In 1993, the godman died in a hospital and his devouts brought back the corpse to his 'Santal Dal' ashram in Sukchar, a village in Hoogly district. The held it hostage for 55 days, claiming he was merely in a trance and an awakening was imminent. The administration served several notices in vain. Eventually, the police broke open the gates one night, confiscated the rotting corpse and took it for cremation.

But the comic aspects divert attention from the real damage potential—the mix of politics, violence and legal immunity. By the 2000s, for instance, Asaram's clout was quite visible. He used to circulate a pamphlet showing chief ministers, union ministers and opposition leaders bending at the waist, palms joined in a salute or touching the godman's feet. 'How can such a man be treated like a criminal? Bapu swayam bhagwan hai (he is God himself),' says a lawyer linked to the ashram.

Such absolute faith soon turns murderous. After Asaram and son landed in custody, new cases emerged—witnesses getting bumped off—and old cases surfaced. Ex-followers turned up to depose about murders, disappearances and occult practices. The parents of two boys who disappeared from an ashram in Madhya Pradesh in 2008 found public support. The Supreme Court recently issued notices to all states to set up guidelines for witness protection in India based on a petition by Mahendra Chawla (Sai's former aide) and the fathers of two complainants. Meanwhile, a probe into Asaram's tantric practices lies sealed with the Gujarat government since 2013.

Spurts of violence both seem to come naturally to cults and also occasionally cause their downfall. In 2013, followers of a self-styled Kabirpanthi godman, Rampal Singh, clashed with Arya Samajis outside his ashram in Rohtak, Haryana. Three people died. A year later, when the Punjab & Haryana High Court issued an arrest warrant, the police could not execute it for two weeks as the godman holed up in his ashram, protected by a human chain of thousands of women followers. A hundred policemen, 70 journalists and 30 others were injured in the clash that followed and Rampal was arrested the next day. The violent streak was in evidence again as his followers disrupted a courtroom while proceedings continued.

Patiala lawyer Harinder Pal Singh Verma, the CBI special prosecutor against Ram Rahim since 2007, once had a car of dera followers hit his vehicle from behind, though he was unhurt. During the trial, a lawyer-follower of the godman also issued a death threat to him while proceedings were on. There are also two murders—of Ranjit Singh, a brother of one of the rape survivors, and of journalist Ram Chander Chhatrapati, who had published the rape victim's letter. Singh's father and Chhatrapati's son are witnesses so the CBI feels it has a good case. 'Ram Rahim's freedom was directly connected with these deaths, so he is being tried for conspiracy,' says Verma.

Senior advocate Anupam Gupta, as amicus curiae, recalled an army intelligence input that had said former military personnel were imparting weapons training to DSS followers. Noting the impending rape and murder trials, Justice M. Jeyapaul too had said the dera should be searched for weapons and its activities monitored. The apprehension came true—it was all live on national TV on August 26.

Similar mayhem was seen last year in a state-owned horticultural garden in Mathura, UP, where a breakaway faction of the Jai Gurudev cult had set up shop for two years—running a country within a country. The original Jai Gurudev passed himself off as Subhas Chandra Bose, drawing on the popular theory that he was alive. Pankaj Yadav took over from him—and Ramvriksh was a malcontent unhappy at being sidelined.

After failed attempts to enforce a 'Netaji' currency, Ramvriksh gathered followers—mostly old tribals and Dalits from eastern UP and MP—and started marching towards Delhi. Midway, he was given space in Mathura. The commune had a 'national song', a school and other facilities but the core team was secretly stockpiling weapons. When police broke through the garden's wall, a gunbattle raged till someone set fire to the huts and those in them. Thus ended the devotion of some. Those who, as Kang says, 'make an investment in the guru's purity even more than the guru', for whom 'anything that impugns the purity of the guru is unacceptable'.

Trouble is, this is a homicidal sort of purity. In Ram Rahim's case, there are older murder cases that may now resurface. In 2008, the godman's bodyguards had fired at a crowd of Jat Sikhs at a Mumbai mall, killing Balkar Singh and injuring others. In 2007, a former driver of Ram Rahim had confessed that the godman had allegedly ordered his former accountant Faqir Chand's murder. The trail had gone dry in both for want of witnesses. 'This one conviction will change things because the courts have ended the state patronisation of the dera,' says Kanwarpal Singh.

While the protective umbrella is there, of course, the ashrams exhibit an enviable GDP rate, often ending like

Maharishi Mahesh Yogi, who is said to have had Rs 50,000 crore worth properties, or any of the southern spiritual 'empires'. Says activist Sreeni Pattathanam, speaking over phone to *Outlook* from Kollam, 'New-age gurus have corporatised spirituality. They jet-set and live lavishly. They use spirituality to create empires. Political powers and big business are beholden to them. Most of them avail tax benefits as charitable institutions. Their account books should be made public. But governments are afraid to touch them because they are afraid of the devotees who make up a sizeable vote-bank.'

And what happens to the dera's mini-empire in Sirsa? The children have control as of now, but after the government and judiciary are done with its assets, there may not be much left. And Ram Rahim's followers may carve out a place in Delhi's Jantar Mantar, squeezing into a tent somewhere between the respective followers of Asaram Bapu and Sant Shri Rampal.

~

The murder trials of Ram Rahim continued after this and on a subsequent trip to Chandigarh, I met Khatta Singh, a witness in the cases against Ram Rahim. Khatta Singh is a former aide of the godman who told me he used to fix his political appointments and perform other small jobs. After they fell out, Singh became an important witness for the CBI. Ram Rahim's operation was large but not on the scale of Asaram's. But there was a great fear factor that muzzled his detractors and former followers. So, Singh, the one man who did want to sing, became an important lead for the investigators.

The law required Khatta Singh to depose in court. The day before his first deposition in one of the trials, he met with the prosecutor and they discussed his testimony late into the evening. The next day, Verma, the CBI's special prosecutor, told Singh, who was in the witness box, to make a statement to the special CBI court and repeat whatever he had told the investigators.

Khatta Singh, Verma told me later, feigned ignorance of any such deposition and withdrew from the proceedings saying he did not know anything. Luckily, he had also deposed a statement before a judicial officer. The court declared Singh a hostile witness, called on the judicial officer and used his corroboration and records to admit Singh's deposition. It caused serious delays and the trial was almost jeopardized because of Singh's turning hostile.

When I met Singh, he said he was under pressure and that he had been issued threats. By that time, he had changed his mind and approached the CBI court to readmit his testimony. The CBI court, Verma told me, had refused to entertain him again and said his testimony to the judicial officer would suffice. Singh appealed to the P&H HC and this entire episode created a delay in Ram Rahim's trial. There were some apprehensions within the CBI that this might be a ground for Ram Rahim to seek bail from the high court while he appealed his conviction and sentence in the high court.

As an aide to the godman, Singh did not have much except some property close to one of his ashrams. The exact size was vague but, years later, he seemed to be doing well and had a swanky real estate office in a developing township of Punjab, close to Chandigarh.

# 13

# Sheep to Wolves

The distinct stages in the evolution of Asaram Bapu start from a cloud around his beginnings. His biography, as published by his ashram, makes him out to be the son that shouldered the family's responsibilities, albeit reluctantly, since he was interested in meditation and a contact with god. But when he had the opportunity, he joined other ashrams till he received deeksha from one guru, direction from another and then set himself up on the banks of the Sabarmati, in Motera village, sometime in the early 1970s—by some accounts, 1972.

In direct contradiction to this lore is the story reported widely in the media (referred to earlier) that Asaram sold hooch in Motera. The bootlegger who supplied him with the illegal liquor came forward shortly after the mysterious death of the Vaghela cousins in 2008. Asaram's spokesperson had a different narrative. Neelam Dubey told me that when Asaram sat on the banks of the river and started to meditate, the only establishment in the immediate vicinity was a hooch den.

The second stage is the 1970s and 1980s when Asaram started to preach to those that gathered there. Those are the years when he first began to expand and one of the few observers from those years is Raju Chandok's grandfather and Chandok himself, who later went on to become a close aide of the godman till they fell out in the early 2000s.

It was in the 1980s that Asaram first became noticeable as a godman with a considerable following within Gujarat. His clout at that time can be gauged from how the ashram in Surat was established, by the accounts of the fishermen in Jahangirpura who clashed with his followers and also the Vyas family, whose land was encroached upon and sucked into the sprawling acreage of the ashram.

This is when the godman also accumulated substantial political clout, so much so that he was able to get a state minister to influence policy decisions in his favour. The 1990s followed with records that showed Asaram increase his business interests into production of puja samagri (ritual ingredients) and other objects that he could sell to the thousands of devotees that flocked to his satsangs. Besides, there was the loan business that began flourishing around this time. The collection of donations in lakhs and crores of rupees (and used in the moneylending business) show how large his following had become.

The 1990s was also the period when Narayan Sai started to appear in various records of the trust and father and son headed westwards. The case of the forged will (as declared by a court in Canada) shows that they had a budding presence in the US and Canada in the early 1990s.

In the early 2000s, middle-class television screens boomed the K-series soaps or the game show *Kaun Banega Crorepati* in the evening. In the morning, the pop gurus spammed television screens with their gyan. Baba Ramdev is probably one of the most successful preachers who revitalized yoga as a form of exercise to the point that air passengers could be seen flexing their abdomen muscles through the entire duration of a flight. Other gurus began with imparting spiritual wisdom and moved on to commentaries on society, culture, Indian tradition, current affairs and politics.

Asaram's televised satsangs were a hit too, and his followers swelled to much larger numbers than before. Earlier, he would sell audio and video cassettes of his satsangs. Even the chants he used changed over time. There are older satsang videos where he would use the chant 'Sree Ram Sree Ram' as a pause during his sermons. That later changed to 'Hari Om' and a staccato chant of 'om, om, om', which is more neutral and would appeal to all sects of Hinduism.

Asaram would also use popular stories from the scriptures such as 'Paap ka Baap' (The Root of Sin) to show the result of greed. He seemed to have stopped using them later when he moved on to quoting directly from texts and commentaries. In the 2000s, he had substantial clout within the government and, in 2013, when Tehelka published a cover story on him, I found a pamphlet at the Kota ashram whose back cover carried a photograph of the godman with several powerful politicians across party lines.

There are several videos, available online, of satsangs where powerful men appear with the godman. Atal Bihari Vajpayee danced to a song, L.K. Advani smiled as the godman addressed followers and Shivraj Singh Chouhan once went up on the dais to be 'godman for a day' and delivered a sermon at the baba's event. In 2008, Narendra Modi appeared to take on Asaram when he directed the formation of the Justice D.K. Trivedi commission to probe occult charges and much more than what was expected spilled out. Many accusations including sexual and other forms of exploitation that tumbled out at the time did not make an impact except to create a perception about the godman.

It was only in 2013, when a minor rape survivor complained to the police about the godman assaulting her, that, for the first time, there was a concrete accusation against Asaram which could be tried in a court of law. Modi quickly dissociated with him in public and asked the BJP to dissociate itself too. RSS groundworkers, such as the pracharak I met in Jodhpur, are still not convinced and feel that this is the persecution of a Hindu saint. The Gujarat police officer, D.G. Vanzara—accused of several fake encounters—was also not convinced and continued to advocate Asaram's innocence. As did a former chief justice of the Sikkim High Court, Justice S.N. Bhargava, who touched Asaram's feet outside the court. At the time, Asaram was still appearing as an accused at the POCSO trial and the former chief justice was there to show his respect. Asaram later said that the man had been his follower for many years. Bhargava had served as a judge of the Rajasthan High Court between 1982 and 1993.

Some frequent questions which I've been asked are: How do godmen acquire a following? How did Asaram have so many followers? What led them to defend his ways despite a conviction? Why are they termed as fanatics in descriptions and debates? What attracted followers to Ram Rahim even though he had been charged with murder, rape and castrating his disciples?

Professor Jyotirmaya Sharma does not need an introduction for those who like to question popular myths about Indian philosophy. When I mentioned this research, Sharma expressed some thrill and suggested a different direction, one that would have to begin with a few years of groundwork in dusty archives but might be worth taking up to see the advent of the twentieth-century Hindu pop guru, the criminalization and politicization of religion through the godman. For now, this book remains a journalistic endeavour and decoding certain concepts and beliefs had to be based on expert opinion, hence the need for a Sharma, who briefly strayed into journalism, and has since been a go-to guy for many journalists for dope on 'Hindu-ism' and Indian religious philosophy.

'Charisma plays a great role in attracting followers and there may be at least three key factors that retain the following. First, the babas don't strain your intellect and do not involve any followers in issues of theology,' said Sharma.

The pravachan (or sermon) at the 'satsang' is like ready-to-cook food or baby food for the soul, which is easily digestible. The godmen do not deliver discourses on schools of Indian philosophy or touch upon issues such as the karma theory.

'In the last two centuries, those who became babas were either ill-trained or plainly ignorant. They just did not have the same level of knowledge as the theologians of the past, neither schooled like them nor trained through tradition,' Sharma said.

A similar parallel may be found in Indian classical music, where one has either inherited a particular gharana from a family of musicians, or else they have studied with a master.

The second factor for the godmen's following could be a result of the end of mysticism or innovation. Mystics contributed greatly to both Indian religious tradition and its influence beyond India's shores. It allowed people to bypass religious institutions, formal structures of religions, priesthood and caste restrictions and establish a direct connection with god.

Sharma pointed out that many of the mystics, such as Ramana Maharshi, believed in the power of 'silent teaching'. This picture of serenity created an ethereal experience for the follower, who revelled in the feeling of being in the presence of someone spectacular. Ramana Maharshi is regarded as the last of the great mystics.

'The appeal was the imagination, a part of which is the extraordinary or the fantastic, and becomes real in the presence of the spectacular person,' Sharma said. 'The most real thing in life could be imagination, greater than any reality. Ancient texts called it manorajyam or the kingdom of the imagination.'

Sudhir Kakar has also written about the imagination and its spiritual dimension. 'An invaluable ally of "seeing" is imagination, which the romantics have always considered to be the basis of reality. Today, we usually think of imagination as the ability to make images, although the capacity to access and elaborate on early memories is equally important. Indeed, it is a complex and often playful combination of the two which characterises a bold leap of imagination,' wrote Kakar.[1]

Ramana Maharshi attracted thousands of visitors in his lifetime, some of whom stayed on and formed an ashram and community around him. He remained near Arunachala (present-day Tamil Nadu) and did not travel around preaching or sermonizing to people.

'Throughout his life, Sri Ramana insisted that this silent flow of power represented his teachings in their most direct and concentrated form. The importance he attached to this is indicated by his frequent statements to the effect that his verbal

---

[1]  Sudhir Kakar, 'The Resurgence of Imagination', *The Essential Sudhir Kakar*, Oxford University Press, 2011.

teachings were only given out to those who were unable to understand his silence,' wrote David Godman,[2] disciple of the mystic and librarian at his ashram.

The babas of today are not mystics, they are salesmen, many of them of the snake oil variety, who never get tired of hearing their own voices.

A more recent school (not more than a few centuries old) of Hinduism in various minor Puranas says that 'naam kirtan' will carry you through the Kali Yug—the 10,000 years predicted by the scriptures as troublesome for the world. This also finds mention in the Sikh religious scripture, the Guru Granth Sahib.

Pop gurus such as Asaram draw their following through satsang, where 'sang' means association and 'sat' is truth, which is reality, which is existence. The satsang was a powerful medium for ancient gurus to connect with their followers, some of whom could even experience 'spontaneous religious sensations' that the seeker strived for.

Sadhus are placed at a very high pedestal in India; they are called mahatmas and mere association with them is akin to a pilgrimage. Seva or service to the sadhu is a part of the seeker's practice. For the average Indian householder, attending a godman's satsang and sadhu seva are instruments for connection with god.

When Ramana Maharshi was asked why he did not go around preaching the truth to people, he replied[3] that mounting a platform and sermonizing was not the sole way of communicating with people. He was a great advocate of silent teaching, described by many as a powerful medium of

---

[2]  *'Be As You Are': The Teachings of Sri Ramana Maharshi*, edited by David Godman, Penguin, 1992.
[3]  Ibid.

instruction and a spiritual experience in itself. He often gave deeksha through silence.

The satsangs were platforms for gurus to preach to their flock and when they hit the drawing rooms through television sets, they greatly helped increase the number of followers for godmen. Celebrity endorsements only added to the size of the ever-growing followers and large crowds automatically drew politicians to the godmen, forever in search of ways to expand their own community or following.

Asaram's discourses were not just on god or religion but also politics, common to many such gurus. There are some whose entire discourses are on current affairs and politics, such as a certain guru whose discourse I had once attended in January 2017 when the hot topic was the Supreme Court's deliberations on Jallikattu. The entire evening revolved around his opinion on Jallikattu and how the courts should not concern themselves with these traditions.

'The man whose power is not derived from theology, mysticism or direct intercession with God, such a man will source his power from elsewhere and find an alternative source to legitimize himself,' said Sharma.

'Today's baba first makes a building, gets land, and so on, whereas the development of a genuine mystical tradition was very slow. There was no evangelical thrust to mysticism,' said Sharma.

What does the guru do with land? Ram Rahim said he rehabilitated alcoholics, drug addicts and sex workers; opened schools and hospitals for the poor; and served communities. There are babas who also do what is broadly called 'social service' such as feeding and clothing the poor. Asaram did the same, and also built a sheltered community for followers, many of whom were also homeless.

The third factor that retains a follower is an Indian tradition of visiting samadhis or relics of mahatmas—a flourishing reliquary tradition found in other religions as well. At these memorials, the seeker often makes an offering in return for a wish, which usually includes some material demand—a promotion, a new job, academic or entrepreneurial success. The extreme form of that vow is mannat (a transactional vow) which has now been perverted to offering only hair and nails.

When the seeker asks god to grant a wish, there is no guarantee of fulfilment, but the godman or the baba, as an intermediary, is different and may even promise delivery.

Whether it is Ram Rahim, Asaram or other babas, the urban middle class approaches them with problems ranging from impotence, sexual repression, alcoholism to material success. The guru enters into a transaction to grant the followers their wishes through various prescriptions in exchange for offerings. This becomes the point at which a follower's devotion is put to test.

My conversations with the former followers of Asaram such as Shantilal Vaghela and others show the foundation of their desire to follow a guru lay in their belief that Hindu tradition demanded it. Another follower says that Asaram gave her life direction from the scriptures though she never questioned the source of this knowledge but believed that it 'flowed from the Vedas' and his philosophy was 'Vedantic', the same description stated by the jail superintendent in Jodhpur where Asaram was confined.

A senior police officer once told me of a childhood friend of his, a godman, who had confessed his modus operandi to him. This godman asked the followers (who came to him with various problems) to perform certain rituals and laid down some discipline. Many times, these steps bore positive results for the followers who paid back the godman in riches (direct donations) or organized bhandaras, and so forth. Asaram's follower, Ishwar Naik, had said that he had also paid for bhandaras on the godman's instructions. The followers who get results will keep swarming around the guru searching for more 'miracles', preaching the godman's greatness, creating legends and myths which in turn increases the following.

'Anybody following a godman is not an issue as long as it does not harm the basic fabric of society which is under a constitutional democracy,' said Sharma. 'In India, people build shrines for film stars such as Amitabh, Rajinikanth, Khushboo and others but they do not disturb anybody. The point of departure is when somebody impinges upon my freedom.'

The godmen often manipulate and brainwash their following and then exploit them, as in the case of the two sisters and the several women that the Surat police came across while probing rape charges against Narayan Sai. The testimony of the witnesses against Asaram also showed that he used manipulation too. Many of the followers were in the know of this and some of these charges against the godman have been proved. Not only did the followers continue to believe that their guru was saintly, but also supported the violent attacks on detractors. So, wouldn't these organizations be classified as cults as has been discussed many times in the media?

'I won't call it fanaticism,' said Sharma. 'There are people trying to find security in something, which does not have to be subjected to categories and labels. When a sufi darvesh is dancing in circles thinking of nothing else, we call that beautiful not fanatic. The trouble begins when the sects become criminal and harm others.

'The sects, organized into communities, require influence to "do good" where they are based and people recognize that influence. So, apart from chanting and meditating, the baba can also make a call to admit someone in a hospital. The wiser ones amongst them made gated communities which had schools and hospitals,' Sharma continued.

'The word for such godmen and their following is sampraday (literally, community). Political parties survive by splitting into smaller factions. Similarly, no religious dogma or doctrine has survived without splitting—the eternal principle in formation of the "sect", which is a religious community that has formed around a religious idea or ideas that have formed away from the mainstream branch of the faith. The most obvious reason for the split is ambition,' said Sharma.

There is an example of splitting in this case because Asaram's daughter publicly split from the godman and started preaching by herself after the godman was jailed. Many of Asaram's followers have started to attend her satsangs. Several journalists in Gujarat, who have covered the godman and his sect, told me that they would not be surprised if she eventually became Asaram's true successor, a way for Asaram's legacy to continue.

In Asaram's case, the charges also bordered on occult practices and 'tantric' rituals, exorcisms and various other 'instruments of evil' in the form of 'black magic' and voodoo.

'Tantra is of two kinds—right hand and left hand. Occult falls in the left-hand category which includes black magic and sex rituals. Many of these gurus are hatha yogis, and many tantric practices require knowledge of hatha yogic practices,' explained Sharma.

Exorcism, as also seen in Europe, is an alternative or indigenous form of psychiatry. Till today, it is not uncommon in India to find villages where a person with mental health issues is treated through alternative, indigenous psychiatry to 'exorcize demons'. It is an extension of the belief in miracles, faith healing and medical remedies through 'magic'. Evangelical faiths that have come later to India have also taken up this form of shamanic healing during public programmes.

Sharma's book[4] on Swami Vivekananda extends beyond well-researched commentary on the preacher who established an order based on Sri Ramakrishna Paramhansa. There are several references to the mysterious school of tantra, well explained beyond common misconceptions that arose out of its defamation by several scholars. It drove me to look at several sects that had chosen this path, such as the Kartabhajas of Bengal. Why that becomes important in a book about Asaram is that many have considered Asaram and his son, Narayan Sai, to be tantrics.

There are witnesses in the Justice D.K. Trivedi commission who have sworn (both to the authorities and later to me) that they believed that father and son practised the dark arts. Mahendra Chawla told me, the courts and the Justice Trivedi commission about how he saw Narayan Sai bent over what Chawla assumed was a human body one night in Madhya Pradesh, while he was still a personal assistant to Narayan Sai. He even suggested that Narayan Sai had taken him to a teacher in Rajrappa, Jharkhand, to train him in tantra. The teacher turned him away but the narrative has stuck.

There is another myth that has often been repeated in the public domain that Asaram's alleged voracious sexual appetite was a part of his tantric practices, a form of sacrifice.

---

[4]  Jyotirmaya Sharma, *Cosmic Love and Human Apathy: Swami Vivekananda's Restatement of Religion*, HarperCollins, 2013.

The protracted defamation of tantra has given it a negative reputation for various reasons. Its followers were made a minority by loud evangelists of other belief systems and philosophies, which have shrouded it in mystery and the rituals are very different from those practised under what is called Vedic Hinduism.

Popular culture has not helped the image of tantra. In the 1951 Telugu fantasy potboiler, *Pathala Bhairavi*, former CM of undivided Andhra Pradesh N.T. Rama Rao played the strapping protagonist, who as the 'poor boy' had to kill the evil tantric to acquire a relic of the 'Patal Kali' which then bestowed him with enough wealth to marry the king's daughter. The marital bliss was short-lived because the powerful tantric was resurrected by his apprentice and reclaimed his position as the villain. The vile tantric reversed the protagonist's fate because he wanted the girl but the protagonist was as clever. He shaved off the tantric's beard which had held all the latter's power, and this act restored good over evil—binaries that are oversimplified for Indian philosophy.

All of the pop cultures that denigrate tantra draws upon Kali (in her various forms) as the goddess who enables these evil men who lust for power through occult practices and black magic. Kali is the first of the ten Mahavidyas, the sect of the feminine, the order of the goddess. The other nine are Tara, Tripura Sundari, Bhuvaneshwari, Bhairavi, Chhinnamastika, Dhumavati, Bagalamukhi, Matangi and Kamala. Matangi and Kamala are also better known as Saraswati and Lakshmi respectively.

The temple in Rajrappa, Jharkhand, is one of the few temples to the Chhinnamastika goddess in India. The other is in Chintpurni, Himachal Pradesh. Both of these sites are described as sthanas (established seats) for tantric philosophy and practice. The idol of Chhinnamastika, or Chhinnamasta, depicts a terrifying scene. The goddess holds in her right hand a blade with which she has decapitated herself and balanced in the palm of her left hand is her own head. Three streams of blood gush forth from this head, one back to her own throat and the other two to the mouths of her two attendants, Dakini and Jogini. And this blood fest continues while the goddess stands on the back of Rati who is lying atop Kama in an act of copulation.[5]

Such a description alone should conjure up an image of wanton sexual practices and blood-drinking that has become synonymous with the negative optics accorded to tantric philosophy and practices. This image is not some sort of snuff pornography but has a deeper philosophical meaning—one that has been explained by several researchers and experts. In a school of Buddhism, Chhinnamastika is Vajrayogini, who, amongst other things, provides an accelerated path to nirvana. The offerings to Chhinnamastika, as per some sources, include meat, alcohol and sexual intercourse, but not rape or sex with virgins as many seem to believe. To push a person charged in multiple sexual assault cases into this sphere without evidence is a disservice to the many practitioners and believers of tantra.

The godman of today derives his power by distorting an ancient Indian custom by which the master taught his students the secrets of life and the universe coded in the scriptures amongst other things. The crimes of Asaram, whether he is charged with or convicted for them, pertain to misuse of the guru's position. It is akin to a schoolteacher sexually abusing or exploiting a student.

---

[5] Rati and Kama are the goddess and god of love and lust respectively.

# Acknowledgements

During this reportage, I have covered the work of law enforcement agencies and their investigators. I ventured a little further, wherever required, to connect some dots. I have relied on documents, some in public domain, some not, and generally followed, wherever possible, the rule of verification with at least three sources—a standard set decades ago by Bob Woodward and Carl Bernstein, titans of our time.

The many police officers and government officials I met and interviewed were kind enough to spend hours with me. Some meetings began with 'I have ten minutes . . .' and lapsed into hours spent from their off-duty time while they patiently answered all my questions. I have to withhold their names on request.

Investigative journalism has a stable ally in Swati Chopra, who conceived the idea behind the book. She has worked tirelessly behind the scenes, helped in keeping direction and gallantly survived the hundreds of tiny heart attacks triggered by disappointments and delays that we reporters are used to.

I have learnt a lot from friend and author Sudeep Chakravarti while assisting him on one of his books. He warned me in advance that reporting and writing a book were lonely processes.

I was able to venture briefly into the spirituality aspect thanks to Professor Jyotirmaya Sharma who was generous with his time and mind.

The senior advocate, Anupam Gupta, has closed the door on journalists but held it wide open for me, even late at night.

My absence was tolerated very generously by my family while they passed through several crises. It is difficult to live and deal with a person concerned about safety and secretive about their work but my parents, Uma and Ashoke, and my partner-in-life, Saloni, survive it regularly. The latter also relaxed our deal of cooking on alternate days so that I could finish writing. Reporting in Punjab is always a breeze thanks to my parents-in-law, Suman and Ashwini Mital, at whose home there's always the best meals, great company and a spare key so that I can sneak in after late-night meetings.

In Jodhpur, P.C. Solanki and his family received me warmly and apart from a bird's-eye view on the POCSO case, gave me the best view of Jodhpur from their terrace. Solanki's conviction and courage is infectious—the records speak for his qualities as a lawyer who is meticulous about detail. Lalit Parihar helped set up meetings in Jodhpur and ferried me to most of them, in one case, despite potential danger. He spiced up the boring and long waits with the best stories and the tastiest kachori of Jodhpur.

Priyanka Dubey was very helpful with connecting me to several key people and her incisive narrative on Asaram for *Caravan* is an example of why she stands out in a crowd. I am grateful that Vinod Jose, the magazine's executive editor and a remarkable journalist, generously let me extract a crucial portion from the piece.

Nirjhari Sinha always has warm food on her table and a sharp memory that provided leads from a decade ago. She connected me to her associates in Jan Sangharsh Manch, which she helped found. Her son, Pratik, doesn't hesitate to share resources whenever I reach out and their help proved invaluable for some chapters.

Paloma Dutta has the eyes of a hawk and doesn't let any errors slip through the cracks. She is the rare editor who respects the descriptive verb and has a better one handy.

Several other journalists and friends enabled the last-mile connectivity to key persons, including Shantanu Guha Roy and Divyesh Chavada in Surat. Uday Mahurkar was one of the first journalists to report on Asaram when the godman was still highly influential. He personally spent time with me to explain the context of many things.

My colleagues at *Outlook* were very sporting about accommodating my long travels. I have maintained the same level of editorial due diligence that I have learnt working with some of the very best in Indian journalism. The magazine was also kind enough to let me reproduce a 'cover story' I had written on godmen.

I was impressed with the state-owned and operated bus service in Gujarat that has great staff and infrastructure, regardless of the class of travel.

Some of the witnesses in various cases and former devotees of Asaram trusted me despite security concerns. Many of them, such as Shantilal Vaghela, relived their agony to enrich the reportage. Mahinder Chawla had been invaluable when I had reported on Asaram's cases for *Tehelka* and *Outlook*. The ones who did not grant exclusive meetings had left sufficient material in their depositions and interviews. Above all, it is necessary to appreciate the courage of the women and other witnesses who have come forward despite the danger.

# Notes

## CHAPTER 1

Details from jail based on author's interview with Vikram Singh, DIG, Gujarat prisons, additional charge: Jodhpur Central Jail; interviews conducted by author in Jodhpur in April 2018.

Details from investigation based on interviews with investigating officers conducted by author and from verdict of trial court.

## CHAPTER 5

Reconstruction of raid based on primary interviews conducted by author with investigating officers. Additional material sourced from:

https://www.youtube.com/watch?v=ifYxuG0WlQY published on 27 October 2013 and accessed on 10 July 2018

https://www.youtube.com/watch?v=Q2JrPU35CNE published on 26 October 2013 and accessed on 10 July 2013

## CHAPTER 6

Narration of interactions between police and Narayan Sai, Monica Aggarwal and Janaki Devi based on interviews conducted by the author with multiple policemen of various ranks, all of whom were in Surat police during the probe leading to the charge sheet presented to the Surat court.

CHAPTER 7

Decision of the high court of Gujarat at Ahmedabad in Special Civil Application No. 1266 of 2017, re: *Ulhas Securities Private Ltd vs. Deputy Commissioner of Income Tax*, delivered by Justice M.R. Shah and Justice B.N. Karia, decided on 13 February 2017.

Decision of the high court of Gujarat at Ahmedabad in Special Civil Application No. 4916 of 2017, re: *Pratius Merchants Pvt. Ltd vs Deputy Commissioner of Income Tax*, delivered by Justice M.R. Shah and Justice B.N. Karia, decided on 26 April 2017.

Decision of the high court of Gujarat at Ahmedabad in Special Civil Application No. 5483 of 2017, re: *Dhanpati Marketiers Ltd vs Deputy Commissioner of Income Tax*, delivered by Justice M.R. Shah and Justice B.N. Karia, decided on 26 April 2017.

CHAPTER 8

In the high court of Gujarat at Ahmedabad; Criminal Revision Application (Against Order Passed by Subordinate Court) No. 77 of 2015; Justice Sonia Gokani on 31 July 2015

Provisional Attachment Order no. 02/2015 in ECIR/01/SRT/2018, accessed by the author in June 2018

https://www.indiatoday.in/india/delhi/story/gujarat-cpos-unearth-asaram-bapu-and-narayan-sais-shady-business-nexus-287220-2015-08-09

PAO further confirmed by adjudicating authority under Prevention of Money Laundering Act within stipulated time period. PAO further used by ED in filing prosecution complaint on 27 June 2018.

Further facts collected and verified by author through interviews conducted with multiple sources in the police department, income tax department and directorate of enforcement in June and July 2018.